Perception Is Truth

Myself… Indulgence

Matthew P Mc

I'd like to dedicate this to my wife, my family, my friends, and anyone who's ever been a part of my life. This collection of works is all thanks to you.

ISBN 978-0-578-01804-1

All contents copyright © 2009 Matthew P Mc. All rights reserved. No part of this document may be reproduced or transmitted in any form, by any means (electronic, photocopying, recording, or otherwise) without the prior written permission of the publisher. That's a big way of saying show your friends what you like but if they want a copy please ask them to buy one.

Table Of Contents

Introduction
...Thanks for coming

Days Of Yore
...The power of ignorance

Creation 1
Creation vs. Evolution 5
Enigma of Time: Keeping Track of a Riddle 7
Poetic Responses 10
Remarks On Marshall 15

Middle Ages
...Learning Begins

12-Dec-02 17
14-Dec-02 20
22-Dec-02 23
23-Dec-02 26
27-Dec-02 28
31-Jan-03 30
Causality 32
Edgar's Esoteric Explication 36
Heretical Reason 41
Perceived Truth vs. Proven Reality In Mental Disorders ... 50
Seasonal Differences 57
Simplicity 59
Technology Opinionating 65

Electronic Revolution
...Searching for identity

A Confession 68
A Rant Without A Date 70
Admonition Against Apostolicism 74
Afterdeath 75
Am I Labeled Correctly? 79
Another Letter to OTR 84
Astral Projection 89
Balance 90
Confused 91
Cynicism or Outright Fear 94
Does God Exist? 97
Does Hell Exist? 100
Does Hell Exist? Pt 2 101
Epiphanic Cervidae 104

Epiphany	109
Equality: An Introduction	110
Ethnicity	111
Everything Is Wrong	113
Everything Is Wrong Pt 2	116
Farewell	123
Freedom Isn't Free	125
Fuck Karma	128
God is my Co-Defendant	129
Heaven and Hell: A Response	131
Hermann Goering	133
Homosexual Christian	134
Inconsistencies and Ironies	137
Is American Idol Aptly Named?	140
Is It Worth It?	143
Life and Death in the Golden State	144
Lifeboat or Executive Decision?	146
Materiali$m	147
Mistakes vs. Regret	151
Over the Rhine: Greatest Band Ever	153
Perception Is Truth: An Introduction	157
Perception Is Truth: Opinions	158
Perception Is Truth: The Beginning	163
Petra	166
Reincarnation and Skeptics: A Response	168
Religion	171
Religious Claim Jumping	173
Religious Claim Jumping Pt 2	177
Reminiscent of a Memory	179
Response to the Abortion Discussion	181
Sci Fi vs. Fantasy	184
Scientology	187
Separation of Church and State	189
Sexual Harassment/Discrimination/Deviance	193
Straight Talk on D&D?: A Response	195
Suicide Is Painless	210
Telepathy	214
The Greatest Power	216
The Love Letter	217
The Source of Biblical Confusion	218
V.A.S.T.—Jon Crosby Is My Hero	224
Violence	226
War of the Words	228
Warfare on the Religious Front	233
We're Growing Up To Be Wimps	238
What's On My Mind?	241

Which Part of the Bible is Valid? ········ 245
Why I Like Music ········ 247
Why I'm Grumpy ········ 250
Why Religious Music is Better ········ 253
You Big Asshole ········ 255

Latter Days
...Intellectual Teenager

Debates, Debacles, or Debaucheries? ········ 258
Disclaimer ········ 261
Evolution vs. Creation vs. Other ········ 262
F You, Black Friday ········ 265
Is Heaven Real? ········ 266
Is Heaven Real? Pt 2 ········ 268
Mixed Messages From Gloucester ········ 274
Pride ········ 279
Superman Sucks ········ 281
The Bible Is Relevant ········ 283
Whatever You Say ········ 284
Work ········ 287

References
...When I kept track

References ········ 288

Introduction

Everyone thinks, but not everyone considers their thoughts. We are a reactionary people in a reactionary society, forced to make split-second decisions without the courtesy of a moment. When supplied with the moment, we react on emotion more than logic, our perceptions clouding our judgment and what would normally be considered wisdom. We watch the news, read the paper, browse the Internet, all in a vain attempt to educate ourselves to the current events of our world, and in doing so ignore the history of it. We perpetuate stereotypes by disdaining them; we further the cause of hatred by claiming racism at every twist and turn. We are no better than we were a thousand years ago and further. We merely repeat the cycles of history with new circumstances.

We are at a turning point in history, though few would admit how drastically. Those who claim to see the future are psychics or advisors, experts in their given field. Still, things happen that even the experts could not foresee, and we continue in our ignorant bliss while the world turns the same speed it has for millennia. What we still fail to realize is that the universe will go on or end as it is destined to do, whatever we as people want to happen or choose to believe. We have no significance in the furthering of total existence besides our own, and we squander even that with the paltry day to day complaints of money, religion, and entertainment. We cast aside as a people anything truly related to knowledge. We don't really want to know anything; we just want to believe what we're told by people who have enough charisma to tell it to us.

For me, the start of my joy in writing began in high school with a poem. I had created some semblance of literature in the sixth grade, but those were introductions to a poetic style and barely worth the ink that I wasted. I also managed a short story which was worth even less. It did show me that I could think, but it did not prove to me my thoughts were more than the mental ramblings of an eleven-year old. I would finish out my primary education believing that while I had a slightly more realistic grasp on the English language than one of my teachers, I was not someone who should look at writing for anything more than completing a school project. Math seemed to be my stronger suit at the time, and I do believe that some would wish I had kept with that particular topic if only for the head and heart aches I have caused.

Once my secondary education began, I was introverted and terrified of the world

- Introduction -

around me, as any classic geek of my age. It was half a year before I was loosened from some of my issues, much of which I still hold onto like a stapled teddy bear. It would be into the next year before I put together a single poem for a class project. It would not win me any awards, nor would it see the light of day beyond a yearbook, but it would open quite a door in my own mind. Other projects would allow me to spread my proverbial wings and be "sky writin' with the smoke of life" as Mark Heard once sang into my ears. For the middle years of secondary, I wrote several short stories and a small collection of poetry. They were primarily focused on events we were studying which included history and religious beliefs. Others were Petrarchen in nature. Unrequited. Those days are long since behind me, but the experience has never left me.

    I have dabbled with tertiary education, but finishing college does not interest me as much as spending what little money I have learning more and more about other things. I have taken classes that I have enjoyed thoroughly, but in almost every class I have found disappointment; except from one instructor at the local community college. He was a business writer. At no point was he paid for fiction or even entertaining non-fiction. He did, however, understand one of the problems my work has always had (and struggles with to this day): pacing. I learned not only how to write clearly and concisely, but in doing so I had a great deal of appreciation for writing on a greater scale. Further, my appreciation for reading increased exponentially. My words at that time went from basic whining and reading of comic books to a greater sense of need to research and to create strong points and real purpose in my work. I am still, unfortunately, ruled by my emotions and this is apparent in my words even to this day. But I am growing.

    That's what this collection of works is hoping to display. Growth. Any great work has a protagonist and an antagonist, a good guy and a bad guy. In those stories, the reason we like or hate characters is because of their growth. I hope to show that I, as a writer, have grown and changed over the years. I hope to show that I am the character in this tale, and that I have allowed myself a great deal of change in the way I think based upon the more I learn. I have written much in my high school years, much of it you will see is terrible. My spelling was obsessive but my usage of the almighty comma can be a tad excessive. I have had several weblogs over the years, some of which turned out pretty decent if I do say so myself. I have had journals of pen and ink, papers that I have written for college, and whatever other random act of literary ambiguity I happen to put forth. It's not all worth reading but it's worth thinking about.

I am glad that you are here for the journey, and if you have come this far I am flattered and hopeful that you will enjoy the rest of the ride. Just know that my ideas evolve daily and that I call things as I see it with the information I have at the time. This often makes me reactionary, but I strive for facts and hope that you will do as I have for many years: question everything.

-Home, 09 December 2008

Days of Yore

Creation

Have you ever looked out at the stars, and wondered how they got there? Has the thought ever occurred to you that maybe they were just part of some cataclysmic explosion that mistakenly created the universe? If so, then you have believed in a farce. The creation of the universe can not be associated with spontaneous generation, or the big bang theory. Simply put, it was designed, created and watched over by God. Science likes to claim that there is no God, but they have been proving over and over again their philosophies have been incorrect, and something must have happened. The only problem they keep coming up against: it has to be God. Only God could have created something so magnificent and so unbelievably extraordinary and huge as our universe, and only Satan would try and tell us that it was all just some mistake. Thus, the enemy could spread his lie that we have no purpose, that our existence was all a matter of time and chance, and that we have no value in the big scheme of things. He keeps pushing his lies that we have a futile life span, and that we may as well believe what the deceived scientists are telling us: we are nothing but time and chance. We are nothing if we believe in that farce.

Now, how does one come to that conclusion? Easily, just look around you. Do you see the trees? Note how extremely complex their process of photosynthesis must be. Consider for a moment how intricate their branch work, how precise their leaf patterns, how strong its roots may be. God did not create this tree as a mistake. He did allow it just to happen, but He gave it thought and time. Although no one may ever know just how long it took Him; for me it really doesn't matter. Just knowing in my heart that God created us, and not believing that my world and my life was a mistake, is all I need to be concerned with.

- Perception Is Truth -

One thing I have learned from science as a whole, it likes to argue. If it is not fighting over how the earth was created, it is arguing as to how long the earth has been here. Christians, atheists, all argue the age of the earth. Some believe the day-age theory, other feel it could be only ten to fifteen thousand years old. Honestly, what does it matter? Look around you, does it matter to God how old His creation is? I highly doubt it, so why should we quibble over something that is basically irrelevant anyway? We were created by God for a purpose: to live for Him, and to worship and have a relationship with Him. He did not want for us to argue over our creation, but praise our Creator.

In taking various sciences, one may learn of the many, many ways in which God proves His power and His love for us. He cared enough to make us all different, to use our different brains in different ways. He created substances, He created the smallest particles known to man: the proton, neutron and electron. In His infinite wisdom, God used these three particles to create a universe so vast the human mind is still having a hard time comprehending the awesomeness of size. In all the understand of electron configurations, of the human anatomy, of how our own solar system works, we still have a hard time comprehending the little we really do know. There is so much more to learn, but for the most part, we merely squabble over the scraps of knowledge God has allowed to fall off His table.

The human body is so much more complex than we can imagine. Although the stupidity of man seems to be a recurring theme, just give it a minute to sink in. Man has become so vain in thinking the human body is the most complex machine, and then say humans were a mistake. Appalling statement, true? Humans are no more a mistake than Christ's death. God knew exactly what He was doing, no matter what others might say. Even atheists have little to back up many of their thoughts on the existence of the universe, and yet they keep showing the biblical accounts being true. How infuriating for them, huh?

Our anatomic structure is too incomprehensible, which is why there are so many different specialists out there. You have a doctor, who is merely a jack of all trades, and yet a master of none. You have a cardiologist, who specializes in the heart. You have a podiatrist, who specializes in feet. There are chiropractors, dentists, reflexologists, and so much more to prove the complexity of the human body. There are very few, if any, who can say they have extreme knowledge in all the areas of the body, especially the brain. It has been said that humans may use around ten percent of their brain in a lifetime. It has been said by some Christians that Christ used one hundred percent of his brain while hwas on earth, and that we have that potential. But, we have got to see past the scientific paradigms given us. We have got to understand the full potential we were created for.

This paper has been the thoughts and ideas of a not so educated man who only has the exceptionally little knowledge of his finite mind, and his faith. But if faith is all he's got, then maybe faith is all he needs. People have faith in science; they believe what the scientists tell them to be true. They go forth with the idea that their government is telling them the truth, at least half the time. They are told, and many believe, that the religious right is responsible for so much damage to our nation, and the reason we haven't tried to focus our attentions on the universe's "true" creation.

What people are having such a hard time understanding is that they do need science, but not for science's sake. I firmly believe God intended science for the glorification of His creation. The understanding of electron configurations, of how they may move within the nucleus, of how every living thing has the element carbon within it, was all meant for proving God's ultimate power. His creation is testimony of how the devil lies to us. He tells us our existence was never meant to be, and that we should just do whatever we are going to do; it doesn't matter. God meant for us to be real, nothing He made could have been a mistake. There is too much we have learned to prove that if creation was just some freak accident, then God is either dead, or never was. Everything about everything is so precise, that no accident ever heard of could have created such awesome repercussions.

Can you deny the existence of God, without looking around you? No. Because, just the fact that you can close your eyes without having to have some machine do it for you—if we were all just freak accidents—is proof enough, not "should" be proof enough, but it is proof enough that God made us, and He wants us to study His universe to give glory to Him, and to have more reasons to praise and honor Him, not so we can say we know this and we know that. In a thirty year old song by Ray Repp, "All creation shows the glory of the Lord. The earth proclaims its handiwork, the sky cries out

His Word". This song sums up creation into one fact: creation shows God's infinite glory. Life itself is evidence of His existence, and His creativity. Who we are, as foolish and empty-minded humans with finite lives, to question someone who has no beginning and no end, who is the first and the last, who is who He is, and nothing more or less? This may seem like a salvation call, but it's really just trying to point out that we are nothing if God isn't real. We would not exist if He did not want us to. We owe all the knowledge we have to Him. Nothing is ours, but it is God's. He just wants us to praise Him for it, and it that means some people become scientists and teachers to prove His creation was His, then so be it.

Creation vs. Evolution

By definition, creation is the act of creating. But, the Creation is the beginning of the universe as created by God the Father. By contrast, biological evolution is the theory of the beginning of life and the slow process of organisms becoming more complex. Two views so conflicting in interest, it was bound to strike up heavy controversy.

Creationists believe the universe was conjured up and created by God. He decided to create man in His own image.

Taking six days out of His busy schedule, God created everything our five senses can possibly take in. On day one; the heaven and the earth, the light and darkness (Gen 1:1-5). Day two involved the firmament and the waters (1:6-8). Day three, the land and all the plants (1:9-13). Four, God created all the celestial bodies: sun, moon and stars (1:14-19). Five brought about the first mobile life: fish and birds (1:20-23). The final day of Creation, day six, land animals were form, as well as man (1:24-27, 2:7, 21-22). Day seven He rested. We, as Christians, believe in Creation rather than evolution.

Evolutionists, on the other hand, believe more on the Darwinian prospects of life. By chance and time, man came into being.

Evolution itself is cut into three sub-headings:

Theory of Beginning – Although unclear in this book, and disproven, this is just the idea of the universe's creation. Not by anything Divine, just accidental. A 'mishap of gastric anomalies' if you will.

Theory of Biological Evolution – Sometimes called organic evolution, this theory deals with life on Earth. It proposes life from spontaneous generation – which was proven incorrect by science some time ago.

Philosophy of Evolution – Thought that all things are progressing toward a future perfection. This teaches things are improving.

The entire Australopithecus segment of humanity was proven to be merely several types of apes – one of which is extinct. Homo erectus is mostly made up of insufficient data, while the rest is a hoax. The only one that has ever existed is homo sapiens. All three – Rhodesian, Neanderthal, and Cro-Magnon – could have been three different races. Even in the same period of time. Not over millions of years, but maybe hundreds or tens.

- Perception Is Truth -

Although evolution, a scientific theory, is proved incorrect and basically a pointless and futile gesture, not to hear it from the pc-media, Creation has never been proved wrong.

Scientists have gone out to prove the Bible wrong, only to prove its correctness.

Enigma Of Time: Keeping Track Of A Riddle

Since we're on the topic of Back To The Future II, I may as well go through my theory on the flick. In the movie, Michael J. Fox and Christopher Lloyd venture to the future to change it. In this future, Fox buys a sports almanac for the past 50 years. But, Lloyd convinces him to trash it. Biff finds the almanac and realizes that Fox and Lloyd are from the past. He takes the almanac and the time machine, and then he ventures to the past and gives the almanac to his younger self to make himself rich.

He brings the time machine back and hides until Lloyd and Fox get the time machine back so they can return to the past. But the past has changed.

In Their Known Timeline (TKT), during the present, they traveled to the future. In the future TKT, Biff went back in the TKT to the past and alters the TKT, this creating A Tangent Timeline (ATT). Fox and Lloyd return to the present, but now it's the ATT. So now they have to put time back into place. Fox suggests returning to the future to prevent the time-switch, but Lloyd explains that they would be journeying to the ATT future. They have to travel to the past to prevent Biff from altering it.

I have my own theory. The reason they couldn't go to the future is because the DeLorean was only able to travel through one timeline. Even though we have two up above, it's still trapped within one timeline at a pop. They were in TKT future, then traveled to TKT past. They then went to what they thought to be TKT present, but time went tangent in the past, thus altering the present to ATT. Now, I think the time machine was still bound by time, even though it could travel through time, it was bound by one linear universe at a time. If Lloyd could've made the time machine to break itself down into tachyon energy and actually merge with time, become one with the time stream, then they could've actually gone to TKT future from ATT present.

Now, let me explain. Everything in the Old Testament through Acts had to happen for God to establish His promise with Man, and Christ's death, and the church's establishment. But after that, decisions and choices altered time, creating billions of other timelines. But, when the time comes, all the timelines become one to fulfill Revelation.

As far as Isaac Newton thought, time was absolute. In 1687, he declared that time "flows equably without relation to anything external." We now know, rather theorize, time is "tied to motion and space itself."

- Perception Is Truth -

Einstein blew our original ideas of time in 1905. In his theory of relativity, Einstein declared that the measure of time intervals are affected by the motion of the observer. Two years later, Herman Minkowski, a mathematician, proposed a new form of geometry, one that adds time to the three dimensional, four-coordinate system, and is referred to as space-time. The "geometry of time" is accepted as an efficient way to simplify Einstein's formulas.

Let us use an example given me. Ever been in a train and notice the one next to yours moving? Strange, isn't it? Which is moving, your train or the other one? You're not really sure until you see a third reference point. That's known as relative motion.

Similarly, time is relative. But, unlike normal relativity, there's no ultimate frame of reference. We don't notice the differences. The reason is that they are infinitesimally small. Time relativity is significant at great speeds, such as the speeds achieved in particle accelerators. PAs produce velocities near that of light. Physicists verify "special relativity" daily. Due to this factor, relativity of time is one of physics' most widely confirmed theories.

The idea seems simplistic enough, but consider the implications – flabbergasting, huh? This means – new example already given me – "that rapidly moving clocks tick more slowly than clocks at rest." Let us say you have a clock on a spaceship and the ship is traveling at 87% speed of light, such speeds are beyond our current technology. Know what? The space faring timepiece would tick only half as fast as a clock on Earth. We have tried similar experiments – atomic clocks sent into orbit – that have recorded smaller differences repeatedly.

Peculiar? Indeed! Princeton physicist John Wheeler – a "pioneer in quantum theory" – measures time by billionths of a second or billions of years, testing the edge of our understanding. Ever heard "receding into a black hole"? He coined that phrase for those "collapsing stars that crunch not only matter but the space around it, bringing time there to an end." "Time cannot be an ultimate category in the description of nature," he declares. "'Before' and 'after' don't rule everywhere."

Since we're on the subject of stars and black holes, let us continue. Last year we learned that the closest star's light – Alpha Centauri – takes four to four and a half years to reach Earth. And that's at light speed! Now, let's say it went supernova – you know

¡BOOM! – it would take four years for the event to be announced to us. But to the stars and other celestial bodies in between us would know sooner. And those past us would know after. So, you could say "time is relative to the observer," stating time is relative, changeable.

But here comes a curious question in and of itself. "Can time be reversed?" Well, the answer – simply put – is no.

A: The 2nd Law of Thermodynamics rules that out.

Isolated systems move from order to disorder.

B: We'd have to be God to do that!

We do not have the capability – in our timeline – to travel forward or backward through time. And even if we could – what would really be the point? Half the scientists who might produce time travel would probably alter time. But I'm sure that there are those out there – myself included – who would just observe. But, I don't think I could go pre-Ten Commandments era. Exodus 33:20, "'But,' he said, 'you cannot see my face, for no one may see my and live.'" And God was all over the place! Too great a risk.

Closing statement from John Wheeler: "We will first understand how simple the universe is when we recognize how strange it is."

Poetic Responses

"Death of the Day" Walter Savage Landor

This poem is simply two quatrains put together to make a rather decent poem, considering his opponents. Although this poem really has no "point", Landor does a good job of hiding that fact. His poem is about nightfall, and he refers to the night coming as the death of the day.

A fairly simplistic poem, but what is the theme? Much like Bryant's "To a Waterfowl," this poem is about something in nature. Yet, they both seem to tie in something spiritual with their failing topic. With Bryant, it was the "Power", and with Landor, it seems to be the mentioning of "Death". For Bryant, this would either be Providence, or God, while Landor focuses on Death, or Satan if you will.

Although most of the Romantic poems have no real "point", they do actually have some kind of underlying theme, although it is only prevalent in one line.

"Death Stands Above Me, Whispering Low" Walter Savage Landor

This is a most interesting poem. I really am not entirely sure what the whole point is, but one thing is for sure: he had a brush with death. If he was welcoming death or not, I do not know. I am aware he was discussing something with death, but there was no fear in the words Death spoke.

The connotations in this piece are somewhat elusive. It seems to me as though he was interested in the concept of death. The only reason I can give is his mentioning of the strange language of death, and it spoke nothing of fear. In my mind, that means Death and Fear are not one and the same, but two different concepts, that come at different periods, whether they are together or not, they are two separate entities.

"Dying Speech of an Old Philosopher" Walter Savage Landor

Mister Walter Landor has impressed me to no end! Although he is not one of the larger, more popular authors of this particular time period, he should not be overlooked.

A friend wants this poem scrawled on his epitaph. It is a man's outlook on life, and the promising contemplation thereof. In the first lines, it sounds he was discussing being single, or he had very few friends. Either way, it seems he was a solitary man. He ponders the two great loves of his life: Nature and Art. Unfortunately, life is nothing of importance, at least to him. Life really is nothing more than a flame, which stinks.

"England in 1819" Percy Bysshe Shelley

Probably the finest piece of political thrashing I have ever seen. Not only does Shelley acknowledge the state of England at the time, but he goes on to venture his own opinion. One of those rare poems that the author is the speaker, he certainly was not very patriotic toward the King, or his sons.

What is this about uniting Ireland to England in 1801? I can't say I blame Shelley for slamming the Act of Union, if that was what he was slamming. The referral to the King and the Princes "leechlike to their fainting country cling" reminds me of our own time, from a certain point of view. This country is fainting, falling apart, and our leaders are trying to hold onto it by sucking us dry. Republicans and Democrats alike are the "Rulers who neither see, nor feel, nor know."

I wonder if this could be sent to the Senate and not considered treason?

"Epitaph" Samuel Taylor Coleridge

The is an extraordinary poem considering the obvious lack of meaning in Romantic poetry. I know I have blasted the Romantics for not really being relevant, there are those poets, or just writings—poems or prose—that do have a meaning. This is one of them.

This is the poem I would like to have on my grave, obviously with the changing of Coleridge's initials. This is also a great tool for evangelizing, I think. If you happen to find a secular poet who likes this stuff, you can give him this poem. As he tries to discover some hidden, spiritual meaning, all he's going to come up with is that he found something to die for while alive, and to live for while dead. God willing, this poet will ask you what this man means, maybe just to see if you agree. The doors are opened!

Inquiry, was Coleridge a Christian, or just a deist?

"Eternity" William Blake

A very curious poem, with a seemingly clear theme, but I am still puzzled. He uses a bird to explain joy, and fairly well, I might add. But, where does he want the reader to take this picture?

Blake says, to a certain extent, eternity's sun rise is when you kiss joy as it flies. Is he referring to it flying over you, and then past you? Or is he referring to the joy of man as it flies, as it soars? The reason for my confusion: his first two lines. The opening of this piece tells of grabbing onto joy, and it destroys life. What is he trying to say? Better to have a short period of joy than a lifetime of joy? Or better to have a short period of joy than to focus on one thing to make you happy... idolatry?

What's the point?

"Lines on Ale" Edgar Allan Poe

I have tried to avoid this author for personal reasons, but I feel I am prepared to touch upon his eccentric, yet exceptionally poetic and inspiring poetry. I have heard him dubbed as "evil", but I consider him "a man after Death." Still, it is pieces such as this that I love; those that bewilder. I do enjoy his many stories of terror, suspense, death, but this poem has nothing to do with anything most people would relate to Poe.

This poem, all about his estranged fascination with liqueur, is a sort of light-hearted look at the peculiar substance. I can picture him at a seat in his den, much like the paintings of "The Raven" in the green anthologies. He sits with a glass of ale in his hand, between thumb and forefinger. As he stares at the glass, he slowly turns it from side to side, studying the many facets of alcohol. He finds his pen, and a pad of paper, and smiles. He dips the pen into the ink bottle, and the words flow from his drunken stupor of a mental state.

I find it truly intriguing the ways people can get inspired. I have many completely opposite ways of getting inspired, and yet it happens, as of late quite frequently. This is one of those rare glimpses into the heart of a poet. Albeit smashed, it's still a piece worth sharing with those cynics of Poe.

"The Bells" Edgar Allan Poe

I would laugh, but I guess this is supposed to be some sort of classical poem? Now, I know many people seem to make mistakes, but to have one considered one of the finest works of American Lit? What luck this guy had... Actually, it's not a bad piece, it just worries me that a poem lasting for so long could be about something so insignificant, and be hailed as great work. Still, I have some poems people find quite good, but I don't think they're all that swell.

Anyway, this is one of those poems without a point, as far as I'm concerned. I have not bothered to read it a second time, but I probably should. It could be put to an intriguing beat of a drum, and read by someone with a monotone voice, or something like that. It would have gone over great in the seventies, but today it would probably get you arrested or shot. Either way, it is just one of those works you need and acquired taste for. Kind of like drinking coffee, or something.

Well, that was a lot of mindless babble just to say that you should probably not show this to a Poe cynic.

"The Destruction of Sennacherib" George Gordon, Lord Byron

II Kings 19:35-37 was the inspiration for this brilliant piece of biblical interpretation. I have not located many of these kinds of pieces, but this is one that is truly a "poem". Unlike many of the other writers of this time period, Byron captures the meaning of having a point in a poem.

This poem tells the story of Sennacherib, the king of Assyria. He had attacked Jerusalem with his army, until the time came when the angel of the Lord struck eighty five thousand of his men dead. He withdrew to Nineveh after this occurrence. While worshipping his god, Sennacherib's two sons killed him.

The poem tells you this story, in a rather round about way, but you get the idea God did not want this man to live anymore. He had gone against God's children, and he was going to pay for it. The final lines depict the theme of the poem as far as I am concerned.

"And the might of the Gentile (Sennacherib), unsmote by the sword,

Hath melted like snow in the glance of the Lord!"

"To——" Percy Bysshe Shelley

A touching piece of work, or is it just interesting? I have difficulty deciphering the meaning of this work, but I enjoyed it nonetheless. A piece about love lost or something to that affect, I felt as though I could relate to it. The title is either a "fill in the blank" title, or it is just to remain anonymous who it is he is speaking of.

Pictures of death fill this work, as Shelley captures the spirit of a broken heart. "Music, when soft voices die… Odors, when sweet violets sicken… Rose leaves, when the rose is dead… Love itself shall slumber on". All great visions of something wonderful that has died. Music, violets, and love, seemingly alive and spirited objects, all die "when thou art gone".

A great work that even Petrarch would have been proud of.

"To A Waterfowl" William Cullen Bryant

It seems to me as though this time period was basically about nothing in particular. If forced to compare this poem to the ways of life at the time, if this was a correct portrayal of everyone's thoughts and feelings, I would be tempted to agree with a friend that this time period was all about "fluff".

There was really no point to this poem, and I would rather refer to it as a mindless babble. I have poems like this that I have not let a whole lot of people see, merely because there is no point, they are just my thoughts about a subject. Provided, I may find them somewhat important, stressing "somewhere", but for most others they would be considered "fluff".

The idea of someone writing a poem to a duck is sort of reminiscent to a tree hugger's anthem. Kind of a new-age, Greenpeace, EPA sort of writing. The only thing to negate this notion is the mentioning of "a Power". Although he gives no direct reference to God, he does consider Providence to be at least somewhat involved with this bird's flights, as well as his own.

Other than that instance, there is really no use for this "poetry". In my opinion, of course.

Remarks On Marshall

McLuhan's statement was not absolute. The medium is not always the message. In fact, the medium should not be the message. It's the message that should be the medium, it should define the means by which it's sent. Whether on a computer screen dulling your senses to its colorful and unrealistic quality. Or if it's a crumpled napkin with chicken scratch scrawled on its rough surface. The key to all messages is the message, not how it's sent. It's important that it's viewed; by the masses or the common man or even your neighbor's dog! It's important that it's viewed, and only nominally important how it's viewed. To get a statement seen or heard, you have to make it happen. How many writers have the best computer on the market, yet their passion is still to use a typewriter? How many poets find their joy in simple paper and ink? For some, writing is treated the way Vince Lombardi spoke of winning. Writing should not be a sometime thing, but an all the time thing. The messages that are written and published are the ones the masses cry out for. What about those spoken and never published? What about the thoughts of these people that are never written out? Are these thoughts any less important? Just because they may never reach us, is that important? Why the hell should it matter if "we" the consumer see it? Are we so bent on clinging to those already famous that we have lost our ambition to be ourselves? Have we become so dependent on our own entertainment, but most find it in and through the lives of others? Why can't we remember we know what makes us laugh better than any comedian? How fucking hard can it be to remember what made us love somebody we never expected? Have we lost our own sense of being? Of self? Of God? Are we, as Americans, simply fascist-communists without a willing leader? Do we simply refuse to express our society's true feelings because it would look treasonous? Why can't we be real any fucking more? There are so few people who allow themselves to be real with the outside world. Their closest friends. Themselves, for Pete's sake/ Shout! Laugh. Get angry if that's what you feel. Stop wasting time on appearances. Live your life honestly and openly. Don't let something as basic as fear get you to deny yourself of your greatest asset. Don't allow anyone to tear you down because of who you are inside. Who you are defines you, not somebody else. Don't let your friends tell you how to live your life. When you're finally free from the parents who birthed you and raised you, don't let them tell you how to live. Respect their advice as learned experience, but the decision relies solely in your hands. Love God with all your heart, but you find Him. You can't live on your parent's faith, nor can you blindly accept everything taught you. God is real and He loves His creation. Don't deny God the opportunity to love you because of your own stupid pride. Don't let your own hardships dictate your present setbacks. Don't allow your past mistakes or forced upon situations hold you back. Live your life! Work, don't work, it doesn't matter. Respect the laws of the land, but don't allow yourself to fear them. Be happy, be sad, be quiet, be mad. If you can

Middle Ages

12 Dec 2002
This, being my first entry into my all-new website, should include something warm and witty about my life and where I am headed. It should be something akin to a thesis for college, or a mission statement for Corporate America. The intention of this section(s) is for me to get things out of my system that I wouldn't otherwise write down. I love to pen my own works; I love the paper, the imperfections of the pen strokes, the way the ink bleeds through the sheets. I love the experience of actually creating something almost from scratch. Seeing the way I scratch out words and overwrite them, the way my writing is slower than my thought and how my misspellings mean bolder and larger letters to take their place. It means the simplicity of thought given in its simplest form; the form not intended to be carried out in, but the form it has become most popular.

The typed word that you see before you is nothing more than binary code-splitting pixels across a screen made of cathode ray technology or some form of liquidated electronic display. It is not the form that has been carried down generation-to-generation, the form by which our books are written by and give us the knowledge needed to "conquer the world". The education of entire races depended greatly on their ability to read. The way industry and technology has achieved so much is through the written works of others that have come so many times before them to conquer what is in their time "unthinkable". The great religions of the world are based upon one simple precept: a book. Without these books; the Bible, the Torah, the Koran, the Talmud, etcetera ad infinitum, we would not have had the vast written histories that we do. An entire race's existence is generally based upon a book, but a similar book can also be blamed the deception of the world for several hundred years. However, in the latter instance, it was due to a lack of literacy in the common peoples.

- Perception Is Truth -

The ability to read, to take that which is written or typed or printed, is one of the greatest powers this world will ever know. It seems so genuinely foolish to think about, but when you look back and consider how few people knew how to read in how many cultures, it becomes no surprise to me where many of these people have ventured off to. I have watched for many years, as people within America, supposedly the most literate and well-educated and powerful country on the planet, are not made to read. I know people who have graduated high school with a 4th grade reading level. However, they know how to get past the system, to make it appear like they can do everything else, and they are set forward on a path to doom. They can do basic math and some comprehension of facts, which means they have a decent enough "grade" to move on. For what end, I always wonder? I would imagine it would be to their end.

The inability to read is more than just the ability to speak out loud the sounds a word should make when you convert from visual to audio communication. Reading is about knowing what the words really "say" and what they mean and how they feel when they come off your tongue. When you are not able to read, you suffer through the usual torment from others about how stupid you are, mostly from peers and I'm certain from teachers during their meetings. Some of them genuinely feel bad, but there are always the ones who have burned out and teach because they don't know how to do anything else. Not only do you suffer personal degradation from your intellectual state, but there's also furthering yourself. You'll not get very far if you are unable to read. Sure, a good construction job; it pays the bills, makes you fit, makes you fit the mold of what a "guy" should be. Or, in the case of the stereotypical female without an education; the pregnant home maker. I bet ladies all over wake up daily and strive to be the wife to a drunken construction worker who can't spell his own name half the time, raising little clones of just such an attitude. And I actually do know guys who wake up wanting to be nothing more than a steel worker, making good money, working with their hands.

Forgive me if I've come down harsh on the construction field; it is not my intent. Without construction, there would be no factory to build the computer that I type on right now, in the house that I so welcome when I leave my work for the day. All I am referring to is the stereotypical personage that is uneducated and cares little about it. They are content with their ignorance, and like nothing better than to be left alone with much of the world's problems.

That, in my opinion, is an example of your "good American". Most of America, it seems to me, cares more about what kind of clothes they wear than about the people they work with, the people they grew up with, the people they live with and share their everything with. We have become a selfish people, and I am not blameless in this respect. I, too, have fallen prey to the "almighty dollar". Most of it is out of simple need for the silly paper product that is almost as malleable as single-ply industrial toilet paper. Some of it is out of a desire to use the paper product to purchase, and allow me to bring to my home, things for which I have little need for, but am told I need quite repeatedly.

America is not about free enterprise; it is about capitalism and consumer spending. Without these two buzz words, we would be more of a socialistic state. Hell, if the person(s) we voted into power had any say, we'd be under the thumb of the rich and ruling class(es) anyway. But, that's all my opinion. However, being in America is not without its merits, do not misunderstand me. Without the freedoms this place allows me, I would not even have this forum with which to speak my views. Chances are I would have had no choice on my vocation. Chances are, I'd still be wearing glasses, but they'd be much worse than the ones I have, and I would not be able to get new ones.

For as much posturing and complaining I may do, much of it is not without merit. But, much of it seems over dramatic and somewhat silly; for that, I shall apologize right now. However, if you have read this far, clearly something has kept your interests, and you are already a part of a (hopefully) growing constituency or people I like to call my readers.

14 Dec 2002

I would like to start my entry by stating it is almost 1am, and I am feeling most tired. Forgive me, o faithful readers (should there be any), for any mishaps, missteps, or misspellings that you may have to endure. I do not do such things intentionally, although I have been known to use a cliché in mixed company without the forethought, or afterthought, of an explanation for such usage. Perhaps you will see them here.

In my effort to attain my writing abilities back, I will attempt to make this particular part of my life as daily an exercise as is physically and/or emotionally possible. I suppose there's a certain sense of inspiration involved as well, but I feel that should I continue to write what I think and feel in a given day, then my inspiration will be awakening from slumber. I will be "awakening my creative juices" during these times, so I ask those who bother to visit and peruse and observe, to please… bear with me.

So, the thing that has been on my mind the most, as of late, is work. My work keeps me quite busy, both mentally and locationally (I know it's not a word). Traveling between three states for the purpose of furthering 1,000+ employees' ability to do the work set before them can be a huge pain in my buttocks. However, it also gives me a chance to meet new people, or see people that, it would seem only I and the few others in my department even know. It gives me a chance to really understand them and get to know them; it allows me to understand if they are truly challenged in their thinking, or if it is perhaps I who is unable to communicate with them properly. It's a chance to get away from the "office" and all its current triteness. Of course, the impending immensity of intense vocational interventions will shift the cumbersome daily chores to that of fantasy once again. Alas, I shan't get into detail about my vocation, for that will spoil the surprise(s).

I have, however, determined some fairly disturbing pieces of information. Such information in my possession is a poor place for it, but it has challenged me to do something I never thought I would do: talk to my boss about my financial status. I have worked with my current supervisor for two years at this job, and for almost a year at a previous employer; we worked in separate places for approximately 6 months in between. I feel that I can share with him my ideas and my concerns without fear of backlash or feelings that I have insulted or otherwise injured the friendship we have developed in that time. It seems topical to most, since we mostly discuss work, but we have talked about other things, and have been involved with each other's personal life. But, all at a limited degree, and those days are more or less over, or at the least few and far between.

Of course, everyone complains about the pay where they work; it's part of being American. However, it came to my attention what a previous employee was making working within our department. Rather, he was present in our department, but worked under a different supervisor, and therefore lived by different rules. That is part of the reason he is a "previous" employee. I have learned that the employee in question was making over 10% more than I, and he was doing less work. Also the position in question was entry-level, while I had to work many moons to achieve my pay scale. It is not necessarily that HE was making so much more (although that is an issue), I am more concerned about the implications. Does it mean that they look at the person more than the position? Or does the position determine how much the person makes? For, if it is the latter, I may have to sign up for less of a job, if only for more pay. If it is the former, I will have to lodge a complaint with my supervisor.

If it comes down to the amount of time worked, then I should be the second-highest paid person in the department. My commitment to my work and to that whole establishment is something of legend. Not being a revenue-generating department, however, we get overlooked by management as to our degree of importance. That would also seem indicative of my pay. I also think it is fascinating that I do most of the traveling, along with another fellow who makes even less than I, and works almost as long.

It is unfair to the workers of such tenacity. I find it somewhat insulting to myself and to my other(s). There is no reason for such treatment. Especially when there is someone else in the office that has been there over 5 years, and makes much more than I do. However, his usefulness is, as far as I am concerned, coming to a quick plateau. Soon, he will not have anything to do, for his abilities to fix problems that he creates on his own for himself is, sadly, next to nil. He spent most of today, for example, attempting a seemingly simple task, to no avail. When asked if he had followed the directions available to him, he said no. Not locating said instructions and following them properly wasted his day. This is not a first offense. There are others, but there is little need to exact my typed vengeance on all of them.

    I feel that if work indicates pay scale, than I am due for a raise. If it does not, than perhaps I really am due a change of venue. One can only wonder. One can only hope that whatever decision my supervisor is forced to make, it will be good for me. I realize that this may sound selfish, but I have not been truly, or perhaps properly, selfish for a long time. I learned differently growing up; that it was always about someone else, never me. Well, things are due for a change. Not out of greed, but out of self-respect and pride. My abilities at my work and my commitment to both my supervisor and my work are exemplary, and all I am asking for is some monetary appreciation. I do not feel that is too much to request. Do you?

22 Dec 2002

Well, I missed an old friend's birthday today...

Something has overcome me, yet again, and still I know not how to describe it. I really don't know if I even understand the strange emotional states I happen upon while in that state, but rest assured something's different about me. It overcame me suddenly, and I couldn't sit in the house anymore. My girl and I drove around, looking at Christmas lights. It wasn't for very long, but it was enough for me to get outside for a while.

I've been feeling like I've lost a part of me for some time now. It grew hard for me for a long time to come up with any creative thought beyond what I was going to tell the user over the phone. In what creative way could I tell a user why they can't login? "Umm," I would fumble, searching my mind for every possible conclusion, "You're spelling your user name wrong. Try your last name. All lowercase. There you go." Instead of just saying, "Well, do you know your own damn name? If not, call HR, don't call Me." *CLICK* would be sure to follow.

I live my life as if work was all of it. I do other things; I run a Star Wars RPG campaign for my brother and one other friend. I can't handle more than that, because I'm so interested in proper detail and making them feel a part of that world... Too many people and I get lost. I have my girlfriend, whom I care about deeply, and I honestly and truly love her. However, it seems at times she detracts from my ability to just let myself go. Her desire to spend every chance with me she gets, while very sweet, is very limiting for me.

The only real time I get to myself is the time I use to write in this journal; which I hope to do more often, but we shall see, my humble reader. I only wish I had more time to do more of the things I wish I could do: read, write, think. My job, while fascinating in its implications and job functions, is something of monotony. I'm overly capable to do most of the work given me. Don't misunderstand me, I am challenged, but not in the way that I had hoped to be using my mind. I wanted to write, which I do now, but I wanted to really write.

Write.

I don't think I could have placed any more emphasis on that. Write poetry like I used to. At one time, I could rattle off poetry just because I wanted to, not because I was inspired. Of course, if I didn't have a scribe or a tape recorder, the true nature of my would-be texts was lost forever, and I would be forced to create an abridged version. All the while hoping that the damn thing would have the same impact; very rarely did that work.

I find that tonight my biggest issue is that I am restless. I feel like I can barely function, like I'm all wound up inside. And out. I just want to shake till it all goes away; I want that feeling of emptiness to leave me like so much wind. I want it to vanish in the same fashion that it came, a feeling. I want that feeling of urgency to flood from my soul and let me be. Or, I want it to reveal itself in my heart and in my mind, and let me deal with it in the way that I know I must. But, I can't deal with it until I know what it is that is wanted of me.

It's very trying for me to think clearly. I am staggering to listen to new music, whilst pouring out my soul to this imitation notebook. I was once able to create lyric at the drop of a rock, stating some witty little quip relating to how "a stone's trickle during its fall is silenced by the trickling of the falls". Something about how the sound of the water lapping over the rocks is soothing, while the lapping of a dog's tongue can be a scary concept.

I also am realizing that much of what I say sounds as though it comes from an amateur; an amateur of thought, mostly. But, then again, I've always felt that my more "poetic" works were never quite up to snuff. I just wanted to be able to respect myself in my work(s), but even now I'm not certain if I can do that. The other thing I want is for others to respect my work, but I'm so concerned about actual publication. I like the Internet, there's a certain level of security in "publishing" my works here, and it's cheaper. It spreads my words faster, but I don't know where they end up, if they go anywhere beyond the four-ish walls of my home.

I read a quote recently (about 10 minutes ago, in fact), from one of my favorite band's websites. They collect quotes and other sundries that amuse and boggle my mind. One such quote is from a musician named Joy Williams, who I have heard of, but am not familiar with. "A writer loves the dark, loves it, but is always fumbling around in the light." A simple quote, but can be approached on many different levels.

Being a writer at heart, I do love the darkness. I've come a long way in recent months to adapting to actual darkness, but I feel that's not exactly what she meant. I imagine she had some deep, spiritual meaning. But, there's a certain truth to that in a physical aspect.

In darkness, one can focus on what they are almost able to see. In absolute darkness, you can only focus on what your other senses allow you to. If you want, however, you can focus on nothing but the insides of your mind whilst in the darkness. Darkness in your soul, in your very spirit, can create a cloud of confusion that you can't even see through it enough to recognize its presence. When your mind is clouded, it can prove to be a wall, and you don't realize you can just walk through it.

A wall needs to be broken, but a cloud needs to be passed through. The hard part is telling the difference, because they both yield the same result in following your path; obstruction.

23 Dec 2002

Well, the Christmas shopping is complete and the wrapping is finally done. Actually, my shopping was complete last week, but I was awaiting gifts to arrive. Which, I am still waiting for one more gift, but they are not expecting anything, so it being late will not be a problem.

You know, up until recently, I was being rather a humbug about this absurd holiday. You see, it seems to me that a holiday that supposedly celebrates the birth of a religion should be celebrated every day. In the heart of the Christian, Christmas should be celebrated every day. The concept that only once a year we should show help to our fellow man; that somehow the coldest part of the American year is the only time people need help. Understood, I am not much better than my fellow man, but I do see the hypocrisy in such a statement.

Merry Christmas is exactly that: the one time of the year where people should be happy. Well, if consumer markets have anything to say about it. And yet, this is also the busiest shopping time of the year. A time of year when we are all focused on buying, shopping, and consuming. This is the fattest time of the year for many people. Diets are off, as it's "the holidays". The inexorable excuse is that suddenly it's okay to eat like a glutton. It's fine if I gain 5 or 30 lbs, it's "the holidays". Well, I don't know about you, but I think that even at Christmas time a heart attack can arrive.

Hmm... I seem to be rambling again, with no clear distinction as to my point. Well, basically, I'm trying to put together a nice Christmas CD for the long haul I have to complete during the snowstorm on Christmas Day '02. So, please forgive me if I seem distracted, my humble reader.

What it comes down to is that I really have disliked this holiday somewhat intensely for some time. It's taken me a little bit to really appreciate how irritated it makes me, and even longer to really see why it is I get so upset about it. Mostly, it's due to a family dynamic that I've struggled with for so long: a whole family. See, unlike the perfect ideal of what Christmas time should be I get to deal with a whole host of problems: relatives who don't talk to each other, never having met half my cousins, and a dysfunctional immediate family. Those three factors have made for a cynical attitude towards this, the most sacred, holiday.

- Middle Ages -

Now, I admit that most of my silly existence is lost to my memory, mostly out of my own desire to have it that way. But, that doesn't mean I shouldn't have a healthy, happy remembrance of the happiest day of the year, right? Well, I don't remember many happy Christmas days for me, at least not in the accurate sense. Sure, I got cool toys, or I got very little. The one thing that I didn't get and I soon realized that I would never have, is a whole family. Not that I do now, at least not exactly, but there's a whole different list of psychoses that will have to wait until some other holiday.

But, with things seemingly better for me, at least in the way of the woman that I love, this holiday season hasn't been so bad. Sure, I've been as grouchy and standoffish about this day as ever, but it isn't so bad. I got my shopping done early. Of course, I don't feel it's nearly enough, but I make dirt (as mentioned above). I am getting a decent amount of gifts, which I suppose doesn't mean all that much. When they're wrapped, it's about the quantity, when they're open; it's about the quality.

27 Dec 2002

So, Christmas Day is over, but Christmas itself is not. At least, it is not for me. My girlfriend and I are going to traipse about somewhere in Maine at her recently rich cousin's house. It will be an event with her family members for whom I know the least, and will probably see the least. As far as they are concerned, at least to my mind, I am just another boyfriend; hardly worth a second mention. I'm quiet when I am around them, for they are much older than I, and I get the impression that someone younger than them is of little interest. I, as always, am "too young to understand" the challenges of adulthood or some such nonsense.

I will admit that I have not lived the same life as many of them, nor do I have any children, as many of them do. However, that doesn't mean I have not observed hardships in my own experiences, and in the experiences of my parents and friends and friends of friends. There is enough hurt in this world to pass around to every single person. There usually aren't enough people to recognize it, to be able to help people through it, to be able to express it in ways that others cannot. It is a truth of this world that pain is real.

I actually received more gifts than I gave, which while not impressive on my end, says a lot about the family I will potentially become a part of. I received clothes, toys, winter clothes, and movies… I got my hands on lots of material possessions that I liked or needed. All in all, I made out like a bandit. For a long time, and still to an extent even today, I've found Christmas to be a hoax and a lame joke perpetuated by the commercialism of America or any system evolved around Free Enterprise. I understand the true meaning of Christmas, its origins and Hallmark Greeting Card incarnations. I get Norman Rockwell and Bing Crosby. I get the Toys for Tots and the Soup Kitchens all over America. What I find the most fascinating about all of it is that this really IS the one time of the year when people truly give. And yet, without this holiday, I wonder how selfish we all would really be.

We've been taught since children to respect Christmas and what it can do for everyone. The Spirit of Christmas is supposed to last all year, but we as people really don't care about any of that. All we really care about is our own stuff and what junk can we get. It all comes down to the ME. Now, I realize I'm not speaking for everyone at

Christmas time, but look around you.

I did all my shopping online because I had worked retail one Christmas, and I'll never do it again if I can at all help it. I'll also avoid the malls like a plague until sometime in January. Which, I have to say, avoiding the mall or any other large store from Mid-November till Mid-January isn't all bad. It made my shopping experience peaceful where others found it difficult. I wasn't party to, nor was I a part of, pushing people aside when the last video game console was shown to the panting populace. I was sitting comfortably in my boxers and robe, hoping the site would just accept my bankcard as a real credit card. Some of them did, others required information that my bank did not supply me with. A little improvisation later, and I was calling someone with an actual credit card, and then giving them the cash that same day.

While I am still waiting for a couple of gifts, thankfully they are for someone who doesn't even know they are getting any.

Still, I don't know how I really feel about this holiday. I'm too cynical to just enjoy it for what it is; an excuse to give/get gifts. The trading of presents is a cherished event, mostly because we're a selfish society. We like to get things, and only give them because we feel we must. For the precious (not few, per se), giving is actually an exercise in happiness. But, they are precious, after all.

Sleep overtakes me, and I must bid my humble readers adieu. I wonder how many, and what type, of readers could have stumbled upon me at this point anyway. Hmm. Do I have a fan base? Much like the Tootsie Roll Pop… "The World May Never Know".

31 Jan 2003

Well, I'm not certain if I have been insulted recently, or merely observed. I was told that a friend of mine said I was "anti-everything".

Now, provided, I understand that my idea of fun is different from most. I don't smoke, drink, dance, or anything that is necessarily the norm for my age bracket. I'm a much more pensive person than I suppose I need to be, but I find it to be soothing and relaxing. It can be amazingly stressful and I find that I lost much sleep due to my overactive mind. However, I enjoy it immensely.

And yet, it got me thinking about myself and about the way I act around other people. About the way I think and feel. About how when it comes right down to it, I don't even know if I like myself, if I like others, or if I like much of anything. There's a careful bit of selfishness in the way I am, but it's not unheard of or even unnecessary. We all think about making ourselves happy. But, I wonder day after day what really makes me happy.

Is it my girlfriend? She does do a fine job of making me smile and making really think that love and beauty and happiness are not far away; that they are really attainable goals, but I linger. My mind and my heart wonder and wander to them self. Am I doing the right thing? Do I really want to do this to myself; to her? Is she, is THIS what I want to be when I grow up?

Is it my work? Provided, my work does challenge me every moment of my day, and it can be very rewarding. However, I find that the stresses it causes me can be unbearable sometimes. I yearn for a time when I truly feel appreciated for my work through the monetary means we all venture to attain. But, at my current place of employment, I find that it could be impossible to reach such a lofty ideal.

Is it my friends? Since I've started to see my girlfriend and get serious about other things in my life, such as furthering my mind and my personal work(s), I find that I do not see them as often as any of us would like. Attempts have been made, rather fruitlessly I'm afraid, to get me involved with them and to do things with them the way we used to. We had a lot of fun, I laughed a lot. We spent time together, and I felt like I really belonged. In some ways, I was the ringleader, someone they all looked to. But, I realized we all looked to each other, because we needed each other's company to really persevere through life. I know I've been a bad friend, downright selfish. I don't return phone calls; I don't hang out with them when they ask me. Hell, one of them could die and I probably wouldn't know it for months. I realize that is a drastic way to look at it, but it is true. If they do not leave me a message, I literally do not know what's going on.

Is it my writing or other hobbies? They do relieve much of the stress for which I feel from day to day, but I think that my writing is possibly the best thing for me. The music is definitely up there also, but it's still a close second to the release I feel from writing. True, I'm sure most of what is here is unfit for actual publishing and sale, but I don't care about the almighty dollar when it comes to my words. All I care about is getting them out there. See, with work it's different, because it's work. With writing, it's a fun time for me when I get to really be alone with my thoughts, and I can observe them and laugh at them or scoff at them. I choose very infrequently to edit my work, but that is a matter of laziness more than anything else.

I suppose I do not know what truly makes me happy. I think it is a combination of all these things. Talking to my friends can be, for the most part, a joy that I yearn for every moment of every day. Work is a reward all by itself, when the financial constraints of my life are stripped from the arithmetic. My writing is definitely something that gives me pleasure every moment I do it. Except, of course, when I have to critique and edit and rewrite. Then, there is my girlfriend, a woman of great beauty and love I cannot imagine a life without her. To look into her eyes is to see a calming sea, but one so blue and full of life you have to swim in it. Not just once, but for an eternity.

Causality

Every decision we make, every choice we have, every thought in the expanse of our minds, has a consequence. Everything that has an effect begins with a cause. Everything that is a cause will have an effect. The key to understanding this is not very hard; just open your eyes. Opening your eyes is a choice that you make, and the consequence is, for most, vision. It's a matter of light reflecting off the surface of objects, giving them appearance, color, and the illusion of density. On the other hand, one may open their eyes at the wrong time, and see things that they would not like to see: someone being killed, a scary moment in a movie or the love of your life lifting slowly the suitcase with their meager belongings and walking out the door that had once been home. Never let yourself be fooled into thinking that a decision you make will not have a consequence. But, take heart, and have hope that the choice you make will be the one that you want to see, the one that brings a smile to your face, or a tear of joy to the eyes of someone, anyone. Be mindful, however, that our decisions, our choices, our causes, should be made with a careful balance of emotion and reason. Without thought, a decision will often be incorrect in its outcome. Likewise, if you make a decision without considering the emotional impact, it may damn you in ways both physical and emotional.

Some decisions are simple, and are made with nary a second thought. Waking up, for example, is a decision that comes naturally. In all honesty, there seems that there really is no choice in terms of waking up. Often, it is because of some noise, such as an alarm clock, and its effect is waking us up from a dream. Yet, the decision to actually get out of bed and go about our day can be very hard for many people, and for many different reasons. Some have no hope of having a good day; many expect it to be a terrible and bleak passing of the sun. Others are physically incapable of rising from their bed, but in their hearts and their minds they might wish for nothing more. Others still may decide not to rise because they would rather not go into the office with their ties and their societal constraints; they would rather stay at home where they can be themselves and not be punished for it.

There are, of course, those decisions that we make out of necessity, like going to the bathroom. If you feel the urge from within to relieve yourself of that which your body has determined it cannot use for nutritional value, we all know from a lifetime of experience that if we do not listen to the nagging of these muscles we will make a terrible mess of ourselves. Provided, some cannot control such actions, but they may not wish anything other than some physical control over such functions.

Another choice made out of necessity is work. This choice is made for a variety of reasons, but many people simply do not like to work. It isn't the typical "I hate my job" mantra, but something deeper, something that goes beyond the scope of disliking ties or thinking cornflower blue is a terrible name for a color. It delves into the very soul of the person, who would wish for nothing more than to sit on a boat, casting their lines into the lake that may or may not have fish worth catching. The effect of not working, however, is not being able to afford the materials and the tools necessary to make the primary dream a reality.

Furthering the concept of work, the types of jobs that people do is often based on necessity. Many people have the given skill set for a variety of different job opportunities, but they may not have the "paper" to back that up. Someone may have a vast amount of skills and knowledge in the technical market, with prior experience and good references. Often, good workers are overlooked for those who have had an education, who have paperwork that suggests they have been taught the proper way to do things.

When I was in high school, I had a friend who insisted that I would have to go to college in order to get a good job. At the time, the computer market was beginning its upward climb, the "Dot Coms" were making it big down on Wall Street, and technical jobs were plentiful. I told him he was mistaken, and I made it my purpose not to enter college. The effect of my decision, my choice, my cause, was that I would be overlooked at many better paying jobs because I did not have the degree they would have preferred me to have. I was able, however, to get into a decent job, with a vast amount of knowledge poured into me on a daily basis. I realized that my decision not to acquire a degree would hurt me when it came to getting a decent raise, or finding work that would pay me for the skills I have developed. I did not realize at the time of my decision what would happen, and indeed I had hoped to be making more money than I am now: cause and effect.

There are, naturally, those decisions that no one wants to make. These are the choices that we leave to people who are more important than we are, or whom we have chosen to be our leaders. There are decisions that must be made for the "greater good", often at the sacrifice of others. War is the perfect example of this. War is a choice that few would make, but it can be necessary in order to solve an issue, or sometimes it is used just to prove a point. It is generally agreed upon by people that war is the last choice someone should have to make, especially since the consequences of such an action could lead to a further unforeseen catastrophe.

Every decision, every choice, every cause that we make has an effect, but it doesn't stop there. Every effect then becomes a cause for some other effect. You're hungry; you eat. You're tired; you sleep. But, it doesn't stop there. The consequence or effect of your eating means you get full, so you stop eating. The effect of your sleeping generally means you dream. Dreaming is one of those curious activities that may or may not be directly connected to your waking up. If you're having a bad dream, often you will be woken up by a particular image, or moment or the culmination of whatever nightmare has overtaken your sleep. On the flip side, if you're having a dream you l like, you will often not desire to wake from it. That's where the alarm clock comes in. The effect of your setting the alarm clock means you are disturbed in your sleep, and you are awakened; cause and effect.

Our decisions, therefore, are not cyclical, but connected, or interwoven. Cyclical denotes repetition, or a repeating pattern. But, we make different choices every day, every hour, every minute. Certainly, it's possible that much of your decisions are based upon a time frame: you sleep at a certain time, you work at a certain time, or you eat at a certain time. However, these are decisions you yourself make, indicating that it's your own choice whether to eat at the same time. While it may appear to repeat, it truly is your own decision whether or not you want to stick to that schedule. This may be affected by other situations in your daily routine that may alter what normally occurs on a given day.

Many of the choices we make cannot be felt by ourselves, but are connected to the choices that someone else must make. Simplest example is shopping for food, or clothes, or almost any other type of ware. We're aware that other people have to make these items, and other people have to distribute them in various transports. But, we don't realize that the decision to purchase such things really do keep other people working and making their own decisions. Our choice to buy things from a store where someone has run a machine that puts together the item, that choice allows someone to make the decision as to what food to buy, what clothes to purchase, and where their family should live. We're all connected in that fashion.

Our causes have an effect on everyone around us, not just ourselves. But, the decisions that other people make affect us, too. We may not realize it, but it works in the same way. Without someone else making a decision to utilize the services that your place of employment offers; you might not be working. Therefore, you might not be in school. But, your folks might be paying for your education, and they are affected in the same way. Without someone using their employer's services, there could be no job, and no money for school.

The world around us, the way we grew up, what we learned in school, how we work, who we spend time with, who we date, or who we marry, all these things and more effect the decisions we make. They alter the reasons why we make certain choices, and those choices affect future choices we make. What we eat as a child determines much of what we like as an adult. Some things change, but the basics are still there. Some people do indeed change their tastes or their attitudes, but many seem to cling to that which is comfortable, those choices that are easy for them to make because they've been making similar choices all their lives. Choices are sometimes easy, sometimes hard, and sometimes impossible. But, every choice must be made. Even indifference is a choice.

Edgar's Esoteric Explication

Poe turned vernacular into colloquialism, but he was not limited to the verbiage of his own language in constructing his tales. As a youth, Poe was orphaned but his adopted father brought him to England where Edgar "showed his proclivity for languages" (Clute 769). This he would use in such famous tales as "The Cask of Amontillado" and "Berenice", but he would not limit himself to just the addition of other languages. Poe would also dissect the English language, his native tongue, and create words that have since become something of esotericism. Works such as "The Tell-Tale Heart" and others already mentioned would contain word usage that we of today allow only to literature and "the saintly days of yore" (Gmoser, "Raven").

Poe, "one of the most important figures in the development of the US short story" (Clute 769), had a driving force behind his work, a "unity of effect" (Charters 907), which would cause his works to contain no forced phrase, no unnecessary syllable, no term that did not serve some greater purpose in the whole of the piece. Poe believed "that this unity [of effect] cannot be thoroughly preserved in productions whose perusal cannot be completed at one sitting" (Charters 907). Though, in truth, Poe was referring to "the limit of a single sitting... can never properly be overpassed in a poem" (Gmoser, "Philosophy"), he still believes that "with deliberate care, a certain unique or single *effect* to be wrought out, ['a skillful literary artist'] then... combines such events as may best aid him in establishing this preconceived effort" (Charters 909); this leans, of course, to a longer piece like a short story. Poe also didn't want there to be any "external or extrinsic influences" (Charters 908) to deter a reader from becoming entrenched in this effect. This would be Poe's philosophy in all his writings, and an indication as to why poetry would be "his first love" (Clute 770).

Poe used words like "immolation", "imposture", and "absconded" (Charters 700 - 701) in "The Cask of Amontillado"; words which gave specific meaning and clarity to the sentences, paragraphs and pages they existed. "Gesticulation" and "ejaculated" (Charters 702 – 703) are also terms that Poe used in to give the reader a clearer sense of action. Poe seemingly created words in "Berenice" like "monomaniac" (Gmoser), but they were merely more of Poe's embellishments to draw in those who dared put eye to paper. "Dissimulation" (Charters 705) from "The Tell-

Tale Heart" would fit into this category, while other words as "pulsation" and "dissemble" (Charters 707 – 708) could be surmised by today's reader even without a dictionary alongside his "Tales of the Grotesque and Arabesque" (Clute 769).

Poe also had a liking for other languages, at least well enough to place them perfectly within his tales, as though their lack would cause the whole of the effect to be missing. *"Nemo me impune lacessit"* (Charters 702) and *"in pace requiescat"* (Charters 704) added style to "Cask", and it reminds us of the prevalence of Latin in the educated masses (Pulju), especially in Poe's time. Other words of the Romantic Languages would pepper throughout "Cask", but their ultimate purpose was to place the reader in a time and place of great revelry in Italy or France or other similarly bourgeois location. In "Berenice", Poe turned to the French of Mademoiselle Marie Sallé with *"que tous ses pas etaient des sentiments"* (Gmoser). While he was speaking to the movement of Mlle. Sallé, for indeed she was "one of the most prominent dancers of her time" (Andros), Poe's primary character was eluding to not only his feelings, but to another French phrase, *"que toutes ses dents etaient des idees"* (Gmoser).

It is evidenced in Poe's work that he intended to utilize the foreshadowing technique, but it is equally evidenced in his own criticisms that foreshadowing was not on his mind. It is instead that Poe's "singular *effect*" created the need for foreshadowing. *"Nemo me impune lacessit"* (Charters 702) in "Cask" is translated as "No-one wounds (touches) me with impunity" (Astrotrain), and it was a clue of ironic fate that Montresor would explain to Fortunato. We, the reader, would know of Fortunato's fate from the very first sentence, as was Poe's trademark, "I vowed revenge" (Charters 699), but the author insisted on reminding us of the intense hatred and vengeance felt in Montresor's heart. "My smile *now* was at the thought of his immolation" (Charters 700), and while there are various definitions for this word, the one that seems to best fit Poe's intent is "to destroy" (Dictionary.com). Even the imagery on the arms itself is consistent with the style of a medieval coat of arms, but it eludes to Montresor's true purpose, possibly the intents of the family as the whole when it came to the realm of their own pride: "the foot crushes a serpent rampant whose fangs are imbedded in the heel" (Charters 702). Much as Fortunato attacked Montresor with his words as a snake, Montresor would put boot to head. Poe reminds throughout that Montresor is not only intent on the ending of

Fortunato, but as intent as any man can be about a task.

The French in "Berenice", which in Poe's day the title would have rhymed with "very spicy" (Baltimore 2), was "also a vampire story" (Clute 769), which is shown by the phrase *"que toutes ses dents etaient des idees. Des idees!"* (Gmoser), which translates to "that all her teeth were ideas. Ideas" (Baltimore). In the same piece, Marie Sallé is used in reference to the title character with the translated "Her every step was a sentiment" (Baltimore), speaking to the love of the main character. Though, ultimately, the madness within himself bade him to remove her teeth, it is interesting to note that this could have been a trick Poe was playing on the reader, allowing them to soak in the words of love from Sallé, accepting the unusual comparison of Berenice's molars to thoughts, only to reveal the dark obsession by keeping her "ideas" in "a little box... of no remarkable character" (Gmoser). *"Dicebant mihi sodales si sepulchrum amicae visitarem, curas meas aliquantulum fore levatas"* (Gmoser), which means "My companions told me I might find some little alleviation of my misery, in visiting the grave of my beloved" (Baltimore), does suggest with a level of finality that the deed was done after "Berenice had been interred" (Gmoser). It gives the reader another clue, like a little mystery, what is to come.

Poe utilized his own tongue in ways that only a literary giant like himself would be allowed to by the common man. "Superinduced", which means "to introduce as an addition" (Dictionary.com), when read contextually seems to mean a heightened introduction of the "species of epilepsy" (Gmoser, "Berenice"). It allows the mind of those less educated on such a term to ascertain an inference of severity and an awareness about the disease that it generates part of the effect of fear that Poe was known for, specifically when the "epilepsy not unfrequently terminate[s] in trance itself" (Gmoser, "Berenice"); this is Poe's hope for the reader, to be entranced by the fear of her condition.

"The Tell-Tale Heart" focused singularly on the effect of an old man's ailments on his in-house helper, yet the context of much of the words used in "Heart" were clearer than some of Poe's other works already mentioned. "You should have seen how wisely I proceeded – with what caution – with what foresight – with what dissimulation I went to work! I was never kinder to the old man than during the whole week before I killed him" (Charters 705), the main character has already eluded very directly that the proper definition of dissimulation in this sentence is "to disguise" (Dictionary.com). A quick journey etymologically sees that dis-simulation is really a joining of "a Latin prefix meaning... 'utterly', or having a... negative... force", and "a pretense" (Dictionary.com). This joining of "dis" and "simulation" would be "an utter pretense having a negative force" (*Paraphrase*); obviously this negative force would be murder in the first.

"Heart" would continue with the character's primary sense of his own pride, much as Montresor's in "Cask": "The disease had sharpened my senses" (Charters 705), "never before that night had I *felt* the extent of my own powers – of my sagacity" (Charters 705). Sagacity, quite simply, is "wisdom" (Dictionary.com). It is this wisdom, this "acuteness of mental discernment and soundness of judgment" (Dictionary.com) that would cause him, the primary character, the antagonist, the bad guy, to give himself up to "they (the officers) [whom] had been deputed to search the premises" (Charters 707). "I shrieked, 'dissemble no more! I admit the deed!'" (Charters 708); the character tells them to discontinue letting "pass unnoticed" (Dictionary.com) as "they were making a mockery of my horror", because "they heard! – they suspected! – they knew!" (Charters 708). For all his wisdom he gave himself up, all because "the hellish tattoo of the heart increased", yet even after "there was no pulsation" (Charters 707), until "I found that the noise was *not* within my ears... it was *a low, dull, quick sound*" (Charters 708). Poe had to bring his effect back to "very dreadfully nervous I had been and am" (Charters 705).

Poe, as has been mentioned repeatedly, was obsessed with "singular effect", which comes to life in his poetry, short stories, the scant novels he produced, and in his criticisms of others' work. The words and phrases related directly to the imagery and the focus of each individual piece, creating such "heavily Gothic... [allegories] for a descent into madness through an awareness of the terrors of one's soul... with a deep and brooding melancholy pervaded by the... intrusion of the ghosts of memory" (Clute 769). For the casual reader, Edgar Allan Poe's works of madness and horror will make him a timeless author who will entertain and frighten them for generations to come. For the author who reads Poe's works, it is more than mere entertainment; it is an example of such artistry and such devotion to his own philosophical literary creations that he will

- Perception Is Truth -

be heralded as a hero and as a true artist of his craft. It will also be a reminder that language evolves amongst its own people.

"In pace requiescat!" (Charters 704)

Quoth the Raven, Nevermore

ORIGINAL BURIAL PLACE OF

EDGAR ALLAN POE

FROM

OCTOBER 9, 1849.

UNTIL

NOVEMBER 17, 1875.

MRS. MARIA CLEMM, HIS MOTHER-IN-LAW, LIES UPON HIS RIGHT AND VIRGINIA POE, HIS WIFE, UPON HIS LEFT UNDER THE MONUMENT ERECTED TO HIM IN THIS CEMETERY.

Heretical Reason

Introducing a Deity

There are many concepts and realities in our world that cannot be argued. Truth is, after all, truth. Such things as our need for oxygen, the presence of gravity, the sun, are truths that are not only accepted, but are provable by modern science, modern thought. These are the many ideas that we can experience in our everyday lives, without question. There are other concepts that are argued not only for their provability, but even their believability.

The biggest concept that is most notably debated is the presence of God. The idea of God, so intricate in its implications about our world and our own existence, puts Man in a place that they would not otherwise desire to be: not the central focus of the universe. Much of the acceptance of God implies the notion that Man, for all its ability to reason and to understand the universe it exists in, was not created out of an accidental explosion of molecules, but by the specific choice of an all-powerful, all-knowing Deity.

Once the debate has been decided over the existence of God, the question then becomes how to believe in this omniscient, omnipotent being. If you choose not to believe in God, your choice is simple: there's only one way to NOT believe in something. On the other hand, if you accept God and believe that God created the universe, why? What was God's purpose or reason? And what, ultimately, is God?

Some believe that God is, in fact, the universe itself. To a very specific degree, God is all around us, all throughout nature, the stars, the oceans, the passing of bacteria from creature to creature. Others believe that God is in all of us, each individual person. That we, as a whole, make up God, and the essence of what God is has been passed to all of us individually. Others still think that God not only created the Earth and the universe, but also plays an active role in our everyday lives.

The easiest and most vocal groups that discuss the various ideas surrounding God are the hundreds of religions that are right now on the Earth. Christians, Jews, Muslims, Atheists, Catholics, Satanists, and many, many more, have gone to great lengths to get their points across. Who else remembers the Crusades? But, this heated debate is in no way limited to the religious sectors. There are many who have opinions on God, on religion, on the validity of both, and a host of other ideals that have taken people to a greater place in their own lives, or been used to subject them to hardship and tyranny. Not strictly the pastorate or clergy, but politicians and poets and even psychiatrists, scholars and philosophers, novelists and nobodies, will discuss God and the impact of God in their lives.

There have been too many minds that have tackled this difficult topic to even begin to list, but there are a few that in the past 150 years have reached the world through their own endeavors. Not strictly in the realm of religion, these four men used their minds to reach out to a world that sometimes barely understood them, but accepted their notoriety as powerful minds with a lot to say. The depths of their minds can be overlooked, and their most notable contributions the only things that people seem to know about. Yet, their ideas on God, Jesus, Christianity, and Man itself, will live on in the fullness of their works, their ideas, and their goals, for reaching out to the world, and to anyone who would hear. These men defined and defied their generations; indeed history will remember their various contributions to popular thought, whether intentional or misinterpreted.

Dramatis Personae

Friedrich Wilhelm Nietzsche was born 1844 in Röcken, Germany, the son of a Lutheran clergyman. Nietzsche would attend some of the finer German schools, including Pforta and the University at Bonn and Leipzig, later becoming professor at Basle University. During the Franco-Prussian War, he was an ambulance orderly, an experience that would shatter his health. (Kaufmann 20) At the age of 24, he would chair the classical philology department at Basle University until his failing health would force his retirement in 1879. In 1872, his first book was published, <u>The Birth of Tragedy out of the Spirit of Music</u>. His last book was published 8 years after his death, in 1908, <u>Ecce Homo</u>. His final work was published thanks to his sister, Elisabeth, who in 1895 had their mother sign a document that surrendered "all rights to her son's work, allowing Elisabeth Nietzsche to gain complete control of her brother's writings." (atheism.about.com) Given Elisabeth's own history, and of her ex-husband who had committed suicide while they lived in South America, "she proceeded to conceal those writings which she disapproved of and emphasized those which appeared to have a most fascist and/or anti-Semitic perspective." (atheism.about.com)

Carl Gustav Jung was born 1875 in Switzerland, his father being a Swiss Reformed pastor at Kesswil. He would attend many schools growing up, eventually becoming assistant physician at the Burgholzli: the mental hospital at Canton Zurich and psychiatric clinic of Zurich University. After less than a decade, he would become the senior physician at this facility, researching schizophrenia and conducting courses on hypnotic therapy. By 1906, Jung would begin his correspondence with Freud, meeting the psychiatrist a year later. During the next few years, Freud would feel that Jung was his logical successor, their common interests and their lengthy conversations giving him the desire to make that happen. However, by 1913, the two men would part, after some serious disagreements about how best to proceed in certain psychological situations. Jung would then name his particular field of study "analytical psychology," and at the same period resign from his teaching at Zurich University. During World War I, he was a Medical Corps doctor. In 1921, Jung would publish his first work, <u>Psychological Types</u>, and his last work would be published 4 years after his death, in 1964, titled <u>Approaching the Unconscious</u>.

Clive Staples Lewis was born 1989 in Belfast, Northern Ireland. He would go to school at Wynyard School in Watford, Hertfordshire. He would enroll at Campbell College, only to come home a few months after, having developed severe respiratory problems. He would eventually finish his schooling at University College, Oxford. He would join the British Army in World War I, where he was injured during the fighting, but he would be restored and returned to the battlefield. He would become Fellow of Magdalen College, Oxford; a post he would serve for 29 years. During this time he would spend 16 of those years as part of "the Inklings", with other writers including J.R.R. Tolkien. He would host radio shows, lectures, and further books and essays were published. 1919 was his first publication; an article in February's Reveille titled, "Death in Battle," but his final works would continue to be published long after his death. In 1954 he would chair Medieval and Renaissance Literature at Cambridge, until a few months before his death in 1963.

Francis August Schaeffer was born 1912 in Germantown, Pennsylvania. His first attempts at higher education included night school at Drexel Institute to become a mechanical engineer. He dropped out of Drexel, and went onto Hampden-Sydney College in Virginia to become a minister. He would then go on to the newly formed Faith Seminary at Westminster until graduating in 1938, where he became a Presbyterian Minister at various American churches. In 1947, he was sent to Europe as a representative of the Independent Board for Presbyterian Foreign Missions to survey the churches of various countries affected by World War II. This mission of his would last for seven years, until he severed all ties with the Board in 1954. One year later, a chalet was purchased in Huemoz zur Allon in Switzerland, and was named "L'Abri", which is French for shelter. "This home ultimately became an international spiritual retreat center for informal study and discussion of Christian thought, life style, and goals." (www.wheaton.edu) Diagnosed with cancer in 1981, Schaeffer would continue his lectures and his writings, including work with Dr. C. Everett Koop, who was better known during his time as the Surgeon General of the United States. "Schaeffer became known world-wide as a theologian, defender of biblical inerrancy and authority, and commentator on the Christian in contemporary culture." (www.wheaton.edu) After his death in 1984, President Ronald Reagan commented, "It can rarely be said of an individual that his life touched many others and affected them for the better; it will be said of Dr. Francis Schaeffer that his life touched millions of souls and brought them to the truth of their Creator." (www.wheaton.edu)

Defining a Deity

Jung defined God as, "the name by which I designate all things which cross my willful path violently and recklessly, all things which upset my subjective view, plans, and intentions and change the course of my life for better or worse." (Stein 6) Jung clearly did his Bible reading, and paid attention closely to the stories told about God and the various interferences with the human race, or specific humans. Christianity teaches that God is ultimately the One who will decide what truly is best for us, whether we feel that is the case or not.

Jung, the son of a Swiss Reformed pastor, spent much of his life questioning his faith; writing about it more in his later years. There have been general conceptions, however, about Jung's feelings upon Christianity. First, it is believed that Jung was anti-Christian, feeling that Christianity, a belief in an eternal God, was a product of the subconscious, and that it should be replaced by reason, by his own analytical psychology. A second idea that is presented is that Jung was attempting to give Christianity certain modernity, defending the Christian truths by using concepts that were more contemporary in nature. Murray Stein, Ph.D., who has authored several books on Jung, is currently the President of the International Association for Analytical Psychology. Stein defends a different argument about Jung's Christianity, stating instead that, "While he confesses ignorance of formal theology, he shows great awareness of theological issues and tackles some of the thorniest theological doctrines known to Christendom. These are not attacks upon Christian belief and practice, nor do they foresee their demise or suggest their replacement by analytical psychology. Clearly, Christianity meant a great deal to Jung." (Stein 4) Stein continues, "He was a spiritually sensitive man who never left his native Christianity for another religion." (Stein 5)

Lewis had many separate definitions of God, in terms of character, omniscience, omnipresence; enough aspects that it would be difficult, nearly a lie, to state that Lewis had one simple statement with which God should be understood. "God is basic Fact or Actuality, the source of all other facthood. At all other costs therefore He must not be thought of as a featureless generality." (Martindale 257) "If anything is to exist at all, then the Original Thing must be, not a principle or a generality, much less an 'ideal' or a 'value,' but an utterly concrete fact." (Martindale 259)

Schaeffer would define God throughout history, in works and actions and in people. Much like Lewis, it would be nearly impossible to pinpoint the specific definition he would choose for the "Original Thing", that being God. But, he was adamant that the Judeo-Christian interpretation of God was predominantly accurate. He would speak of God's direct involvement in historical moments, political movements, and even the creation and substantiation of the Americas. "John Witherspoon (1723-1794)... Presbyterian minister and president of what is now Princeton University, was the only pastor to sign the Declaration of Independence... This linkage of Christian thinking and the concepts of government were not incidental but fundamental." (Schaeffer, Manifesto 31-32) Schaeffer's primary arguments about God and God's purposes and goals for our country, indeed our very existence, is wrapped up in the ideas put forth by the Bible, and put forth in factual, historical instances. To Schaeffer, God was not merely some force, or some spirit or some being that may or may not have existed, who may or may not play a role in our everyday lives. For him, God is <u>The God Who Is There</u> and <u>He Is There and He Is Not Silent</u>.

Worshipping a Deity

The religion that is most connected with the idea of God is Christianity. Christianity has many sects, many different branches of belief systems. They all seem to believe differently the "person" that God is, and who Christ was, and is, and will continue to be.

"Is not the popular idea of Christianity simply this: that Jesus Christ was a great moral teacher and that if only we took his advice we might be able to establish a better social order and avoid another war? Now, mind you, that is quite true. But it tells you much less than the whole truth about Christianity..." (Martindale 104) Lewis was trying to establish a foundation of thought regarding Christianity without throwing in the dogma surrounding the entirety of it, but he wanted people to understand that there is far more to the religion than the simplicity of being a "little Christ". He did not want people to be confused about his own Christianity, however. He wanted to establish himself as a Christian mind that understood how to speak to people, and how to show them concepts in such a way that they could relate to them, or at least understand them in a fantastical way. "I believe in Christianity as I believe that the Sun has risen, not only because I see it, but because by it I see everything else." (Martindale 99)

Schaeffer also believed strongly in Christianity, but his methods of speaking with others would not cover so much allegory as comparison. "When I say Christianity is true I mean it is true to total reality - the total of what is, beginning with the central reality, the objective existence of the personal-infinite God. Christianity is not just a series of truths but Truth - Truth about all of reality." (Schaeffer, <u>Manifesto</u>, 19-20) Schaeffer had studied the formation of Christianity, its rebellious attitude towards the worshipping of Caesar, whether singularly or in conjunction with Jesus, and its continuance throughout history. "...they worshipped Jesus as God and they worshipped the infinite-personal God only... If they had worshipped Jesus *and* Caesar, they would have gone unharmed... They worshipped the God who had revealed himself in the Old Testament, through Christ, and in the New Testament which had gradually been written. And they worshipped him as the *only* God... All other gods were seen as false gods." (Schaeffer,

How Should We 24-26)

Nietzsche would not be so kind in defining Christianity. In fact, based upon what he wrote, one would find it hard to argue that the man did not have a strong distaste for the religion, perhaps growing into a hatred for it. "What is more harmful than any vice? Active pity for all the failures and all the weak: Christianity... Christianity should not be beautified and embellished... Christianity has sided with all that is weak and base... it has made an ideal of whatever contradicts the instinct of the strong life to preserve itself... The most pitiful example... Pascal, who believed in the corruption of his reason through original sin when it had in fact been corrupted only by his Christianity." (Kaufmann 570-572) Nietzsche's many thought on God and Christ would culminate into one central idea, one philosophic conclusion on the basis of reason, in direct avoidance of the idea of faith.

Killing a Deity

"God is dead. God remains dead. And we have killed him. Is not the greatness of this deed too great for us? Must not we ourselves become gods simply to seem worthy of it?" (Kaufmann 95-96) Friedrich Nietzsche defined one of the facets of humanism most excellently with this essay about a madman running through the streets, seeking a god he had reasoned was no longer alive. According to him Man caused the death of God. He was determined a madman because of his unpopular perspective on God, because others did not understand him. However, he saw it a different way. "I come too early. My time has not come yet. This tremendous event is still on its way... deeds require time even after they are done, before they can be seen and heard... and yet they have done it themselves." (Kaufmann 96) His feelings were that Man had accomplished this task already, and that it would only be a matter of time before we all realized the validity of his statement. Nietzsche, whose final lapse into insanity around 1889, would never realize the full impact he would have on the world. Nor would he realize the rebuttals and agreements that would come regarding this philosophy for the next hundred years, and counting.

Schaeffer, to a certain extent, seemed to agree with Nietzsche's interpretations of that now infamous phrase. "Nietzsche in the 1880s was the first one who said in the modern way that God is dead, and he understood well where people end when they say this." (Schaeffer, How Should We 178) What Schaeffer was referring to was not the physical, or indeed spiritual, death of God. What Schaeffer and Nietzsche meant was the idea of God had died. The importance and necessity of God in the eyes of modern man no longer had any place, given the progress made in science, medicine, industry, and reason in general. Nietzsche's madman did not immediately realize the consequences of this action, and perhaps Nietzsche himself did not grasp the fullness of his idea until it was much too late.

Schaeffer refers to Nietzsche's final years, wherein a venereal disease is most often cited for the philosopher's mental and physical condition. However, Schaeffer adds a different reason for much of Nietzsche's emotional state at the "end" of his life. "If God is dead, then everything for which God gives an answer and meaning is dead... I am convinced that when Nietzsche came to Switzerland and went insane... it was because he understood that insanity was the only philosophic answer if the infinite-personal God does not exist." (Schaeffer, How Should We 178-179) Schaeffer continues to state that Nietzsche had a deep understanding of the toil and despair of Man during these years. He then explains that this sense of despair, this emotional "tension" comes from a spiritual lapse, the then-determined lack of the "infinite-personal God." Without a personal God, Man's inner being cries out for a sense of meaning in this world, and indeed this universe.

"The Middle Ages assumed the absolute reliability of all the New Testament accounts concerning the person of Christ... Modern people no longer acknowledge the New Testament accounts to be absolutely reliable, but only relatively reliable... critical scholarship lays hold of the person of Christ, snips a bit off here and another bit off there, and begins... sometimes overtly, blatantly, and with a brutal naiveté - to measure him by the standard of the normal man. After he has been distilled through all the artful... mechanisms of the critics' laboratory, the figure of the historical Jesus emerges at the other end." (Stein 45-46) Jung's interest in the thoughts of man would allow him to explain Nietzsche's ideas in such a way that was littered with sarcasm, bordering on an intellectual anger, but a deep understanding of what Nietzsche meant. Not only that, it would seem that Jung was upset because Nietzsche was right. Modern man has, indeed, killed this idea of Jesus as the God-man, and brought him to a place that we would no longer consider God and the Son of God to be truthfully Deity and Heir to the Throne.

Conclusion

The search for the eternal Truth rests in the heart of every man, woman, and child. It is unfortunate that more people do not open themselves up to this search, for there is much to learn. So many people attempt to tackle this toughest of subjects, and so many of them have died for what they believed in. It is often disheartening to hear that these men have died in vain, for nothing. Indeed, they died for what they believed was Truth. These men that have been spoken of also died, some of them for their Truth, others because… it's the inevitability of man to die.

They lived so that others could learn from them on a great many fields. They used their vocations to promote truth in many ways, in many different cultures, schools of thought, and in different generations. They each lived their own experiences, going through different wars in different ways; Jung and Nietzsche in medicine, seeing what war does to a man, Lewis as a soldier, seeing war face to face, and Schaeffer, seeing the effects of war on a people's spirit. All of them have seen people die, including those they loved. Yet, through it all, they would stay attached to the concepts that many other men would falter from had they gone through those same experiences.

Today's society marks itself as the generation of thought, of reason. We have turned from the traditions of old, and indeed from those that began this very nation. We have allowed ourselves the complacency of commercialism, and have cast aside thoughts of an Eternal Truth. These men recognized the coming of this from a very early age, and it has been a wave coming for many, many years; its time is here, its purpose is now. We are a people without Truth, but we have our Reason.

"Have you not heard of that madman who lit a lantern in the bright morning hours, ran to the market place, and cried incessantly, 'I seek God! I seek God!'" (Kaufmann 95) Perhaps I am that madman after all…

- Perception Is Truth -
Perceived Truth vs. Proven Reality In Mental Disorders
Truth vs. Fact

What is truth? Truth is nothing more than a statement, thought, or idea that is accepted to be true; in other words, a mass opinion. A fact, on the other hand, is based upon real occurrences. Truth can be said to be nothing more than a logical belief, while a fact must be a provable belief. While this is, in fact, not the fullness of the meanings of either word, it is useful to note this for the purposes of this paper.

Those who determine what is truth and what is not are those who are, curiously enough, the most educated. During the Greek and Roman periods of history, the only thing needed to determine death was the absence of a heartbeat, absence of breathing, and the smell of the dead, or putrefaction. Even in 19th Century Germany, all that was needed to determine death was putrefaction. It was not until the mid- to late-20th Century that brain death had become accepted as true death. Were the Greeks, Romans, and Germans wrong? Was their diagnosis incorrect because it lacked the understanding of what a coma is, or of other possible explanations for a person's "death"?

Most of the scientific community develops ideas called hypotheses, such as what determines a person to be factually dead. While they have some information, some fact, to base their ideas upon, some of the facts they are using are indeed nothing more than the accepted perceptions of other scientists in the same, or similar, field of study. These are therefore not always facts, but often truths. Math is called an exact science based upon the concepts of counting per the particular culture's methodology (Base 10, Base 2, etc). This was, at least at one time, an accepted truth. However, it has grown into a fact of all forms of life. Psychology, on the other hand, is a series of theories that are accepted as truth, but can be argued for or against dependent upon a particular situation. The study of the mind is far from being wholly factual, but it is often truthful. This is not to say that facts are not developed from these truths.

One of the first examples mentioned in David G. Myers' text compares the ideas of Plato and Aristotle. Both are still well respected ancient Greek philosophers, and both did agree on a great many things. In fact, Aristotle learned from Plato before developing his own theories about the mind. However, they differed greatly in their ideas about the existence of innate ideas. Plato, believing in their existence, felt the brain was "the seat of mental processes", while Aristotle denied their existence, citing instead that the heart was "the seat of mental processes" (2004, Inside Cover). We now know that the brain is indeed that which controls the mental processes. While many may argue that the heart controls your emotions, it is still the brain that controls how your emotional states change (Myers, 2004, p. 500).

These are truths that we have determined are indisputable. Theoretically, these ideas could indeed be proven incorrect, but based upon our present knowledge; we do not foresee this occurring. These are, therefore, fact. There are a great many things, however, that are not so easily defined.

Take for example those with Dissociative Identity Disorder (DID), Multiple Personality Disorder (MPD), schizophrenia, and other mental and emotional disorders. I feel that I should clarify my own stance on these matters, as it will further assist in understanding the context with which the terms will be used. I realize that MPD has been renamed to DID (Kennett & Matthews, 2002, p. 509), but I feel it is necessary to continue to use the terms as separate disorders. I need to point out that I have an extensive religious background, having been raised in a "charismatic" Christian home for most of my life. In that time, I have seen many things, and had many experiences, that will not allow me to write such a paper without adding many of the more spiritual theories.

The reason that Multiple Personality Disorder needs to be kept a separate disorder is due to the cause of the disorder itself. In a paper compiled by Christopher H. Rosik, two Lutheran pastors who have worked with persons afflicted with mental disorders recognize the differences between what can be construed as a "religious" understanding of this disorder versus a more "secular" definition. "Is the entity a demon or an "alter" personality" (Rosik, 2003, p. 115)? They also speak of Bible verses that suggest Christ Himself knew the difference between a person and a demon (I John 4:1; James 2:19). This requires a great deal of faith in both spiritual activities and the potential outcomes of such a series of hypotheses. Of course, I am not one to discount the scientific theories either.

An "alter" (Sinnott-Armstrong & Behnke, 2000, p. 303) may commit a heinous act upon another person, or even themselves, without the "host" (Allers & Golson, 1994, p. 265) being made fully aware of it until they "wake up" (Kennett & Matthews, 2002, pp.

510). There are arguments over the existence of DID (Dunn, Paolo, Ryan, & Van Fleet, 1994, pp. 454-457), and numerous debates over who, ultimately, is responsible for any improper actions committed by the "alter" or "host". There are also various persons who may try to abuse knowledge of this illness for their own purposes, such as the Hillside Strangler (Myers, 2004, pp. 644-645). Take a look at one of the first truly accepted examples of MPD, an older woman by the name of Eve White (O'Kelly & Mackless, 1956, p. 27, quoted in Kennett & Matthews, 2002, 510). She is supposed to have had an "alter" present with her from childhood, which has been named Eve Black. White had no recollection of the "alter" Black, but Black knew of the "host" White personality and would put White into embarrassing situations. In the end, it was still Eve who had not only committed the acts, but would be blamed for them by those around her.

Those who suffer from this illness, it can be argued, in essence create their own truth (Allers & Golson, 1994, p. 265). This may seem an unfair statement, but when a "host" or "alter" is in control, it is often that they have differing "early recollections" (ER) (Allers & Golson, 1994, p. 265). "What is significant about these ERs is that they often indicate a life-style which is quite different from that of the "host" or other "alters" in the system" (Allers & Golson, 1994, p. 265). This allows an "alter" to feel justified in their own positions and actions, but it may also be an internal struggle for ultimate control of the body.

It is comparable to selective attention, "the focusing of conscious awareness on a particular stimuli" (Myers, 2004, p. 232); while our unconscious brain is taking in 11,000,000 bits of information at any given second, the conscious brain processes 40 such bits (Myers, 2004, p. 231), just as the "host" is pre-occupied mentally or emotionally on any number of given topics, the "alter" is able to "control the common body." (Brown, 2001, p. 436) The truth of the "host" is that they were sleeping, while the truth of the "alter" is dependent upon what action they've committed. The fact of the matter is that the "common body" took part in an event, irrelevant of who was specifically in control at the time in question.

I think one of the finest examples of MPD/DID is a film from recent popular culture, *Fight Club*. A book first, this movie centers around a man who has what seems to be a happy life. He has a good job, a good home, and seems content with his things.

Yet, you find out later that the individual has inside of him another personality by the name of Tyler Durden. Tyler, you find out, is the "alter" in this scenario, while the "host" has no name. The movie would have you believe that the "host's" insomnia is the cause of the "alters'" late-night activities, but this only sates the moviegoers who want to see a decent film for a high-ticket price. The thing of it is, the movie leans towards the idea that, whether it's the "host" or the "alter" who commits the various crimes played out in this film, there's still only one person behind it all. At the end of the film, it takes a traumatic event to bring these two personalities together.

Was Alice the Hillside Strangler?

> ...for this curious child was very fond of pretending to be two people. "But it's no use now," thought poor Alice, "to pretend to be two people!" (Lewis Carroll, 1865, *Alice's adventures in wonderland*, third last paragraph of Chapter 1; quoted in Kennett & Matthews, 2002, p. 509)

In a paper written by Jeanette Kennett and Steve Matthews, their purposes for the paper include discrediting some of the ideas of their fellow psychologists, Walter Sinnott-Armstrong and Stephen Behnke (2000, pp. 509-510). "...If someone with DID acts in a morally or legally bad way, can we hold this individual responsible when it is claimed that the accused personality is not the personality who acted? Walter Sinnott-Armstrong and Stephen Behnke argue we can; we present reasons for denying that we can." (Kennett & Matthews, 2002, pp. 509-510) There is a moral obligation, it seems, to not only determine whether a person is afflicted with this disorder, but whether they are truly responsible for any actions committed during a time in which they were deemed insane or delusional.

The piece continues by stating their reasons, but first describe two different possible positions of "how many persons" (Kennett & Matthews, 2002, p. 510) are truly inside a person suffering from DID. Although they do note that there is a possible third perspective (Kennett & Matthews, 2002, p. 524), it does not seem to fit with their complete ideas on moral responsibility for the DID sufferer. "Realists would argue that we should treat "alter" personalities as though each was a separate person, because each *is* a separate person... We can regard realists as committed to what we will call the *Multiple*

Person thesis. Those with a genuine commitment to this thesis will occupy the default position that body-sharing "alters" are not responsible for each others' actions." (Kennett & Matthews, 2002, pp. 510-511) On other hand, "We favor what we will call the *Single Person thesis*... So-called alter personalities are not to be regarded as metaphysically separate entities from the person, but rather count as altered states of that person." (Kennett & Matthews, 2002, p. 511)

The facts that they present, while logically sound, still amount to a theory about those who may or may not suffer from DID, and whether they should be held responsible for the actions that they, or their "alters", may commit in a morally reprehensible way. This topic seems to be most significant in court cases, where those involved in the decision-making process must be able to understand what it is the plaintiff claims, versus what the defendant is attempting to delineate. In these instances, the jury does not truly know the facts, but only the truth as presented to them. With the facilitation of the judge, the jurors need to not only understand which part of the law they are attempting to give the ultimate decision for, but they also need to understand the crime, the nature of the crime, and the possible explanations for the defendant's actions.

Is the scientific community correct in the understanding that DID can be caused by a traumatic childhood event, particularly sexual abuse? (Allers & Golson, 1994, pp. 263-464) Or is it caused by the presence of a truly second, or multiple, set of personalities that afflict the sufferer? Or, is it the cause of a demon, or other negative spirit, being introduced to the system by means totally unbeknownst to the sufferer? This is one of the many reasons that MPD is considered attractive to philosophers. (Brown, 2001, p. 435)

Dementia Praecox

Schizophrenia is another affliction of the mind that may appeal to philosophers as well as those who seek to understand and ultimately treat those who are cursed by it. While the causes of schizophrenia may be similar to that which causes DID, the symptoms of schizophrenia are truly different. According to Myers, there are five subtypes of schizophrenia (2003, p. 648): paranoid, disorganized, catatonic, undifferentiated, and residual.

The paranoid schizophrenic is the one that we in today's modern culture are most familiar with. *A Beautiful Mind* shows a man with a brilliant capacity for numbers and codes, remembers specifically having a roommate whom he had never truly had contact with, and did work for a secret government facility that no one else knew existed. The movie indicates that the sufferer would continue to have these people in his life to this very day. While a majority of people will determine that this person suffers from paranoid schizophrenia, it is only a truth that they suffer from anything at all, it is not necessarily fact. Just because it can be proven that such a "person" did not exist on paper or in our own records, it cannot be proven that the "person" doesn't exist at all. The "person" may indeed exist, but may be nothing more than a spirit of some sort, or even the culmination of many years of troubled emotional states rolled into one "imaginary friend."

This is comparable to those with DID, where some would suggest "multiples may claim co-conscious psychological continuity over the lifetime of the human being." (Brown, 2001, p. 436) The major difference between the two is, of course, who determines the actions that the sufferer will commit. For a schizophrenic, it is up to the "host" themselves to make the ultimate choices, but the "persons" that speak to them influence decisions.

Treatment

I would not begin to know the best way to treat those afflicted with emotional, mental, or other disorders. However, it is helpful to note that the many treatments offered to those with these illnesses are also in contention over which one is the most appropriate. Depending on the method by which the origin of the illness is determined, there is generally an accepted solution to helping the person heal, or at the least suppress, the illness. Again, this is not the factually best method, but it can be true that it does help people.

There are many methods of assisting these people in their afflictions, but it seems that the most important thing that anyone can do is to listen to the person, "host" and "alter" alike. (Allers & Golson, 1994, pp. 264-265; Rosik, 2003, p. 116) After it is determined who is truly speaking, be it "host", "alter", or demon, then an appropriate treatment plan can be surmised.

Not every plan will work for every person I would hazard to guess. For as many labels as we create for ourselves, the more rules have to be broken. With more titles come more expectations, and more frustrations. This cannot be found in any simple document; you must live life to understand fully how unceasingly different every person is. If you read enough things, you can find a way to fit anyone's labels. Point of fact, if you delve deeply enough into my brain, one would consider me schizophrenic on a certain number of levels. I believe in spirits, and have indeed felt them around me. I have only seen them in my dreams, but perhaps one day, when I am ready, I will be confronted with the amazing facts of reality around me.

Seasonal Differences

As one sets foot out onto their doorstep, which most people will do on a daily basis, often more than once a day, don't forget to stop and take in all of your surroundings. No matter where your home is, whether it's in the suburbs of a big city, or out in the woods where few but the animals dare to tread, or smack dab in the middle of all the chaos and life that only a municipality can bring, there's one ever-shifting constant amongst all of those arenas: the seasons. Provided, the level of enjoyment for the shifting of seasons is largely dependent upon where your home is, in that each area will experience and deal with these changes in their own way, but there's no stopping it. The changes are going to come, and there's nothing subtle about them. The ways in which the seasons come about are not the mystery they were hundreds and thousands of years ago; we can explain them based upon scientific research. Yet, many people long for the days when there was magic about the seasons, when they were looked upon as a sort of natural allegory, a representation of our own lives.

Setting aside the Gregorian calendar we have all lived by for several centuries, one can look at the seasons, and their changing, and compare them to the way that life as we know it changes. Spring is, undoubtedly, the time of birth and rebirth. With the death of much in the winter, the rains come to wash away that which is passed on, and usher in the beginning of life all over the world. The many clichés placed on this season, most notably love being in the air, is not without cause. There are many creatures that breed during this time, and plant life blooms all around. It gives a sense of hope for the rest of the year. Following spring is the warm summer, which is, in many ways, an example of our growing up, of the formative years that will determine the person we will become. It's a time of joy, of brightness, forgetting the past, and putting off the future for as long as we can. Then comes autumn; a season of change, of passing away all that was our youth, and embracing our adulthood. It's a peaceful time, where we grow into the ones we were meant to be, and we prepare our loved ones, and ourselves, for the time of great passing. Winter is the unmistakable example of death, of the ending of many things, of letting go of all that we once knew, and welcoming the end of our time here on this earth. But, as all good things must come to an end, so there must be a beginning.

Spring, which can be considered a transitional season, prepares the world for life forthcoming. It also allows the passage of winter to be forgotten as the cleansing begins. With the coming rains, comes a somewhat emotional contradiction. When many people think about rain, they are often depressed. The sunlight faded from view, the water trickling down incessantly, and the sounds of the puddles being filled ever higher. It's as if we are forced to watch as nature washes itself off, and we are unable to enjoy nature until it is appropriately cleansed. However, other people look at the rain as a sign of hope, of a peace falling over the world, as it awakens to a new day, to a new beginning. With the onset of rain comes the promise of sunlight, a sunlight that brings with it freshness as it lights the world with its warmth.

Autumn, the other transitional season, prepares the world for rest forthcoming. It reminds us that, no matter how peaceful or how happy or serene life may seem, there comes a time of rest that all must undertake. It has its own emotional contradictions, but they are not as noticeably prevalent as was in the spring. You see examples of the hibernation, or even the death, that nature is itself preparing for. The colors on the leaves are changing as they themselves are preparing to fall from the place they had lived all their humble existence. They are separated from their place in the world to find a new home, a place where they can rest and show forth their own beauty to a world who only knew them in comparison to the roots for which they were attached. Now, they are a source of much joy to a younger people, to the adults who see the many colors and recognize the wonder of this process, and its need. In certain parts of this country, people will travel many miles just to see the vast examples of this change that the season of autumn represents, and the magnificent displays.

On the other hand, while it can be argued that the remaining two seasons are also transitional, it can also be said that summer and winter are the apex of life and death, where spring and autumn are a preparation for them. During summertime, there is little precipitation, if any at all. It is, however, the time of the most warmth and light that the sun can bring forth. During this axial tilt, ever closer to the gas star far away, life is rejuvenated and fed by this object, the health of many often determined by the amount of sunlight they receive.

Simplicity

The sky had opened up to a beautiful azure blue, with few cirrus clouds lining the vast expanse. It was early in autumn, and its evidence could be felt on the breeze. Slightly more biting than the summer currents, the chilliness in the air required a second layer, of which I wore a long sleeve shirt of poly-cotton fibers. I breathed in the freshness of the air, cooling my nasal passages and sighing out in relief that another day was approaching dusk, and I was here to enjoy it.

I went to a small, private high school, which took place mostly in the basement of a small church that had a couple hundred years of history behind it. The school day itself had ended, but my fellow "car pooler" had a project to work on that would keep him there for a couple more hours. I decided I needed something to occupy my time, so I thought I would venture out to the cemetery that rested behind the church. There I could sit, walk, or stand in the quiet where I could sort out my mind from the various chaotic patterns that enveloped the fragility of my teenage years.

I glided gently on the homemade parking area, which was more dirt than anything else. It would not be for three years that the parking lot would be fully paved. I kicked sand up as I walked, but the wind quickly and easily took the now airborne particles and moved them further away from their place. Other sand moved beneath my shoes, the tread marks leaving behind the aftertaste of my presence.

I continued around the back of the building, stepping onto the recently thrown together basketball area. I could not respectably refer to it as a basketball court, as it was no such thing. Much like the driveway, this area was put together with a reckless abandon for the sanctity of the septic tank below. The grass was unevenly grown, sparsely populated, and generally unfriendly to most bugs. It would offer them little protection from sunlight, predators, or people as they trundled along. For those who observed or collected such creatures, however, it was the best place in that area to find some hapless beetle or ant or spider that managed to end up in this anti-oasis.

Beyond the yard was a rock wall that seemed to be seventy-five to one hundred feet in length, and about 3 feet in actual height. The stones were a part of the raised earth it protected, where grass, weeds, moss, and other assorted types of non-edible vegetation permeated its surface. There was a definite pocket of insect life that existed in all the openings afforded them. Many of the creatures made the holes themselves; others found recently vacated cavities to place their nests or their young or just to avoid contact with others.

I found the stones that had fallen from the rock wall near a hidden corner behind the church. They allowed me to walk up the wall, rather than scale it, as I would normally have to do. It was not as if the scaling of the wall was all that difficult; it was only three feet tall, and I towered over it at my domineering-to-rock-walls five foot height. I just thought that I would take it leisurely today, and not try to impress my insectoid audience.

The stones did afford them a bit of a show, as one of them wasn't quite level. You learned very quickly how it would move at the slightest shifting. There was no real danger of falling off of it, however, unless you allowed your own fears to knock you down. The stone was sturdy enough, but there was a piece on the underside that, when you stood on the precipice appropriately, would cause the unevenness. It moved slightly under my weight, but I was able to quickly move off of it, almost as if I was an acrobat on the tightrope, or a slightly overweight teenager on an unevenly "grown" rock.

I stepped through the underbrush and weeds that managed to gather up on the rock wall. Those who cared for both the yard in the church and the grounds of the cemetery were unable, and mostly unwilling, to properly cultivate this mess of overgrowth. Many of it was thorn bushes, and I found myself grateful for the denim I had protecting my legs, and the boots that weighed my feet down even more so than my body did. As I did so often before, and so many times since, I jumped about two and a half feet in front of me to get over some of the trampled and thorny shrubs. Here I was, officially in the cemetery.

There were several small gravestones that were set in the path before me. They were the oldest members of the cemetery, and by far the least ornate. They had no style, no fanciful etchings, barely a presence. Although there for at least 200 years, the grass and weeds and sundry roots in the area hadn't made any effort to displace or alter the markers in any way. They had the general color of seaweed and mud, the shape of an overweight brick, and appeared as if a lathe beveled the corners. The face of each stone merely stated the person it was meant for, along with the dates of their humble physical existence. The method used to stamp the letters and numbers onto the discount bricks drew me to believe the dead themselves were forced to make these markers as a final reminder of their life ever ending.

The cemetery was close to the main road, but another rock wall protected it. There was some grass between the road and the homemade structure, about seven feet from asphalt to stone. There was also a large iron gate that kept the dead in and the living out. The lock had rusted permanently over the course of the many years it sat there amidst the elements, keeping it shut from all who would attempt to move it. The wall on either side of it stood a staggering 4 feet tall, making it almost impossible for a kitten to jump onto, and definitely impossible for a puppy to do anything but relieve itself against.

At the furthest end of this rock wall, however, was a second gate. It was smaller in its width compared to the previous opening, being only six feet wide, while the rusted gate was at least ten or twelve feet. This gate was also showing signs of age and wear, but it had been left open one night long ago, allowing people to pass easily in and out. You could see the markings of vehicles that would make the journey to the cemetery through that gate, visiting a former owner no doubt.

The section nearest the road seemed to have the newer sorts of stones, of columns and ornate slabs of worked earth, polished to an unnatural gleam. The columns seemed out of place for this particular arena of age and history, but they still found their way to be accepted with the other, simpler monuments. I could see these manifestations of what I considered to be gaudy epitaph emplacements, but I did not venture any closer to them. In fact, I would never venture to the section nearest the road, for it was too close to the civilization I was seeking to avoid; the markers themselves a reminder of modern times.

I made my way through to the gap of ground that separated the "modern" section with the more homely stones of old. An expanse of ten feet from grave to grave, it could be seen that some vehicles dared climb the uneven, and in places steep, incline from the open gate to the large tree that sat at the apex of the landscape. I was, of course, on the opposite side of the tree, but I could plainly see the trails that made their way towards its massive girth.

The tree must have been at least as old as the cemetery, and perhaps even older.

- Perception Is Truth -

The cemetery itself seemed to grow out of the ground surrounding this massive life. The branches were too high to reach for any good climbing to occur, and it stood tall and proud, as if it were the real caretaker of the fallen souls who placed their carapaces here before their journey to the afterlife had begun.

Other gravestones jutted from the earth with the look of many years, of many seasons. They were grayer than any storm I had ever seen; the cumulous clouds of the thunderstorms that kept you awake at night as a small child were nothing compared to these markers of lives long since passed. The wear on them was so prevalent, and the various repairs to them so obvious, that the names of those they were supposed to display were no longer readable. The softer stone they must have been made from, and their two and a half foot height, allowed the winds and the sands of time to scratch away much of their surface.

I noticed that some of these stones had been irreparably damaged, but their remains were set gently against the base of what had first existed. I later learned that former students had damaged some of these stones, but no one was able or willing to fix them, or pay to have them repaired as other stones had been. It seemed a shame to disgrace those who were there; a people who have come before them were now nothing more than a cheap piece of rock to them.

I walked calmly through the stones, weaving a path not intended by the founders of this cemetery; it was little matter, as neither the living nor the dead would notice my presence. I would be a passing memory to the tides of time that would wash over this place. I smiled at my eternal insignificance and trundled along.

The farthest gate, which laid bare to all, had a path cut into the earth by various sorts of wheeled traffic. It straightway marked the end of the cemetery on one side, but it came to a circular path on the rear of the cemetery, rounding back upon itself. This rear section was also lower; a small hill separated the upper and lower sections by five feet of elevation, and twenty feet of earthen expanse.

On the path that extended from the open gate to the far end was a small wall of stones, maybe a foot in height. I found myself heading towards the wall; I knew I would sit quietly for a time at that place; the furthest from the school proper. As I got closer, something was stuck in the ground that struck me as peculiar for its placement and its

- Middle Ages -

shape. It was a rock, a stone; a piece of large earth that was sitting seemingly juxtaposed with the gravestones. I thought this might have been a mistake made by the crafters and planners of this cemetery. My curiosity was drawn to this rock, so completely different from everything else there. It was too large to be part of a rock wall that may have existed there, and it was too simplistic to be a marker.

I moved unexpectedly towards the rock, and as I rounded its rough edge to face what I then realized to be the front, I was amazed. There was an inset section, with a name etched into it. In fact, not only was a name present, but the dates whereby he lived and died, and the name and date of his wife. Franklin J. Hall was his name, though I was not able to make out the dates. There was a greater sign of wear on this rock, and some moss had eaten away some of the inset and the etchings. His wife, Edith Hall, was also buried here. There was no indication of a family plot; no other Halls were buried here.

I marveled at the humbleness and the workmanship in this gravestone. There was no epitaph, as was present on other markers, no indicators on what he did, or who he even was. It was merely Franklin J. Hall, and Edith Hall, his wife. I pressed my hand against the rock, and could feel the coolness of it. The moss almost rose to meet my hand as I moved to different sections of the stone, but I was careful not to disturb the lichen. It, too, had a place in this cemetery, on this stone, keeping Franklin and Edith in constant reminder that life is all around them.

I wondered about this man, this Franklin J. Hall. Was he a farmer? Was he a merchant? What was it that made Franklin J. Hall live his life in Candia, NH? Who was Edith? Where did she come from? These were tales that, for some reason, interested me. These two people, whom I never met, had passed long before my great-grandparents were considered for conception. What were the issues that they faced? What social ills did they feel need correcting? Did such things even enter their minds, or were their lives already so full that they hadn't the time or inclination to think of things beyond caring for their home and their family?

I sat on the wall facing Franklin J. Hall, and his wife Edith, and I began to get inspired to write a poem. Not in any morbid sense, mind you. I have learned through modern culture that the dead are something you fear; it may crawl out of its grave and attempt to eat my brain. Yet... even in the dark, I knew this cemetery would bring me only serenity, of which I felt very little in the hustle and bustle of my life. This stone reminded me that there were a people that came before me, and they passed with little remembrance. They would not be recalled in anyone's memory, and none would write about them. Franklin J. Hall, and his wife Edith, deserved more than that, in my mind. I wasn't out to correct any misconceptions about their lives, but I had something that begun in me praising the simplicity of this stone, of this moment. I thanked God for this visit of inspiration upon me.

    The cemetery seemed higher to me in many ways than our humble beginnings of an educational institution. Those within this place would see the passage of time in ways none of us could conceive, and they would watch the school and the children within grow and move on. They would wonder of our future as we wondered of their past.

Technology Opinionating

The current philosophy of our American existence involves more technology than seemingly necessary. According to Marshall McLuhan, "If it works, it's obsolete." In terms of technology, he's absolutely right. However, in the speed of which this is accurate, we're also fading away our past, and the humble simplicity of life all around us. I find it increasingly the cases that people who are my age, and more notably, younger people, are addicted to the technology of not today, but of tomorrow.

Wandering through the malls, as I do as little as possible, I am astounded at how much pop culture directs our youth. Cell phones, tight clothes, loose clothes, sideways baseball caps, attitude problems, all of them are in abundance. I see children who are not old enough to drive waving around their cellular phones and calling up friends and family members with reckless abandon. They care very little about what is going on around them or their world; they seem only concerned with the moment. They have to look good, as purported by popular music, the movie and television business, magazines and advertisements, and so on. There's no longer a sense of real belonging, only the sense of appearances.

They are fed the lies of life by the icons of modern pop culture, the musicians, the actors, the actresses, but very few writers, it would seem to me. At least, they do now realize they are affected by those who write the songs and the movies and the television shows that change their views of reality on an increasingly speedy level. For example, they are taught the word "love" by movies and songs, but very few of them understand what that means. Increasingly, our physical lusts have been replaced by the term "love", and no one seems to have noticed.

Instead of trying to solve the problems at hand, such as children feeling inadequate amounts of love from their parents, we give them band-aids to solve the crises they later find themselves in: condoms, "better late than never" education on the dangers of STDs and pregnancy, abortion on street corners. It is unarguable, in my mind, that these are a product of a society gone mad by media moguls, and that we are seemingly powerless to stop them. "Why is it so easy to acquire the solutions of past problems and so difficult to solve current ones?" again, I quote Marshall McLuhan. Although a man who passed away before the first PC was introduced, he had a keen perception of how media controlled the masses.

There are so few people in my generation that seems to understand and appreciate the world around them. When you talk to them about nature or going for a hike in the woods, many would rather hang out with friends and gossip about who's sleeping with whom, and who'll be sleeping with him/her next. They don't want to sit back, look at the beauty of the sky or the changing of seasons, and think about how awesome life and living really is.

When in high school, we went on a camping trip into the mountains, to a place of such serenity and peace that I never wanted to return to the mundane reality I had learned to accept. We climbed the mountain, sat against the natural rock formations, and stared out at the earth below. It was a breathtaking experience that I have tried so hard not to forget.

The changing from summer to fall, the color in the trees shifting to a whole other section of the spectrum, indicating their partial death was again soon at hand. The wind would blow in our face, softly at first, as the stones we lay against gathered up the air. Then, a powerful gust would practically bring us to flight, reminding us of the sheer magnitude of force that nature was capable of at any given time. We would sit and we would smile and we would marvel at the mountain range that lay beyond the valleys below. We knew that each mountain held a different experience of nature, a time away from the cell phones and computers and televisions and radios that kept us away from ourselves.

Yet, I had one friend who did not understand the spiritual significance this held for so many of us. "It's just nature," she spoke callously, radically confused as to what we could possibly gain from this lack of electrical interference. I wasn't sure how to respond to her, and was forced to smile at how easily she turned her back on this, the thing that gives her life each and every day. My amusement at this experience and her comments also fueled my cynicism, yielding forth the radical idea that maybe Thoreau wasn't all-wrong.

Of course, I also learned in high school that Thoreau didn't fully adhere to his own published beliefs. The man himself, who "lived off the land", would journey into town at least once a week for provisions, never truly accepting that life could be lived outside of people, or of the advancement of technology. Whether you refer to technology as things electrical, or as simple as the corner store, all of these are different types of technological progress.

I would like to clarify and state that I am not speaking against technology, or stating that technology will one day take us over and cause the end of the world as professed in so many movies and fiction novels. I am, however, inclined to believe that we are becoming more spoiled by technology, that when it comes down to it, most of us would not have the skills to survive should there be a global power outage, or for some reason we are forced to live as our forefathers. I am no better, being a computer technician and network engineer. My entire livelihood is currently dependent on technology.

There is a danger when we allow ourselves to become wholly dependent on technology. If we allow ourselves to always use a computer or a calculator instead of doing the math ourselves, we run the risk of not learning anything but how formulae work, and not the actual application therein. If we rely so heavily on spell check, but never learn how to actually spell, it would be difficult for us to be taken seriously as learned or educated. I realize there are many people who have learning difficulties, but there are ways and means to help these people, if they have the will.

Electronic Revolution

A Confession

I did something last night for which I am none too proud of, but I'm going to tell you all anyway. I watched the American Idol finale. Normally, I head upstairs and crank out a game of City of Heroes or my recent MMORPG upgrade, World of Warcraft. Well, last night I skipped the first hour, but came down so I could learn if my prediction was correct. I was proven true, though I felt it was much closer than I would have otherwise expected.

This season has been fraught with scandal, on stage and off. It's reminded me why sensationalism is everywhere, and that the three hosts of the show are great at hosting or whatever their individual professions happen to be, but they couldn't act if their lives depended upon it. I will agree with the starter of the more heated scandal for the sake that Paula Abdul looks pretty good for getting paid to sit on her well-tanned ass.

At any rate, the outcome was never in question for me. Carrie had to win. She's the southern farm girl who attracts the working class stiffs and the little girls who actually watch the show. Bo, while a great singer and a true southern rocker, really shouldn't have had the mass appeal that he carried all the way to the end of the competition. I like Bo, don't get me wrong, but Carrie was never in doubt.

Still, I'm wondering how this will all affect Bo and his band mates. I mean, he went on a pop competition TV show, did a horrible rendition of a horrible song by the horrible band Nickelback, and in the industry he probably could have been called a sell-out. What happens now? With the contract I'm sure he'll still get from Fuller the money-making genius behind this incredulous competition, I doubt he or his band will be making music together anytime soon. OR, he gets out of whatever soul binding agreement he's locked himself into and tries it on his own with his buddies. I've heard or read somewhere that this latter option hasn't worked well for former Idol contestants, but I could be mistaken.

Why am I writing about this? Because it's almost as popular on the news front as the failed Jackson molestation trial. It's popular, but no one knows why... At least, I don't.

A Rant Without A Date

I have no words to describe what I feel. I have no feelings with which to describe. I have only the knowledge of doubt, the feeling of nothing, the realization of fallacy. I have the doubt that comes from confusion, the truth made of lies. I have hope, and I have fear. I have love and I have hate. I have a smile... but, I'm closer to tears more now than ever in all my days. I can barely contain the way I'm avoiding my own distaste for the sweetness of life. I would not go so far as to say that the bitterness of death tastes better than the honey that life promises, but I don't feel as if life is everything I've always been lead to dream it as. Even through all that I have seen and talked to and listened with... It seems to pale in comparison to the ways in which I'm supposed to feel. What I know is that the only thing right now that really makes the most sense to me is the woman that loves me more than anything. The only thing that keeps me awake at night dreaming of a better bed, with something more tangible to hold onto than pillows. She's the reason that I get up and even bother to shave. I would have a beard in August if I was allowed to revel in my own filth the way I had before I had her. My parents mean well, but they both have their own problems to contend with. My mother spent some time at the hospital, where her EKG was "a little off". That means something to the effect of heart murmurs, or something equally as aortic. My father, who has addiction concerns, is rationing the medicine that he needs to survive. The keyboard that sits before me is unusual, the keys are too close together, and don't have the same "feeling" as an older keyboard that weighs more than the combined weight of my head. I miss my pen and paper, but an attempt to write out things as they come to me causes more pain in my wrist than it relieves in my soul. All I know is that when I am sad, she cries for me. When I am happy, she laughs and smiles where all I can do is welcome the joy that she is, and she brings, to me. I often think back to the time when I thought I was most happy, but even then there are so many tears and stresses and fears that it's hard for me to wrap my mind over what about my life has been so grand and glorious. Sure, I may be smarter than other people, but that's because I spent so much of my time doing something other than talking to people. I understand people better because I can relate to pain on a few levels, but I admit to having nothing to compare with those who have experienced what can be considered major pain. While, at the most basic level, pain is the same, people are different, and our emotional states and our own understandings of pain are, in essence, different. This means, at least to me, that while some people may think I've had it easy, or I may think someone has had it quite hard, we have all learned from our experiences, hopefully, and have grown into a better, or worse, person. We accept the stimulus in our lives that we choose to, and we process them using the same brains that were given to us by Nature, or God, or Evolution, or whatever you happen to believe in today. We respond through acts of violence, greed, hate, love, passion, fear. The biggest causes of any major event are hatred, love, and fear. Often times, it can be argued, that fear is really what is behind hatred, but it is hard to get people to really explain their reason for doing some things. Some people can read other people's emotions, the way they sew them onto their Kevlar sleeves, displaying for all the world that they have a heart enough to take down the political regime that is strangling a country to death, but making certain that the OICWs are all pointed at those who you swore to liberate, in fear of a rebellion. Our society has allowed for a major denigration in our own sense of value. I have this stigma associated with writing that I won't be able to maintain the finances I've worked so hard to attain. I realize these are very meager means, but they are things for which I should be proud to stand back and think what a wonderful job I've done. Look how hard I've worked, and all that materialism nonsense. What I wish I could do is share my heart and my soul to an audience that may or may not appreciate it. I think I've learned enough of the human condition to be able to share the pain and the joy that only those who really want to live… because once they wanted to die… can really relate to. I talk to people who have had things go so well in their lives, their parents have been together all their lives, they went to good schools that their parents paid for, their first job was to help them buy food while they were away at school. I find it fascinating, and simply fabulous, how they consider a tragedy when they don't get the bonus check they think they deserve. I, on the other hand, consider it a tragedy that they should get a bonus at all. We spend all our time and energies chasing after money, "security" that comes from a home and a family. We don't live, we survive. We wouldn't know what living meant if it bit us in the face. Sure, you could go and live on the streets, doing whatever you want. You could pick pockets just so you can eat, or you could learn to hunt or fish or whatever you need to do in order to survive. Where's the living then? There once was a time that was so basic and so... honest, in our past, that so few people ever think about it. We're always racing towards the future, towards a universe that most likely doesn't want us around. All the while we turn our backs on our past, thinking we've solved all those problems, or at least acting like it. We see the past as something to forget, something to have to move on from... It is this past that makes us what we are today, and tomorrow, and forevermore. We disgrace our history, we look back on the things that we feel are inappropriate, and we just don't talk about them. Space monkeys... Without the sacrifice of these brave and kidnapped chimpanzees, we'd never have set foot on an otherwise placid moon, and stained it with our very presence. To commemorate this, we even left a flag that represents a nation who can barely feed its young. We've been to the far reaches of our known galaxy, and even beyond. We even discover new galaxies at the stroke of the pen, because math, as we see it, is an exact science. Has anyone ever considered that the reason we count the way we do is because it's based on a single principle... ONE. It isn't so much the number one, or the value... not necessarily. What it amounts to is a basis for greed to thrive, one idea, or one dollar, at a time. We as people have this difficult time comprehending this concept, because we aren't ones to think about the whole. At least, not at first. We always think about ourselves first, and then everything else second. And, when we think about other people, in terms of groups, it's because they get labeled. "Retards" or the elderly, the handicapped and the thrown away, the homeless and the needy, the poor and the lame, the fatherless and the widow. These are terms that we create to bring about a sense of sorrow, or often anger at a system that exploits them. At least, this is what we think during the holidays, when we all finally come together and try to help those in need. We feel better about ourselves because we volunteer for one day out of the year so we can pour them canned, year old soup into relatively cleaned bowls and plastic flatware. This is the catharsis for our success, volunteering. I can barely contain my cynicism when it comes to the holidays. I have no answers, I have only questions. The basis for any holiday we happen to have is all steeped so strongly in religion, and yet we've commercialized and monopolized these days "for the good of the children". I love how everything is about the children. For all the races and the creeds that talk about being exploited, it's really the "children" who get used the most in all of this rigmarole we call marketing. It is generally un-argued that this is a good thing, doing things so that the younger generation can live better lives. But, in our effort to not hurt the inner child, we've taken away discipline, a sense of responsibility, and we've set in place a chaos that grows from within the inner cities and spreads to the wealthy suburbs. It isn't a lack of education or skin tone that causes violence. It comes from the same feelings that make me write; restlessness. Some people have their own personal demons, and in some cases they may have actual demons infesting their spirit, raping their soul with each pass of their devilish claws on the skin of the lost and fearful. In general, though, you watch the news, and you see all of the people who have died in these terrible and horrible acts of violence. You learn later that, basically, the people involved in the crime itself had nothing better to do. It wasn't self-preservation, this hunter-gatherer need we supposedly have mostly bred out of our psyche, but a boredom that overtook them to such a degree, that any thought they had on something to do would be far better than to sit at home and imagine another day of watching the local newsman explain how a 4 year old child got a hold of a 45 caliber hand gun and shot their older siblings, killing one and putting the other in critical condition. Why watch the news, when they could go out and make it. Fifteen minutes of fame is still what so many people are after, from all the hit talk shows, to the books, to the constant stream of marketing benefits one receives when they purchase the latest brand name butt plug. We spend our time, and our money, on things we don't need, and indeed, we spend money on things we don't even want. No matter how clever it is to have a singing sock for a holiday that celebrates a fat man who, for some reason gives freely, how many people really look at that gaudy and silly bauble and consider how needless it is... How needless is much of what we let our society dictate to us to be a fact and to be a necessity... Why can't I sleep at night? Why have my dreams grown ever worse lately, most of them ending with the ghoulish notion that the spiritual and demonic realm I was raised to believe in, but shunned from the horror and thriller movies that portrayed these ideas? I wonder sometimes if I should welcome the insanity that comes from a seemingly inane fear. I wonder if I should welcome... anything... sometimes.

Sometimes...

Admonition Against Apostolicism

There must be a balance ☯ between my own theology and ✞ the ones that brought me into being, but I'm going about it in the wrong fashion. I've spent so ✠ much time trying to tear away at all the thoughts and beliefs I've ever ✡ had, I'm not spending any time really trying to evolve my ☪ own thoughts or to study the other religions and philosophies that are out there. I will ॐ do my best to prepare topics that are of my interest, not of my "life is like an onion" madness ☸ where everything has to be stripped away until nothing stands.

Isn't my whole purpose to educate not eradicate? Shouldn't it be my mantra to build and not to break?

Afterdeath

A friend from high school has her own blog, and her most recent articles involve discussions on what is most oft construed as the afterlife, specifically heaven and hell. Now, I do not wish to detract from her views, for indeed any thoughts regarding these places are merely speculation. However, it's been such an issue for so many hundreds or thousands of years that I feel it bears some sort of look into it for purely educational reasons. In other words, there would be no thoughts about it if no one talked about it in their own way.

Heaven and hell have always, and I mean *always*, been described as a physical place to me. In every single teaching or commentary or adage or anecdote about such places, it's always been described in physical terms. Provided, this could all fall into my theory that God has explained things to us or that the Bible has specific concepts put into it in such a way that we would be able to understand it. For example, referring to God as male or as father is ridiculous as God has been described as both male and female. Likewise, if we, man and woman, were made in the image of God, then how can God be either? A simpler example is that of time, which God created specifically for us. Time wasn't around until God created the day and the night, ere go God did not require this event, but gave it to us so we could keep track of our sad little lives. But, I digress.

Heaven is supposed to be the happiest place ever, where we shall live for all eternity. There are many things promised us in this afterlife haven for our soul, yet it's all from a physical perspective. Is this merely for our child-like brains to have a clearer understanding of why we want to be sent there? Is this truly where our forms will go after they've broken free of the shells that bind? Are we actually experiencing heaven and hell right now, and when we die we'll continue to live within it? Will our souls then be free to see everything our bodies have denied? Will we then see everything for what it truly is and not through the blinders that my bi-focaled orbs now blurrily display?

Wow. So many theories running through my mind thanks to M's entries. I can't get these ideas out of my head, for she did open my mind to doors and windows and rivers of thought that I would have never considered. Are Heaven and Hell merely metaphors to keep us in line with Biblical doctrine? Will we experience them physically with our Spirit Man? Does God truly intend on sending those who refuse to believe to a lake of fire and brimstone with someone else that showed pride and disdain for God's rule? Is Satan even real? Are we actually living in heaven and hell based upon our life choices, and then will continue as such when our spirits are separated from our bodies? Will that be our last chance? What about the Dead in Christ spoken of in Revelation? What about the 144,000 Jews who are supposed to ascend into Heaven? What about predestination? Will I win Powerball tonight? Should I even have any answers?

The first thing, I think, that bears the most importance in this regard is what does God, the Almighty, the Creator, the Supreme Being, whatever name you give to that which made us, what is the perspective of our Deity in regards to loving us and caring for us? Where does that level of caring reach? I place the highest level of importance in this area because I believe it's key to know if God cares about us or not that will determine God's commitment to our eternal soul. If God does not care for us, there would be no need for eternal salvation or damnation. If God does care for us, then it would stand to some reason that there is a purpose for heaven, and a similar purpose for hell. It's also arguable that the idea of hell is our own souls living within these human shells, and that when we are living in the fullness of our souls, then when we are no longer blinded by these soft gelatinous spheres we will be in the heaven that God intended for us, which would be some level of ascension, I would imagine.

I have contested for many years that God is not love, but this is based upon the Old Testament. The New Testament covers the idea that God is Love, specifically in 1 John 4:7-12, but that's the New Testament. Besides, that particular section of verses states that God is Love *specifically* because Jesus was sent. I'll correct myself here, it states that God showed love by sending Jesus to die for us. This does not, logically, mean that God is Love, only that God shows love. Yes, it states that those who know love know God because God is love, but that doesn't make any sense to me. Logically speaking, it doesn't work. Yes, I know God's ways are not our ways, but why would we have our ways if God didn't allow them? If our thoughts are God-inspired, then shouldn't some of this stuff make more sense than it does to me? That's like saying those who know chocolate love Willy Wonka because Willy Wonka is chocolate. While it makes sense that Willy Wonka, a truly mythical character, creates chocolate, he is not in fact made of chocolate, nor does he embody chocolate. It's not a valid observation. Am I nitpicking? Probably, but I don't have blind faith anymore.

Aside from that, is it not said that Christ is the same yesterday, today, and forever? If that's true, and the Triune God is truly a single being with three equal parts, then that means God is the same yesterday, today, and forever. Fine. Can someone tell me then why God changed the way in which we were punished? In the past God would have wiped us out and started again. Later on it became necessary to sacrifice lambs or other material goods in order to appease the Almighty. Eventually, God's own Son was sent to be sacrificed so we could stop slaughtering animals. Well, if God's the same, and God is Love, then how is it love to wipe out a planet, to destroy Sodom and Gomorrah because they were immoral? That's punishment, sure, but what do they learn? We believe that punishment is supposed to teach us something, but if God decides to wipe you out, you never learn your lesson. While it can be argued that what Sodom and Gomorrah were used to teach other people, is that love? If so, then love for whom? Love for those who will perform the exact same tasks and immoralities? Why should they get off so easy while the Sodomites were obliterated. Lot's wife is another fine example of God's punishing love, in that she was turned to a pillar of salt for seeing God at work. Yes, she did what she was told not to, but why would God punish her so handily and immediately for going against God's Will and give so many others a break for ignoring the Biblical precepts set forth so many thousands of years ago?

Let's continue on the topic of God's Will, since we're here. God has God's Will, God's Perfect Will, God's Perfect Plan for our lives, what God wants, etc. We have Free Will. As mentioned previously, free will isn't free, it comes at a hefty price. Aside from it not being something we have asked for, we still have to pay for it. It's like being forced to accept a service that we may or may not want depending on the trade-off. Quite simply, if we, with Free Will, choose not to follow God's Will, then hell is the alternative. That, to me, doesn't seem like a choice. Yet, people, myself included, choose every day to live their life as *they* see fit, and do not follow that which God set forth for their lives. What do I have to look forward to? Apparently, no matter how it's perceived, I'll be set away from God, living in eternal torment with no hope for reprieve. There's some debate over that fact as I was saved at a young age and did help to convert someone to Christianity. Technically, depending on your particular brand of dogma, I'm all set. I'll be going to heaven based on what I've already done, not how I live the rest of my life. Short of blaspheming the Holy Spirit anyway. Of course, there's the argument that I can lose my salvation, but I haven't the time to get into the whole faith without works argument.

So, we have Free Will; do as God says or burn in hell. That seems about right. We have a choice, but we should choose to do what is right and proper and precisely what we are supposed to do. Yet, if God has a Perfect Plan for our lives, if God's Will is Perfect and infallible and not even our choices can contradict what God wants, then why lie to us about Free Will at all? How can there be the thought of predestination and Free Will? If God already knows what's going to happen to us, why even bother trying to impress the Almighty? If predestination is a possibility, then why are we trying so hard to do things so right? If the interpretation in Revelation is accurate, and only a large handful of Jews are to go into Heaven, then why are the Dead in Christ going to ascend? What the hell is going on in Heaven?

While it's true I'm cynical because of my own beliefs and my own history within this faith, I still feel that my points are valid and that people, specifically those of the faith, need to carefully consider some of these arguments. Souls are not won by spouting Scripture, I'm sorry. I didn't convert someone to Christianity by preaching to them, but by talking to them and answering the questions that they had. I cannot come back to Christianity, to the faith that I was raised in, until certain questions are answered. I don't see that happening.

Well, it seems there are some answers.

Am I Labeled Correctly?

So, I've been hearing a lot about labels and stereotypes and name calling and such in the news of late. It has troubled me greatly for a number of reasons. I'll do my best to recall the labels I have heard and the given context, for indeed context has also become something of an awesome argument of late. I'll also be forced to edit much of these words as it is not MySpace friendly, but you'll understand what I'm getting at.

Let's start first with Don Imus and his sideways comment about female basketball players. Was it an absurd thing to say? Absolutely. Should he have gotten in trouble for? Nominally speaking, yes. A fine or sensitivity training or having to put up with Sharpton or Jackson on his low-rent talk show for a couple hours. That would have been plenty of punishment. It's funny that Imus would get fired for such a sideward statement but Stern managed to stay on the radio for years. Sure, he got fired here and there, dropped from certain radio stations, but we was still on the air. Why you may ask? I believe it's the sex he was peddling on a day to day basis. Imus wasn't peddling anything except that which had the Imus label on it; his cancer ranch, his organic food. He was like Paul Newman without the respect. I for one do not miss his presence, but I am annoyed at how he was removed. Take him off the air because he sucks not because he repeats what has found its way into the lexicon of "White America" from "African-American Society" or "Ebonics".

We've been subjected to these racial epithets for so long in sensitivity training and by shock jocks and by the religious leaders and by politicians who seek to end "the racial divide." They seek to end it by bringing it up every damn day. That's not ending it. You aren't going to get people to forget a thing by repeating it every day, you're just going to exacerbate it to the point that it becomes something else, that it becomes accepted in society. The "African American community" uses such anti-black phrases rather frequently in popular culture, if not truly on the street. I remember a neighbor kid in the project where I lived (this isn't true ghetto project, but it sucked just the same), who was black, who referred to an older black kid by everyone's favorite "N" word. The older kid proceeded to beat the crap out of the younger kid. You couldn't do much, the older kid was something of a gang leader in the area and ran the place I lived at. Everyone was afraid of him. Nowadays, it's a joke to use the "N" word at each other, like it's replaced the 70's "brother". It cannot be spoken unless you are one yourself, as it were. The same cannot be said for the Hispanic community, at least it has not been suggested to be as prevalent.

To further the "racial" topic, let's look back at the Imus situation. Fines, yelling, firing. All for a simple little phrase that, once Imus said it, was blown onto every newsstand across the country. Suddenly it was okay to say "'knappy headed hos' because Don Imus said it and all I'm doing is repeating what he said to say how horrible it was". All over the news, the nightly news, the weekend shows, the papers, the blogs, the web papers… Everywhere this "racially charged" phrase was thrown in our faces to show how bad one man was. Well… who's the more foolish? The fool, or the fool who follows him? (That's a direct quote. Anyone? Anyone?)

Let's continue on the racial thing as I segue way into homosexuality. Funny how I can do that. It's like seven degrees of separation with me. Or is it three degrees…

Actually, I'm using politicians as the juncture point, or at least politicking in general. There's a woman and a black man running for the presidency and there's been talk about the woman being a lesbian and the black man not being black enough. Let's discuss frankly the fact that the black man, whether or not you believe he is more white in his speaking and his education than black, hasn't the experience in office to assume the Presidency, and I hope this is something people really consider when that day comes. Some will say that he lost because of racism, but those same people would say that race had nothing to do with his winning. Right. Of course there are similar arguments against the female of the species. I, for one, am not opposed to the idea of a female leader of the free world, just not the one I've been presented with. Both of them, along with all the rest of the politicos, have used labels for themselves and their constituents and the undecided and those they wish to curry favor with. In the meantime, everyone's been getting offended by it, but they insist on being labeled just the same.

I made the choice to watch a video by an openly homosexual individual who has a host of these little infomercials about why he's homosexual or why his homosexuality matters or why he thinks this about that because he's homosexual. Listen, I realize the way I was raised I should be mighty upset with the whole concept of homosexuality, and before anyone tries to quote the Bible to me, understand I've already had this talk,

I've already done the research, and I've already lambasted a liberal nut job in my town for trying to use the Bible to back up his point. God doesn't like homosexuality. At the very least, the Judeo-Christian perspective of God is opposed in a major way to the act of homosexuality. Free will be damned... Read Leviticus and I Corinthians, Chapters 13 and I believe 6, respectively. Could be I Cor 9, I seem to be slipping in my old age. But, this is also between them and God, not them and us or whoever. Ye without sin cast the first stone... However, what I don't agree with or approve of is the inconsistency in our society regarding the way that people act.

We call for the head of anyone making a joke or a comment about race or homosexuality who is not of that race or that sexual proclivity. If I were to say "fag" it'd be called hate speech and I'd probably get in trouble. What if I were talking about twigs? Or cigarettes? That particular word has other meanings, it's the context that matters here. However, if I were of that "team" and made a comment about "those fags" it'd be considered a joke because "it takes one to know one" and all that. Sometimes I feel as though life has become one big f'ing cliché. This is part of that thought. Further, in popular culture, the homosexual, specifically the male, is allowed to make crass or otherwise impolite jokes in mixed company and it's considered bawdy but acceptable. An equally heterosexual male making the same joke would be looked upon as a pervert and ostracized from the party he didn't want to go to in the first place.

What everyone is screaming for is equality, and it's just a front. They don't want equality, they want to be better than everyone else. They don't want to be recognized as just another set of people, they want to be recognized as the only right people. They want to be seen as better than the white Christian male, because the white Christian male has subjugated people and persecuted people for as long as we can remember. And they're not far off on the subjugation part, but the Christian and the white aren't always accurate. Africa still has slavery within some of its countries, genocide occurring in numerous areas, Iran persecutes their own people, Islamists blow us up every single day. Before I get too far ahead of myself, and before I get attacked for being anti-Islam, step back. Not all terrorists label themselves as terrorists, but all the terrorists we've been hearing about have been Islamists. Allah and Mohammed is His Prophet spread the word by the sword, in violence and subjugation. The Jews did not commit such heinous acts. The Christians... That's another story altogether. Back to my point, there are countries in the world where "atrocity" occurs on a daily basis. Human trade, be it for sex with children or for body parts, goes on tacitly accepted in Southeast Asian countries; catch a few high-profile "predators" and let the rest go through unscathed. It's a money-maker, after all. Some countries women are forced to wear things or are beaten in order to malform their bodies to be more acceptable for their own society. This reminds me of my argument that morality is defined by the majority, by the "religion" or the society of a place.

But, I digress from my point about labels. We assume that just because someone fits into a label they'll be the kind of person we expect of them to be. To say someone were Christian would mean certain things on a societal level. For me, it often means someone with a superiority complex who believes that they're right and that everything that I do in my life that they don't approve of is not of God and therefore must be of the Devil. Catholics are expected to be this pious bunch, but really all they have to do is go to confession and they're free to sin again. Mobsters are good Catholics, aren't they? To say that someone is "religious" is to do them a great disservice. To say you are "spiritual" is to make something of a joke. I've known people to say they were "spiritual" and really they just use it as a line to make themselves look deeper than the puddle of oil their personality really is. You talk to them and they can discuss some base-level religious theory with you, but when it comes right down to it they use what little they have to try and pick up chicks. It's a sad world I live in.

We give ourselves labels to keep people from talking to us too much. I've been labeled "melancholy" on more than one occasion. That's fine. If it keeps people from asking me too many questions or from assuming that I'm going to smile just because they ask me to... You have to understand that just because I smile once in a while and seem all gloomy the next doesn't mean I'm depressed and it doesn't mean I'm going to be happy all the time or even more of the time. I'm wired this way for a reason and I'm not inclined to start changing my polarity just because "life" happens. I've always believed there's more to life than living, there's more to living than surviving, but I'm not sure how to live any more than I can just survive...

We use clichés and words and phrases that we all know because it's become part of our vernacular. I appreciate that growth is good, that the evolution of our language has helped to improve our way of life and has given us great strides in technology that we wouldn't have been able to achieve if we hadn't thought beyond what we knew… But we've lost sight to what the words really mean or where they come from or that slang really isn't a language. We've lost sight of the fact that what we say has an impact but that it shouldn't have as big an impact as it does. The only people keeping racism alive are the people that perpetuate the stereotypes and the people who are too ignorant to realize the war is over. Needless racism and hatred is still among us, but by pressing it into our face every day it's not going to go away. Don't preach diversity, live by it. Don't force the idea down our throats, just let it happen. It's funny that the same people who argue that God is being shoved down their throats are the same ones trying to shove their ideas and their morals down everyone else's throat. If you can't beat em, join em? Or at least use their tactics?

"If you tell a lie big enough and keep repeating it, people will eventually come to believe it. The lie can be maintained only for such time as the State can shield the people from the political, economic and/or military consequences of the lie. It thus becomes vitally important for the State to use all of its powers to repress dissent, for the truth is the mortal enemy of the lie, and thus by extension, the truth is the greatest enemy of the State."

That was from none other than Joseph Goebbels, Minister for Public Enlightenment and Propaganda for Hitler… We complain our politicians lie to us…

We're allowing our world to head into a cesspool of whatever passed for morality for a thousand years, and we're doing it willingly. When you stand up to say anything, you're a dissident or a traitor or unpatriotic. Because someone agrees with the war or doesn't agree with the war, depending on which side of the fence you're on, makes you unpatriotic. Plenty of examples in today's news about people being called unpatriotic when they're just saying what they believe. It's sad when even the words we say are labeled. Why can't our words stand on their own anymore?

What will I be called when someone who doesn't like what I have to say reads all the way to the end…?

Another Letter to OTR

I would like to begin this email by stating that I came into knowledge of you guys during a show in which you opened for Vigilantes of Love. I'll get into that later. I would also like to mention that I've written quite a bit about you guys as a band, and as an inspiration. However, I've never shown such works to anyone, ever. The last time I wrote anything was when I picked up Films for Radio, but I'll get into that later, too.

First, I'd like to give a little review of the album I just picked up this afternoon, Ohio. On the surface, it's everything I've come to expect from you guys. It's heartfelt, it's raw with the solemn emotions that have come from you in recent years.

It has the sadness of Good Dog, Bad Dog, the taste of Patience, a dash of Amateur Shortwave Radio, and the essence of a Grey Ghost story. It's a piece of musical literature I will treasure with the rest of my library. The thing about you that has really got me to stay ever interested in whatever work I can put my hands on is your ability to grow. In everything you do, no matter what the situation or the song or the context, I respect your growth most of all.

While it is true your sound has changed, indicating your growth in your combined musicianship, the power of Karin's voice and her words have really shown through with a wonder I cannot express with words the way she can by opening her mouth and releasing all the feelings she's ever had… In a single note… Linford's musical ability has exploded in recent years. My amazing appreciation at both of his albums (though I admit to loving I don't think… more than Grey Ghost Stories), I think, really got him thinking about music more, and how to make it flow even more intensely than any album before.

I see that on Good Dog, Bad Dog, and even further with Ohio. It would be a travesty to say that Ohio is your best album. In fact, I think it should almost be considered and insult. The fact is that you have allowed your music to display a growth, as though it has developed beyond its own teenage years and blossomed into adulthood. I think the albums of Over the Rhine really stand the test of time as a testament to how expressions grow with each passing year, day, hour…

I understand of course this is becoming something of a tale, rather than a simple review. I also realize that much of these thoughts are repeated or may not flow as perfectly as Karin's voice when she soothes me to life again with such songs as "Bothered" and "Go Down Easy". I appreciate any and all who sit here and trundle along through this seeming diatribe praising a band we already love.

I wish I could see you guys while you're in my area next week. Alas, I have class, and will be unable to attend. The CIS department has a policy for missing class, and it's none too friendly. I am toying with not being at class, but I already have to miss class a week prior to your show because I'll be in a class for work. It's a long story, but I was supposed to be in Waltham, MA, the night of your show in Cambridge. Well, the schedule changed, and now I won't be there that week. I'm trying to work out a solution, but my situation gets more complicated as the days go on… I'll try, though. Really, I will.

Now, for the real story, at least the best I can remember… The first time I ever heard Over the Rhine.

It was 1996, I was a young, Christian teenager, and my ideals were higher than I realized. I used to have the poster for this tour… But it was destroyed during my most recent move… Sadly, it's one you stopped offering at your website. It was the boy falling in the pool, "Go Down Easy" hovering above him. It was the Gordon College show.

Anyway, I went there with some friends of mine from church who were on a first name basis with Bill Mallonee. They were on the guest list, and I was their stowaway. We arrived early, as all good concert goers should. But, I got the best treat of my life; I got see Karin during a sound check. Linford was at his keyboard, she was standing before her mic with her acoustic guitar in hand. At the time, being a good Christian boy, I was very much into the lyrical basis of all music, secular, Christian, otherwise. I had the "us and them" mentality Mark Heard spoke about. I was no different than anyone else I thought I knew.

When I heard the voice of this beautiful blonde, with seasoned poet laureate behind her, I remember specifically, verbatim, the words out of my humble little mouth. "I don't care what they believe. I'm buying one of their CDs." I stared in a sudden awe, through the feedbacks and the grunts of the engineer. It turns out the show was moved from the auditorium to the cafeteria area, for reasons I'm still not sure about. Something about us being bumped because there weren't enough people to fill the area. It ended up making for the best concert performance I'd ever been to, ever heard of, ever imagined. I've been to a few concerts since, even worked at a few, but they all paled in comparison to the feelings that were shared throughout this tight-knit group of Christians and secularists alike who had come together for one common goal: music.

It's difficult for me to recall all the emotions that coursed through my veins that night, but I was excited the whole way through. I saw the light at the end of the tunnel, I saw the train coming for me, and I embraced it. I allowed my fears and doubts about music to die that night, and I was opened to such a larger world beyond the realities and the heartstrings that religion had placed around me. I'm not saying I became an atheist, but I felt... free. I was so touched by the ways and the words and the musics and the sounds... If I had tears to shed, the beauty of it would have bade me to drown in the River of Love that I saw and heard and felt that night. It was the greatest gift I could have had.

I got everyone's autograph that night, from all of Over the Rhine, and the incarnation of VoL that existed for... A couple of albums, anyway.

Years later, I'm in a relationship I'm actually fairly pleased with, things are going well. I ventured into the local Newbury Comics (where I purchased Ohio, incidentally. Don't worry, though, I want the collector's edition direct from you guys.), noted the Back Porch release of Good Dog, Bad Dog, but I saw behind it a wholly different thing. At first, I was so happy and amazed to see you guys were out of the attic and into my back yard, that I wanted to run to the register with Good Dog, Bad Dog, just so I could have Track 10. But, I looked to see what person had placed a non-OtR CD with the rest. Thinking perhaps it might be Eve, my attitude adjusted slightly. What I found in its place was an album that further changed me, Films for Radio.

There was an incoherent truth that was shared between myself and my CD player that night, one that inspired me to write words of such length and wonder... It tied in the emotions I had felt that first night, with the love I thought I knew at that very moment. Things truly did not work out with the person I was in the relationship with, but my love for Over the Rhine hasn't shifted with the breeze. I hope to find that slip of paper, which I know I have in a box someplace, and I'll send along the unfinished masterpiece.

- Electronic Revolution -

I'm in college now, after a few years of being in the work force, but I'm told I have a wisdom and a vision of men twice my age. Well, almost twice my age. I see things differently than most people I associate with, and I've always wondered why that was. I wrote a paper recently for my English Class, and of those in my class who edited it, not a single person came away with their own thoughts. The idea of the work was to show them a place that had been a great inspiration to me, in such detail that they could really see what it was I was trying to share, but not spoil it with my own emotions. I wanted THEM to feel something, to draw forth a stirring of something more important than themselves. I failed somehow. It seems that none of them were able to ascertain my "point". It was as if they wanted me to tell them how I am supposed to feel, but I couldn't do that. That would cheapen the reasons for writing the piece.

I think that this is summed up by the greatest lyricist I have ever had the pleasure and the honor to have experienced. His music is ever fresh every time I throw the CD into the player and let the laser act as the needle as it scratches the surface of my metallic album, vibrating the sounds to my always welcome ears.

"Maybe those inclined towards the arts are so spiritually retarded to a degree that we must go through the whole process of cathartic expression just to discover how we really feel." Mark Heard

That's one of the things I love about Over the Rhine, and people like Mark Heard. You guys don't pull any punches, you don't cater to the system and what you're supposed to do. The commentary on Good Dog, Bad Dog, where you were described as "undiscovered". The problem is that you weren't undiscovered, you just weren't saying the things that everyone wants to hear. You were saying what you felt in your heart, not what you felt you "had" to as musicians. I have such a deep respect for the pictures and the poems and the ways in which Linford and Karin both share their hearts and their talents, and dare I say I have a love for them because of it?

I'll be getting married next May, and my love and I are toying with putting together a CD with different love songs on it. I was a bit hesitant at first, knowing her more "mainstream" musical tastes. Not that she doesn't appreciate Tori Amos or Sarah McLachlan, but I've always struggled with people really understanding my choice in music. I'm pouring through the albums and the lyrics to pull together a couple of OtR tunes, but I'm forced to consider what people would really think of as a "love" song.

Sometimes I don't know why, the context of the song doesn't entirely fit the mold... But I think that "Happy To Be So" is one of the most beautiful songs I've ever heard. The way Karin's voice moves melodically throughout this piece just buckles my weakest joints, knees and all. It's a song that I have to listen to with as little distraction as possible. It explains in some detail the way I feel about the one that I love. My heart's trapped, but I don't care. It's on its own deathbed, clamoring for the life it once had, but I'm willing to let it die. I want to be in her arms forever, and I hope that I can show that to her in everything I do.

I just want to thank you for all the work... hmm... all the feelings you project in your... art, for lack of a better term. I think sometimes that the term "art" or "artist" leaves behind a stigma... an attitude of higher intellect or of loftier emotions. I think the reality is that many artists really know what it is they are feeling, and can show it forth in ways most people are too afraid to try.

Thank you, Linford and Karen, for being a constant source of pleasure and inspiration to me. I hope that your music and your own personal love with last beyond the realms of life and passion.

Thank you, for taking the time to read this lengthy and possibly cumbersome writ. But, to quote a great poet: "And once again, we find ourselves with homespun pieces of reality. Memory markers in the meanwhile. The same story. Which, if you've read this far, obviously involves you."

Astral Projection

Here's just a quick thing to ponder… Please be forewarned that my knowledge of astral projection is wholly limited, though I do believe I have experienced a portion of this ability in my own life. Naturally, my belief is not strong enough in this idea that I have any sort of control over it, or that I truly experienced it. Yet, I have found a rather curious reference in the Bible that suggests this is a possibility.

Revelation 4:2 (NIV)

"And immediately I was in the spirit: and, behold, a throne was set in heaven, and one sat on the throne."

John the Apostle, not to be confused with Christ's cousin, spent some time on the prison isle of Patmos, paying for his crimes because of his faith. Either through delirium or a chosen adventure by God, he was able to see heaven in its fullest, and view what has been described as The End Times for as long as I've been alive.

The reason I point this out at all is because of the Christian concept that such an act is not of God. Yet, I have heard many times of people being taken up into Heaven in their dreams, or have seen Heaven upon their very deathbed before being brought back to life. Spiritual movement in that respect is astral projection, as I understand it. If it is natural for our spirits to leave our bodies when we die, then is there any way we can control such an ability while we're alive?

Balance

I'll have to add in quotes and verses and references later, but I know I've heard lots of areas where the idea of balance and moderation are religiously prevalent. This partially coincides with my other talk regarding materialism, but there's a broader sense of balance that really ought to be achieved in all things. Work, play, money, etc. Everything should have some kind of balance.

I'm not referring to some kind of points system, wherein you can go a little over or a little under your quota, as long as everything equals out to zero. I mean you have to consider what you're going to do before you do it. Don't react, think. This can be true of any situation you find yourself in. Don't accuse someone without some facts, and don't defend yourself in such a violent way if there's a possibility that you could be wrong.

We live in an age of violence and pride, greed and power. We run around and protect ourselves from that which may not be there. We stereotype and hate and suspect people for absolutely no other reason than they wear their hats backwards or their parents are from a country that hates us but they've grown up in Southie all their lives. We ignore the old adage "Don't judge a book by its cover". We want what we want when we want. Burger King, "Your way right away". It's a catchy slogan I agree, but it's exactly what I feel is wrong with our society. There's no patience, there's no penance. There's no concern for our fellow man unless it's thrust in our faces.

Confused

Our life is littered with distraction after distraction, and I find myself looking around trying to make sense of it and decide what to focus my efforts on. My desire to be a world-famous and overpaid writer isn't going as well as I want because I'm not focused on finishing what I consider saleable works or at least finding someone willing to pay to read what I have to say. I mean, what really makes me stand out beyond the rest? What can I say or do that will make someone interested enough to come and read more of what I have to say and/or be willing to then pay for such drivel?

While I try to figure that out I have to work to upkeep my lifestyle and the lifestyle my family (cats & wife) have become accustomed to. I can't just up and quit and be one of those starving artists who'll write for food; I have to maintain a standard of living because that's the world in which I live. I live in a world where monetary wealth and the ability to earn money is vastly more important than thought or the ability to spell correctly and in proper context. Don't believe me? I cannot help you then.

I think about all the labels and the names of the manufacturers of our goods and how important it is for us to be shopping at this store but not this other store because they're just not hip anymore or because they lack whatever draws in customers. They're old news. Time to move on to something younger and sleeker who'll advertise better. I blame this perspective for the recent resurgence in Apple Computers, but naming names isn't why I came here to…day.

We have people who dwell and obsess over their lives or their childhood and all they do is wallow in their own guilt or self-pity. We have people who can't handle the pressures of the day-to-day so they shut down emotionally but go about their day and accomplish at least what they need to survive. We have people who are concerned with what they wear and how they present themselves and work to maintain the appearance of wealth if not the actual capital. There are people obsessed with money who let their personal lives fall to the wayside so they can conquer the world by amassing more of this money I keep bringing back up like a bad Chinese leftover lunch micro waved for too little time. We have people obsessed with cynicism and talking about why the world is doomed to the wasteland of emotional and intellectual emptiness I've grown accustomed to. We're obsessed with politics and music and celebrity and religion and science and we don't stop and stare at the world and wonder what we really should be doing with our time.

We see the world advance further and further into an unknown future with eyes wide shut and brains on fire. We have no clue what the future holds for all our posturing and fortune-telling. We have no control over the direction our society goes anymore. We gave up on that when we gave up our identity by casting aside religion in favor of thought. Don't get me wrong, I'm all for thought, but no one actually did any thinking when they decided we didn't need God. No one bothered to fill the void in our societal hearts and minds, so we fill it with whatever vagaries we possibly can, all fueled by those who endeavor to be famous and manage just enough fame to make an impression.

People who every single day do things for others are overlooked because they don't have the sense God gave to Satan; they're not in it for their own glory, they're in it to help people. There are truly selfless heroes that no one notices unless there's a camera in their face. We have reality television about aged rock stars trying to find true love in a foray into lust, pure and simple. There's no love on these shows, only opportunity and lucrative television contracts. Our obsession with this "genre" of television has gone so far as to include meter maids. For some reason I find this the lowest form of this already ridiculous sub-genre of narcissism. We live in a world of people who say "Who Cares?" but we can't wait to see Lindsay Lohan get out of jail or finish her public service at the morgue or if Britney will get her kids back.

We enjoy when people of privilege get their "come-uppins" and we laud those celebs who try to do what's right; if they're one and the same then we just make fun of them for treating us so stupidly... Yeah, after your third drunk-driving offense we no longer care if you're going to devote your life to helping AA. You're just another liar. Go make another movie so we can pay you millions to kill yourself on the nightly news. We'd rather watch about the hurt and pain in this world then learn about the good in this world. We're falling apart as a society because we want to, because we're learning from the media that it's the right thing to happen. It must be, otherwise why would they constantly show us the destitution our world has reached? This must be what life is all about; misery and mockery.

I don't have any answers. I keep questioning things to a point where the only logical solution is to drill a hole in my head or play video games till I drool myself into a coma in some Japanese cyber cafe. It happens. I'm one of the lucky ones to have such a wonderful and loving wife to at least share this life with, no matter the outcome of our futures. At least I have her. Could I get by in life without her? I'm sure I could but why would I want to...?

It's a conundrum, for if we live our lives blissfully ignorant things will happen to us by the rulers that we decided against choosing because it offended our sense of morality. But if we obsess over such decisions we fall into the possibility of an early grave through stress and heart failure. If we don't take care of our bodies properly we'll die and if we over stress our bodies while trying to take care of it we'll die. The old adage of death and taxes doesn't apply; it's strictly life and death. All these things shall pass, right? Taxes. Surcharges. Rent. Mortgage. Chanel. Eddie Bauer... We have to make decisions about them because we live with them, but do they matter? Stability and durability matter, but do the names matter?

What is it that matters in this world and does anyone have a real answer that I can't argue out of how to live our lives? Or, better yet... Does anyone really care about this rant?

Cynicism Or Outright Fear

I've heard there's been some issues with Mr. DeLay of late, but I admit I've been ignoring most of it. I did finally read this particular article because of what I felt was sheer audacity on the part of the House Majority Leader.

This is one of those pieces wherein I do not know if my cynicism is what sparked my imagination and concern, or if I am correctly fearful of the implications of what this man has suggested. Specifically,

We've got Justice Kennedy writing decisions based upon international law, not the Constitution of the United States? That's just outrageous. -From the Article

This sparked my further researching of a comment made by Noam Chomsky in regards to the United States blocking various UN Resolutions with their veto power. Specifically, observation of international law. From what I found, and indeed this was a brief search, in 1982 the US vetoed a resolution regarding development of international law. For the next 4 years they would continue to vote against such a notion, culminating in 1986 with their veto of all nations observing international law.

So, now we're in a place where international law is "ridiculous", according to the House Majority Leader of the United States of America. And why not? We're the greatest superpower in the world by most accounts, so why should we bother to observe any ideals or thoughts or feelings from other countries? We've been denied extradition to and from other countries because of our acceptance of the death penalty, we knowingly assist a terrorist nation on a daily basis, and there's apparently a problem when a Supreme Court justice takes some initiative and does his own research. A terrible cloud of idiocy has fallen over a nation when trying to gain more information on a topic is "just incredibly outrageous".

I haven't studied civics in quite a while, so I was a tad unclear as to the story mentioning the House has "no power" over the Supreme Court Justice process. Well, it seems that the Legislative Branch, or the Congress, while consisting of both the House and the Senate, only allows the Senate to confirm those judges appointed by the President.

This means that the comments made by Senator DeLay, whether right or wrong, are mostly irrelevant. Except, perhaps, for this one:

However, DeLay has called repeatedly for the House to find a way to hold the federal judiciary accountable for its decisions. "The judiciary has become so activist and so isolated from the American people that it's our job to do that," he said.

-From the Article

He goes on to further explain how he means to implement such an amazingly brazen idea:

One way would be for the House Judiciary Committee to investigate the clause in the Constitution that says "judges can serve as long as they serve with good behavior," he said. "We want to define what good behavior means. And that's where you have to start."

-From the Article

Well, that's one way to get around the fact that he has no legal right to stake any claim in the judicial process. It's one way to work around having a judge who observes law in forms dissimilar to his own. It's one way to edge that much further from a population-led democracy...

Clarification

Every time I read this particular entry, I find that there's something missing: clarity. My perspective is somewhat lacking here, except my distaste for the words uttered by Tom DeLay. Big deal, a small-town computer tech disapproves of the ideas of the House Majority Leader. Well, that's exactly the point. I disagree with his perspective for a number of reasons, but I also must point out that my opinion is mostly irrelevant. I'm not a member of his constituency, I don't live in his state, and in fact I've already forgotten what state he represents.

The reason that my opinion SHOULD matter is that we live in a democracy. Truly, I feel that we haven't lived in a true democracy for some time. Of course, I'm also not a poli-sci major, nor am I heavy into politics aside from what I see in the paper or on the news. It is my understanding that a democracy is supposed to be the voice of the nation, not those in power. Are there others who are screaming for us to change the ways in which judges are chosen and allowed to stay in office? Did this idea of his suddenly come to him in a dream? Was this idea fed him by an image consultant or from lobbyists throwing money in his face? Or did this actually come from some little old ladies who are actively concerned about the future of law in their country?

That's a question I never hear: Where did this idea come from?

I also feel I should be specific about why I find his method for skirting the judicial system as disheartening as I find it abusive. "Good behavior" is rather confusing verbiage, completely unhelpful in legal matters, for it indeed allows for interpretation. I learned what good behavior was from my parents, teachers, and those that I found to be role models or examples of what I was supposed to be like. However, my life was certainly different than the Senator's. Naturally, this means his perception of what good behavior is will be in severe contrast to my own. Never mind from a political perspective, but certain things that I would overlook as "human nature" he would see as "rude", and vice versa.

The true point of this is that the people who oversee our country and indeed our day-to-day lives have power unimaginable. Their ability to create laws and their vast experience in hiding such decisions from the public has become something near miraculous. I feel as if it doesn't matter what people say or do anymore, we're not truly a democracy. Sure, we decide who's in office. Yay. Who decides what good they are? Why is it we hear about third-world nations conducting real grass-roots democracy and it's celebrated all over the world, and is indeed lauded by a nation whose rights are repeatedly breached in the name of "national security"?

When will we, the nation, the true voice of democracy, be able to determine what "good behavior" is?

Does God Exist?

There have been many instances where this argument was raised in schools, churches, homes, other places where dialogue may or may not have been necessarily permitted. The idea of being an agnostic or an atheist is not unknown to me, but I find a certain ignorance to it the likes of which I shall explain here. I should also warn the casual reader that I am not a church-goer and find myself question friends and family of their faith in trying to get a better understanding of it and to see that they have a clear enough understanding of their faith to believe in the things they claim to believe in. In other words, I like to help them find direction, whether it's towards their faith or away from it... It's not my place to make them choose, merely to answer the questions and concerns they have.

I've seen and spoken to many people about the topic of Creation, the Big Bang, evolution, etc. I'll further be honest to say that these are not always learned people; though some of them are learned in one way or the other, pro-Creation or anti-Creation, as it were. Most of whom I talk to are those with whom I would like to educate or help direct; the uneducated like myself. This is all personal interest and while I'm not concerned about the future of my soul, I am concerned how people spend their spare mental cycles here on Earth. It's important to have a solid foundation with what you believe in. It helps others to believe and even respect you for your knowledge and belief in your faith. Of course, you'll still have people who just call you stupid. Those people I've stopped trying to reach out to.

I've seen where people have referred to a banana as "the atheist's nightmare"... Yes, this is Kirk Cameron. I was appalled to watch this video with Growing Pains star turned Christian zealot and continued actor in a short documentary about proving to atheists that God existed. This was a complete farce and I found my face turning redder and redder as it continued. Normally it's not what they were saying that mattered, but the message they were trying to convey. This was not one of those moments. This was such an embarrassment to anyone who's ever legitimately found God and wanted to be a servant. They continually compared the creation of cars and buildings and Coke cans to the creation of mankind; if these things are created, how much greater a creation the human body?

- Perception Is Truth -

I get your point, Kirk, but comparing me to a Coke can is a bad fat joke wrapped in a short guy reference (but I'm not short...), and looking at a building and seeing how God created the world is just a bigger leap of faith than is really necessary. The video later moves on to talk to atheists about how they are bad people. Well, one of them kept saying that if you're using the Bible to determine if I'm bad or not, then yes, I'm bad. Kirk didn't get the point, and this is a point I've made to my mother for years and years; not everyone plays by your rules. So, if you want to get people to believe in God, you have to hit them where it counts, you have to meet them where they are or where they are coming from.

A coworker got me hooked up with a series of MP3s that were copies of a poorly recorded session between two experts in the field of Christianity and Atheism. Actually, only the Christian was an expert, the Atheist here was merely a scientist who took up the flag of no God. It started off with the Atheist making some very interesting points but about halfway through it he lost every single argument and every single point he made was just ludicrous and lacked in the logic he was so vehemently touting.

Unfortunately, due to time constraints of the debate carelessly flouted by the Atheist, there wasn't ever a proof that God existed, but everyone with half an open mind walked away thinking that there very well could be. Why you may ask? Simple: logic and reason.

The good Christian doctor played a very interesting card that I had never considered fully the implications, though his method was one I'd worked on for years: use their own words against them. The atheist kept referring to logic and reason and alluded to the notion that the human mind evolved into what it is today because of the need for logic to survive. I would argue this point but I'll do that later. The fact was the atheist could not answer where this logic came from. I do not believe for a second that logic and reason are what got us to where we are today. At least, not from a historical standpoint going way back.

Fact is if you believe in evolutionary man than you must also know that all we needed to climb to the top of the food chain was will. The will to do whatever we had to get on top of everyone else. The will and the cunning. I would argue that this is still humanity's true nature; to do what we had to in order to be greater than ourselves. Even if you believe in Genesis and Creation... Adam and Eve did what they could to be like God. Look back on what the Serpent told them; they wanted to be like God. Will.

In my opinion, no matter how you look at it, people are not inherently good or evil, but are akin to the animals in that our instincts are to survive and our ability to reason is nothing more than our willpower to be cunning to get powerful. All have sinned. Never forget that.

So, uh... Don't do drugs. Seriously. They suck.

For us to have logic and reason and even my ability to sit here in my skivvies because it's 90 and I can't get the AC to mount in the new windows properly without breaking something or losing the AC down into the driveway is testimonial to the fact, not truth or opinion or any crap like that, but the FACT, the REALITY, that God does exist. Does this mean the Christians are right over the Jews or anyone else? No. I still don't think God is worshipped or understood properly...

Does Hell Exist?

Hard to say... For now I'm going to say that my current beliefs answer this as a "NO" question... Forgive the emphasis but a quick skim will give the casuals an easy read. It's my argument that Hell was not really a place but something symbolic and has developed into the idea of a real place... More to come on that topic in later sections based on my research.

Part of the problem is that Sheol is the Second Death... But I think that Sheol is the place where souls go to eternally die. Not burned continuously, but just away from God forever and to never know of anything... In essence, when you die, your soul goes to Bema, the judgment seat. There you are told to go to Heaven or Sheol. Heaven puts you in with God, while Sheol puts you nowhere. Prepare to die, heathens! TWICE!

Seriously, if Hell's initial interpretation was literally to be outside the presence of God, than Sheol is simply that.

It's funny then... The next question would be how do we know we're living in Hell... But the next installment will cover various ideas of hell from numerous sources. One is NEVER good enough. I'm not an intellectual monogamist.

Does Hell Exist? Pt2

Here it is, the barely-anticipated sequel to my hardly audible previous installment on the above topic where I declared proudly that Hell did not exist; and I still adhere to this concept today. I hope that throughout this probably very brief conversation, I'll convince some of you of the same fact. As always, none of what you see here really ought to be viewed as radical or somehow original. It's not. I have few original ideas it seems, but those that know me oft do not have the same ideas or have heard the same bits of information that I thrive upon. Please know that what I'm trying to do is enlighten and teach, not to destroy or speak against an entire religion (well… I'll come back). The fact is my heart is changing the more I read. Don't expect me in a church anytime soon; they're not teaching you what's accurate in Christianity. They're teaching you merely what they want you to think, whether it's of God or of man. We'll discuss that in brief throughout.

This is scattered information taken from a singular source. Much of this data I also have in books in my collection and online research. It's out there; just got to look…

Hell itself has gone by many names, some of them apropos and others, well not so much. Review your history, learn the facts, don't just let them stand up there and tell you that Hell is a place of eternal torment and punishment. This is the key to my free will argument. Right here. This is why free will is a hoax plagued upon Christians and those professing to be of the Christian theology. With this knowledge, I begin to see why free will isn't as big a lie as I suspected; there are other lies being perpetuated.

The first supposed representation of an afterlife is that of the ancient Egyptians. Priests of Heliopolis composed texts for the pyramids of the V Dynasty. This was roughly 2400 BCE. It is further suggested that these texts, this very invention of an afterlife of heaven & hell places were for subsequent moral control and its function was to support the monarchy. This concept was used to control the people in support of leadership. Staggering, isn't it? Wait, it gets better.

Often there are Bible "scholars" or teachers who discuss Sheol, which has been referred to as Hell in the Old Testament. This is not correct. This is merely a place below the ground of silence and forgetfulness situated below the ground. This is information available in the Old Testament if we just read it. Further, while Sheol is a place where the dead souls go and are cut off from God, the Almighty is not absent from this place and can deliver souls from here if desired. The minimal references in the New Testament are of Sheol and the power of death. Not much else.

In the New Testament, the word "hell" translates more directly to the Hebrew word "Gehenna", which meant "the valley of Hinnom". Hinnom was outside Jerusalem where children were sacrificed to Moloch. Later, Gehenna became a place of eternal torment and unquenchable fire that was to be punishment for sinners. The eternal factor was not present until the New Testament times. In the Old Testament lesser sinners were believed to be delivered from the fires of Gehenna, much like Sheol.

Other types of Hell exist, including Hades and Tartaros in the Greek, even the Koran has its own belief on Hell, which seems to be taken from the Jewish, Hindu, and Zoroastrian belief systems. In fact, some have suggested that the idea of Hell and Satan were not originally part of the Jewish faith either, but was brought in through the middle eastern connections with the Zoroastrians. Strange how history works.

It wouldn't be until the Roman Catholic church that Hell would become a place of such eternal damnation and no hope for deliverance. Further, some of the "treasures in Heaven" we had grown up on may also be a falsehood that the Church used to push their agendas on the undereducated and illiterate of the Holy Roman Empire.

In summation (I know this has been brief but there's still a lot of material to go over), Hell was little more than a symbolic place that grew into a real place and has gone beyond even that to be not only real, but a really place that you went if your soul was damned to it, then to such an extent the damnation that not even God can take you out of it.

The reality is that Hell is anyplace that is outside of God. This does give Hell less of an edge, but the implications are staggering. That would mean that Hell may not be a place for souls but a concept, and idea that anything outside of God is Hell. We could literally have a Hell on Earth by avoiding God or running from what is asked of us. While this doesn't seem like much, well if Sheol is a place where souls go when they die and are effectively cut off from God (as long as God wants; though you may be delivered which I do not understand how that would work), this raises some key questions and again destroys an argument I'd had for years.

This is proof that God is merciful. This proves that God isn't the omnipotent four-year old that I've been harping on for so many years. This proves that God does want nothing but the best for us, and when we're bad we're put in a corner (if any one of you even THINK "no one puts Baby in a corner"... ...dammit...). This may be for eternity, or it may be just long enough to learn our lesson. The afterlife is the key to any major religion and I think Christianity has become so skewed on where it's taken our souls that we have no idea what we're doing anymore.

This also creates a conundrums for any Christian who believes that God is Love. This has never been accurate I do not believe, and even what I've found here does not assist in that argument whatsoever. God is Just, God is Jealous (which I still think is a crock), but God is Merciful. Also, God created evil. There, I said it. God is the cause of all evil in this world; hands down. Rather, God has permitted the existence of evil to perpetuate from our first selfish decision to accept Original Sin all the way to today when I cursed at someone for driving like a kitten killing a retard (don't ask). I'll avoid any talk of fate or predestination as this is not ground I'm willing to enter into yet. I'm looking over the waters into their murky fields of mud and the foggy skies above, but I'm not ready to face that yet.

Be careful what you're taught and what you read. If you're willing to just accept it blindly then I worry for those who venture to Bema to be judged for their life. What if we're all wrong? God may be Merciful, but God also destroys people when they do not heed the Almighty warnings. Sheol awaits. Being cut off from God can be just as bad as eternal torment, especially if our souls need God for sustenance...

There may be no Hell, but there is still judgment.

What do souls need with streets of gold and mansions and crowns? Nothing. This is merely a response to the lust of our flesh, wanting "the good life"...

Epiphanic Cervidae

So, tonight was another night where I felt this need for the wind in my hair and the tunes in my head; I went for a long drive tonight. A good couple hours even. It's all part of really how I meditate. Some people learn yoga or how to meditate the transcendental way, staring blankly into candles when a flickery Lite Brite will do just nicely; though this exercise may explain part of my optic nerve damage... The driving is something that I do to help and center myself again; really sit back and find something to focus on, or nothing I suppose, but just to get away from everyone and everything and envelope myself in melody and try to get as lost as is possible.

The prospect of getting myself lost without going VERY far north or just over the border in MA, which I don't want to get lost in, is a difficult thing to achieve. From having driven many of the roads in this state, especially surrounding Manchester and much of Concord and even some of Portsmouth, it's not so simple for me to really find myself without direction. Tonight, tonight I finally got myself "lost", for which I was pleased. There was no annoyance in my losing myself, for it allowed me to drift ever further into the music and the mind. It caused me to continue down the various roads as I have often done in life, aimlessly and inertial, bouncing this way and that, headed in whatever direction I happened to be heading in, waiting for something to bounce off of to turn me on my heels.

For those who know the area, I decided that the best thing to do was cut a swath through Bedford, head out through New Boston to Goffstown or is it vice versa? I ventured down a road I haven't been on for ages and ages, so long ago that while there should be some significance to me, it just isn't reaching the right synapses. Before I took this little jaunt I grabbed a bottle of Mountain Dew, certainly the worst thing I can think of to do to myself besides getting some late-night La Carreta, threw in some extra sugar-free mints (I still have a thing with mints) and was on my way. My tongue is still all tingly from the Dew/Mint explosion that I put myself through, but it seemed the right thing to do tonight.

Anyway, I did my best to avoid the main roads, 101 or 114 specifically. I wanted to go "between" them; the whole swathing I was after... that should read swath thing... swamp thing?... So, I ended up on the Donald St Ext, came upon a set of lights that looked awfully familiar, for indeed I drive that way a lot to get to my folks and to my sis-in-law's house (Weare and Goffstown, respectively). Hmm. Well, I didn't want to turn left for that returns me to the awful 101/114 intersection. I didn't want to turn right, that being 114. Though there was that time when a few of us came across some runaway bovine near the Jehovah's Witness hall... That was a good time. RUN FREE! or MOO! MOO FREE!... I almost hit a skunk tonight, glad that little scavenger got across the road when he did. That would have sucked. Stunk. Something bad.

Oh yeah, the lights. So, I went straight across. What is that, Bedford Rd? St? I don't know. I stayed on this road for a while. I passed Tirrell Hill, which I used to know someone who lived down there, and passed a lot of other roads that I knew and thought I recognized but my mind doesn't remember why. I even passed an Air Force Base in New Boston. Uh. Don't recall that ever being there. Must be new. In the past half decade or so anyway. Full moon, nicely clouded. Saw a woman walking her dog. Odd thing for that time of night, but maybe she was doing what I was trying to do; find some focus, some escape. I don't think I ever got mine tonight. I tried and tried and just kept changing the tracks. Enya to Over the Rhine. The night had started out with Rage and moved to Harrod and Funck and jumped ever-so-briefly to Mark Heard, but ultimately I decided to drone out to Enya then on the way back home it was Over the Rhine.

During my drive I ended up on Chestnut Hill Rd. I remember this because I saw the sign at Horace Greeley indicating where I had come from. Well, this is also where I turned around the first time, to go back UP the hill. For I had seen something that I wanted to see again. At the top of what I surmise to be Chestnut Hill, I saw a field that was pretty open up until the tree line down a little hill. Within this open field I saw a deer. Either a doe or a fawn, it had no antlers to speak of. It seemed a tad large to me to be something young so I presumed an adult or near-adult female. I know nothing about deer, you see, but I know if it doesn't have horns it's not male. At least it's not supposed to be male... Hmm...

So, I decided to turn around at Horace Greeley and come back up the hill to see this creature in the night again. I pulled off the side of the road and just looked at her. I stared deeply into the eyes of nature, the docile gaze peering back at me. I wanted to feel something primal, something inspirational and poetic. I wanted to feel what you see in the movies or you read about in books or hear about from people who claim to have such moments. I wanted that. What I got was a clearer understanding of why L doesn't eat meat. I found it ironic that all this was happening just across the street from a tiny place called Wolfe Rd. Ahh, irony tastes better with A1, doesn't it?

A few minutes later and it seemed that the deer went about what she was doing in the first place; milling about the field looking for somewhere to go. A car shortly thereafter ruined things for me as the deer found the obnoxious sounds and the louder paint job to be predatory and took off for the aforementioned trees. I was annoyed. I turned around and went back down Chestnut Hill.

It got me to thinking, though. It got me to wonder about things that I've thought about for years or experienced or wondered or wished. It got me to do the thinking I wanted but it wasn't the focused questions I had hoped for. The deer reminded me about how I seem to care more about the animals than people; which is funny considering I get rabid when the mandarin orange steak tips come out. I couldn't ever be a cannibal. The sheer mention of the word and I get queasy.

Seriously, though, my callous nature and my cynical growing up has led me to deny much in the way of human compassion. It's almost as if I feel that they deserve it or had it coming to them; that God has chosen to send a message that, as always, no one will heed. In other ways it reminds me of a theory I have had and it gave me some new meaning to it. I have said before that I thought Earth was really for the animals, that God didn't really intend of putting Adam and Eve here. Or that we were put here as a joke. Tonight I went a step further to say that Satan put us here.

I had been taught growing up that Satan couldn't create anything, only corrupt what God had created. See one of my previous entries regarding the creation of evil for some minor clarification or at least a further point on this topic. I realize that the notion that Satan created Mankind is a farce given my logic, but what if God created Mankind and Satan put them here. God gave them Eden to live in, but Satan actually convinced God to put them HERE in the first place. Does that make sense? Satan put us here to be the Corruption of Creation; look at the harm we cause our world.

Some things can be argued, including global warming. I am opposed to the notion of global warming for there are scientists on both sides who are world renowned experts arguing for and against global warming. I think I just cut my eyeball with a fingernail... Hopefully the eyelid took the brunt of that assault. The climate of our globe has changed drastically in such ways that I find the idea that we are affecting it to be another example of human self-centered-ness in an odd ironic way. The thing that no one's talked about is if global warming is real and melting the ice caps and that we are polluting our sky and our very planet, what about the melting after the Ice Age? That seems kind of drastic to me and when there are still things frozen all over the world... Something's missing from that argument but I don't know what it is. I still can't tell a cumulus from a cumulonimbus, though I think one of them brings rain and the other one looks like the intro from The Simpsons.

Anyway, I've felt bad for a long time that we humans are here gobbling up the earth around the animals when they have no real means to defend against us. If we wanted we could wipe out an entire species of animal without so much as a thought. Look at the dodo, not that you can, or certain whales or birds or cats or other "endangered" or "extinct" species. Yeah, for our survival, sure, but are we supposed to be herders or hunters? What is it God intends for us to do with the animals? Farm? Breed? Eat? The Torah's pretty explicit about what and how to eat, but meat's still on the menu... I don't know. I still say humanity's a cruel joke played upon Earth because whoever knew that our inner flaws would ultimately lead to the destruction of everything we believe we hold dear, and then some.

The thoughts then moved on to what I've done for this world or for myself. All I see when I get like that are the things I've done wrong. Trivial things like speaking out of turn or getting yelled at all the way up to how I've lived my life the years before I got married, before I got serious about being an adult. I'm still getting serious about that, but certain things lose their grip on me every day. Pun intended. I think about the "fun" I had being single and living alone or at least out of my parents' house. The games I played and the women I "dated" was mostly just about me. There were a scant handful of them that I had real feelings for and even fewer of those I loved. Had my heart broken a lot, but I've broken more hearts than I can remember. Was it all in preparation of meeting and marrying K?

I won't got into the details of the adventures, but needless to say I've received some compliments about my "success", mostly from those of a less-than-moral nature. Others are just disbelievers and that's fine. I don't have anything to prove. I just wonder of late what I really learned during those couple years of debauchery. There was very little life-changing moments during this time and though the experiences are behind me, they are still a part of me. They are still a part of who I have become and part of why I have what confidence I have. I also count my cynicism and my still burgeoning attitude about people's opinions of me going south as part of why I am who I am today. There are few people who's opinions of me truly matter, and I find that I'm still a touch nervous around those people and can't surmise even the slightest conversation without having them start it. What's frustrating is when they don't really like or want to talk either. I don't show up with planned material; throw me a bone :p I might be interesting someday.

Unfortunately, I have no conclusions. The solution for the notion that we're not supposed to be on Earth would be human genocide, which is easier said than done, for one thing; it's also not the best idea someone can have. The solution for the problems in my head and heart are not something easily tackled; I don't like to make rash decisions. Except to leave a job because I hate hate hate it. That ends up working out for me pretty decently so I can't complain too much about that. But buying a house wasn't the smartest thing I could have done. Should have waited.

So, I returned home feeling as frustrated and somewhat empty as when I had left. The cats were crying for their dinner so I fed them and rubbed them and came up here to type this. My wife came home from her outing and I just finished putting her to bed so I came back here to finish this for my loyal readers. So far I seem to only have redheads subscribed to see my words, and I get comments from only one of them. So, either I'm writing too much or it's not worth the time to come up with something snappy. Either way I see no need to discontinue the madness that is posted here and maybe one day I'll edit them for publication or just to make it legible. Stream of sleepy conscience is NO good. NONE!

I bid you all adieu and I trust that your nights are filled with frolicking sheep and the occasional drunken dromedary. Be well.

Epiphany

It seems that I have no readership, for I haven't exactly 'advertised' my presence. It also seems that those who are aware haven't the time nor the inclination to give me a modicum of time. That's fine, I understand how important time is to everyone and how unnecessary it is to give my rants the personal observations that they probably don't deserve. This, you would think, should give me clearance to say what I want about who I want. I don't feel the same. It's that one rare instance in which someone Googles and mistakenly happens upon my website that I must maintain some sense of sobriety and honesty and sincerity. Naturally, I could just say fuck it and curse a blue streak in ways I used to only imagine. I wonder if I talked about things that created controversy that would make what I say more interesting. Talking about the news and about music I'm listening to that no one else cares about clearly isn't getting my point across, and I'm too concerned about people stealing my ideas about my world that perhaps I'm holding myself back. After all, there's only a handful of people reading this or any of my sites anyway; I should just release the reins and aim for the cliff. So to speak…

Equality: An Introduction

Do we really understand what we're talking about when we reference equality? Equal pay for equal work and equal access to medical help and equal this and equal that. What are we really talking about? In our society we're just talking about money, and we're not really tackling the problem inherent to the system. We're talking about equality as though it's the solution, but really it's part of the problem.

This premise that exists about equality recognizes a failure in the system by ignoring that failure, but it does exacerbate the divisions in our society by bringing them to the forefront.

If we want real equality, start thinking that all people really are equal and not that they "deserve a chance". Let it all be equal. Equal money for equal work, equal money for equal skill, equal everything out. Let everyone be married, let everyone be who they're going to be… Yeah, we don't want equality, we just want certain groups to feel equal. To feel equal. The illusion of equality is what we want, is what we'll allow.

It's tiresome. Our only inequality is that some of us can have children and some of us grow more muscle. Yay. It's not the same for everyone but we treat what's perceived as most common as being "right". Well, if you truly believe in that premise, if you break down your stupid ideas and you really sit there and stare into a small cup of water or at a candle, can you really tell me that everyone in this world who doesn't live or think like you do are wrong?

Stop trying to grant equality and just see everyone as equal.

Ethnicity

I'm not certain where I expect to end up with this one, so please bear with me for as long as whoever you happen to be is mentally and emotionally able. I was listening to Imus this morning on the radio, which is a rare feat indeed. However, when he said the word "African American", it touched me in a way that I never before imagined. I think that the most prevalent reason we have allowed racism to pervade our society isn't because there are actual racists. I don't want to down play real racism, I just feel that the problem of true racism from the Klan or the Black Panthers has subsided to a greater extent. I think that a true understanding and a re-naming of certain American subcultures has assisted greatly in this area. I also feel it's the reason we may never truly be rid of racism.

I realize that there are movies and books and random acts that have already suggested this. I would not dare to infer that this was an original idea of mine. I believe that this idea is not taken seriously, that we look at it in movies and other modern media outlets with a certain level of disdain or disbelief. It isn't possible for racism to go away if we allow ourselves to consider such an idea a falsehood. This goes beyond positive thinking in my mind. This goes right into the realm of altering our perceptions. We're raised to be "tolerant" of other people. Tolerance isn't a good thing, it is merely acceptable. People sometimes discuss how much pain they can tolerate in a given situation, or how tolerant we are about terrorist actions. Typically, we are *in*tolerant of such activities.

This also touches upon the media and the news outlets and their inability to phrase anything in a manner which is more proper and suited towards shifting ideals in the population. They create new phrases and new ways to be perceived as "politically correct", but all it does it create a new label for an old stereotype, or allows us to stereotype people in new ways. We have labels and sub labels to everything from yogurt and rock music to world cultures and the subcultures that live within them. We have high-rises and low-rent and ghetto and trailer trash and afro-centric and metro sexual and alternative rock and faded jeans and high-definition TV and reality bites the heads off of cockroaches… It never ends.

I further realize that what I'm about to suggest is impossible in my own lifetime, because ignorance breeds and complacency is a commodity. Still, it would be nice if we did away such monikers as African American and Latin American and Tiger Woods altogether. I used to be a guy, a person, a male. Now, now I'm a young professional Caucasian American male. That's a tad wordy. I have a name, too. If you want to label people, why not use the labels they were born with? I think psychology, our now infamous pseudo-science, has been used in ways that are detrimental to the very psyches that the practitioners are trying to salvage.

Just let us be American, or African if you prefer, or how about just be people again? Can't we just be people for a fucking change?

Everything Is Wrong

This is such a huge topic I don't even know where to begin; what ISN'T wrong with the world today? Without getting too deep into my usual philosophic discussions on right and wrong, I'm fairly certain there's a general consensus on what can be labeled as "wrong" with our world with very little arguments, but some topics I know I see things vastly different than the few people who are even aware of my presence, but let's begin.

The Planet. So, we live in a world that's existed for as long as it has existed, and I will not debate the age of the planet because we just don't know. Assumptions are made based upon accusations that were first proven and disproven but most people aren't aware of the facts surrounding these ideas or just don't care. Science has become more of a religion than a tool, but you'll see that a lot throughout this conversation. Global warming I firmly believe to be a hoax, the climate problem or the problem of climate change or however you want to order the words I believe to be an attempt at furthering fear and keeping people in the limelight, but I don't believe they are 100% incorrect either. I don't think we're affecting the world as drastically as has been suggested, but I'll get into that shortly. I also don't believe that gives us the privilege of destroying everything in our world including living creatures and plants to our way of life. I think that we have a responsibility as people and inhabitants of this planet to be mindful of what we do with this place and not take it for granted as we do everything else in our lives. We won't live forever but if we want our kind to live for any length of time we should consider what we're doing and how it connects to everyone else in the planet. Science is helping us, as a tool, to see our interconnectedness, but it's ruining us, as a religion, by spouting out immediacies when there's still a debate on whether it's accurate or not. Gravity is one of those things that's been pretty hard to disprove, but evolution is not hard to disprove yet people still believe in it. Say a lie loud enough and long enough… The earth does not have a fever and we are not in any immediate danger of being wiped out. If we are it's because we're supposed to be and whether you think it's nature's design or God's Will or whatever, it's the fate of all humans to die so be respectful and aware but don't be foolish. We're extending any lives by car pooling or moving to solar energy or chomping on soy bars.

- Perception Is Truth -

History. We don't listen to it. We don't listen to experts we listen to pundits and commentators. We listen to people who observe from the outside just because they're someone supposedly important and not because they know a damn thing they are saying. How many times have we learned that the government knew about an attack or a potential threat and for one reason or another the threat was released or avoided and we find ourselves under attack and blaming the people currently in power?

Humanity. We're idiots. I don't know how to say it more delicately or directly than that. See the above about global climate change. Watch the news. Watch movies. Watch sitcoms. Read the paper. Read a magazine. For as smart as we are and for as wonderful as it may seem to be at the top of the food chain, there's a reason that ignorance is bliss. Give it some thought you'll see why. Or don't give it any thought and you'll probably smile right away. We're all high and mighty and feel superior to everything else but how many grand mistakes have we made? How many total wars have animals fought? I've never heard a story about many thousands of elephants being wiped out during tribal combat or that the tiger finally got the bomb... We do that. And parasites, apparently. Viruses. We don't live alongside the planet anymore we live in spite of the planet. We use science as a tool against nature and it's going to ruin us but where would we be without it?

Dichotomy. Everything is dichotomy to me it seems, or at least everything has a sick balance to it that makes no sense to me. Is abortion, AIDS, and homosexuality nature's way of cutting back on humanity? Is it the way to control the population so we don't overtake the whole planet? Is the planet fighting us as much as we are fighting it? Is it really just the supposed Devil or Yahweh punishing humanity for fun or vindication? We can't agree on anything except that it's bad. Thanks. I figured that out on my own. We seem to have diseases a lot and I don't know how random it is, but we do seem to find excuses to thin the herd so to speak. And those who don't really want to live their lives except for the purpose of using drugs or some other means to destroy their mind... They're just misunderstood and should also be allowed to live. How many people must be allowed to live on this planet? Are we just trying to fill it up so it forces our hand to colonize space? We aren't satisfied with screwing our planet so let's go somewhere else and screw them up, too? Didn't I hear earlier this week evidence of global warming? Doesn't that prove that it's not a problem caused by people? Of course not, now that it's out there no one will recant. Is it just nature's way of cleaning up and starting over? Is it time for our galaxy to stop sustaining life and to let another one do it? What are we living for?

Religion. My favoritest of topics. What are we doing with religion besides abusing it? We use books that are predominantly outdated using translations that didn't work then and they've been rewritten to work even less now. Certain books are not that way because the language that spawned it has not evolved, but we still rely heavily on a book that we feel the need to rip apart and use for our own ends by quoting a "verse" or whatever. I don't think that the writers of those texts ever separated out chapters and verses, but we don't know because no one has original copies, and other writing from that day have not revealed a writing style of chapters and verses so what are we to believe? We don't even know if this stuff is right, there's just enough historical coincidence to make it at least plausible, but there's still little logic to it. Just because the book lasts this long doesn't mean it's right, but if it did what about the books that were removed or the passages that were reworked because they were deemed one thing or another that was bad for the populace? There's no consistency...

I am rambling because I am tired but I also don't feel that there's any good way to clean this up. Everything is wrong and I can't find a reason to think otherwise. Everything is topsy turvy and I feel that we're unable to change anything because no one is willing to make a change. Everything is... just... not right...

Everything Is Wrong Pt2

The first installment of this piece was written while I was well inebriated with sleep (not with drink however), which is not fair to anyone. I should have also spent some time editing that previous work, which did not occur and isn't likely to occur for this installment. I'd like to think of what is coming next as a continuation but I fear it will correct certain concepts stated previously or at least expand upon them in a broader way. Since it seems that everything I do needs to be corrected or edited so that people understand my purpose or my overall point, here we go again.

The Point

The point I am attempting to make here is that the things we are doing on a day to day basis to distract from that which is most important is only going to suit those who would do us harm. We are distracted from our personage and from our own survival so we can play God or Monopoly. Money and religion have been both good and terrible to the existence of all, but no one will believe me. Sure, they'll listen to me with a slight eye roll or will list me as entertaining or over their head, but overall I don't believe a single person is hearing a word I am saying.

I am not surprised by this because most people refuse to accept their choices were ever wrong, or that childish mistakes are no longer being made because they are older now. They are making these logical jumps based upon age and not based upon the presence of wisdom. Wisdom does NOT come with age, wisdom comes with observation and study and willingness. The willingness to be wrong, the willingness to seek out facts, and above all the willingness to look themselves in the eye and believe in all that they are and all that they do that they are trying.

The State Of The World

This should be a simple case of watching the news and not seeing what they show you but what they're skipping. We have to educate ourselves about the world around us, not just accept blindly what the news media tells us from the TV, the Internet, the papers, etc. What we see is biased to a certain perspective. No one is just reporting the news anymore, they are telling us what they want us to know and what they want us to think and what they want us to believe. This isn't a conspiracy theory, this is fact. Watch the news. All they want of us is fear and hopelessness, because that's the kind of news that people like. No one wants to watch a happy story, because no one believes this world is happy anymore and therefore those stories couldn't possibly be the norm. Has anyone considered that perhaps it's a chicken and egg argument? Did the world start going to hell in a hand basket because it was already on its way or because we've become so obsessed with hearing about our world failing that we're emanating this hopeless energy that's spreading like a disease across our planet? Are we the cause of our own failures because we don't believe in ourselves or our fellow man? Must we always look somewhere else for hope and sanity when we should be looking into ourselves and into each other to try to come together? Must we be destroying ourselves because we don't agree on what kind of toilet paper to use or because someone worships their god differently? Must we live in fear that we're killing our planet when our planet gives us life? Must we live believing that our lives are worth nothing because of the harm we're bringing to that which gives us life?

Must we turn a blind eye to the harm we are legitimately causing this planet because if one facet of one argument is wrong then everything they are saying is wrong?

We're hoping that Al Gore can save us from global warming when he couldn't save us from Osama Bin Laden. Do your history, learn about how everyone's favorite democrats the Clintons and the Gores let that one slip through their fingers time and time again. Everyone blames Bush when he had nothing to do with it. Do I like Bush? No. He's a jackass but he's been elected twice so we have no one to blame but ourselves. No one's perfect, certainly not our elected officials.

There are few diamonds in the rough but let's be realistic, democracy in a capitalist system is by design corruptible. We're a constitutional republic, for one thing, but the system that runs this country is destroying it bit by bit. Say bye to your freedoms in the name of security. Say hello to inane and emotional thinking and goodbye to logic and reason. Say hello to fear as a religion and a tool of those in power or those who want to stay in power. Say hello to the failings of our own leaders in the name of the almighty dollar. Say hello to more power for those with more paper. The more dollars we have the less they are worth, doesn't anyone pick up on that fact? We have inflation because we keep printing more money and because we allow capitalism to drive up prices. That makes no sense. Capitalism is supposed to bring down prices until it's almost not even worth it to do business. It's collective greed. It's more than just that feeling of owning your own business or being your own boss, it's about making the big bucks. Just remember: the bigger the lesser. And fear is a religion condoned by the leaders of this world.

Why Religion Helps/Hurts Everybody

This is an opposing statement for me for many reasons. For one, if not for Catholicism, my mother would have never been born. This is a fact. Thus, without Catholicism I would never have been born. That is also an indisputable fact.

But the overall damage done by Catholicism is far-reaching and certainly not worth the lives of a handful of people, certainly not my family. The damage created by the lies of supposed Christianity and the alteration of the Bible is astounding. People should do more research into the history of their belief systems, not just accept blindly what they are told from the pulpit. Until you honestly admit that there could be something wrong in what you are being taught, you will never truly be thinking for yourself. You will continue to sit in those pews week after week, praising a God who may not be there and may not be listening, arguing about the gender of the deity so many people have given their lives to in so many different ways and religious practices. You will continue to debate the tenets of what a particular passage means instead of what it says, never mind not knowing for certain if what you are reading is even the accurate interpretation of what was written. You will continue to believe you are right and superior about everything even though your religion speaks of no one being worthy of any of the gifts the almighty has bestowed upon us. You will continue to believe you are right and that you are better than everyone else in your rightness even though your religion speaks of being meek and coming as a child with honesty and purity in your heart. You will feel puffed up and proud when everyone knows that pride comes before a fall. Everyone I know who is of the religious mindset tell me to read my Bible, but are they? Or are they reading what other people think about the Bible? You don't need to have a degree from a seminary (cemetery) in order to do some research. You just need to have the will to accept that you might possibly be wrong. Simple as that.

I could go on for days in excruciating detail about this, but I don't have the time and I'm certain no one cares. That seems to be a recurring theme of my work and my life; no one cares what Mc has to say because Mc's just entertaining or just wrong or deceived or bitter or misguided or otherwise incorrect in his assessment. I have been wrong about things all of my life and I readily admit to them, but the second you start treating me like an idiot or like someone who doesn't know anything just because I wasn't led around by the nose at some university doesn't make me less of a thinker or less of an intellect. In many ways it has made me more of an intellect, but I will not argue pride with the proud. I have done it for years and I grow weary of the games that people play when they are "right" without knowing anything. I also grow weary of people believing that they are without blame of any kind at any point during a situation in which I am involved in. I have spent my life taking on blame where it wasn't earned and accepting fault when I knew it was not my fault. But we as a people seek out someone to blame for everything. In religion you have the deceiver, Satan, though he goes by many names. There are no facts to support that Satan is our overall enemy here, and besides for all the deception laid on Satan's feet; Adam and Eve still made their own choice to disobey, right? Don't blame the deceiver, blame the ones who accepted the deception when they were given a very simple task. There was no grey area in the order given, even though they perceived one. Don't do what you think God meant, do what God said. Just like the Bible. You want to believe in the Bible wholeheartedly, fine, but maybe you should spend more time worrying about the words and not their intentions. You may be wrong about those intentions. Wouldn't that be a kick in the face to come before God at the end and be told you defied the almighty when the words were plain as day before you...

Religion has caused great focus and caused people to be on a much better path than what life had given them. But at what price? Their souls? It's an addiction like anything else, it's a cultural choice like anything else, it's just another way to live your life. It's just a philosophy. We have no proof that any of it is right, only personal experiences. We have learned that there are some facts in the Bible that can be discussed scientifically and without the benefit of an all-powerful representative sending fireballs from heaven. Sprinkle in a pillar of salt and you have yourself a full-fledged miracle and a war from heaven itself. That's enough to convince everybody you're selling them the right stuff.

- Perception Is Truth -

This week, I have had several people impugn my intelligence and treat me as a lesser. In each instance, it has been from a devout, God-fearing Christian. I have known people who have owned their own business who have told me that the only people that have ever screwed them over have been good Christian people, and one of them was certainly no prize, but that says something about today's Christian doesn't it? Am I taking this personally or perhaps blowing this out of proportion? You're god-damn right I am. I grew up hated by my peers until I got to high school and realized I was an okay guy. It's taken me at least a decade to get this far and I have no plans on stopping. I have no plans on allowing myself to be intimidated by people any longer. I've lived my entire life in fear and I know more about it than anyone of you out there in FB land, so don't dare tell me anything about fear I don't already know. I've tried to live my life free of fear and focused on God but that did nothing for me. Life didn't start for me until I gave up on the Christianity that raised me and started to live in the real world. If you close your eyes to what's going on around you and just spend your time with all the same people the world looks pretty much the same and you'll never see anything beyond your own two eyes. Don't come to me and tell me the world is great on that side of the fence when you've never really taken the time to see people who live on the wrong side of the tracks. Some of you have seen it and some of you have lived it, and that same few have risen from it and become something. I applaud you. You chose religion which is disheartening, but it also worked.

You could have chosen a lesser life, and I know plenty of those people, too, but you didn't. You found something that worked that should rise you above the crowd and turn you into a representative of hope and change. You also found that seeking outward for your solutions was the right thing, when I would argue that it's not. It's merely a distraction from what's really going on inside of you and until you face that you'll never really be free.

There Is A Way Out

It seems that the whole cause of being a philosopher or an angry, typical white person is to have a solution. It's not enough to stand on my high horse on a soap box at the street corner saying the world is coming to an end... and then nothing. I have to give you something to look forward to, something to cling onto so when that final burst of light hits we'll be waiting to go to glory or an eternity in bliss and happiness. I don't have that luxury because I'm not fond of lying to myself or anyone else. I'm not going to sit here in my own little angry prison and tell you everything's going to be alright. It's not. At least we don't know for certain. Some of us believe one way or the other, but both are bound by fear and some just happen to sprinkle their fear with hope. Others legitimately don't care, and I wish I had their stamina. It takes a lot of effort not to care, at least if you know something. If you don't know anything or if you are truly callous, it's easy. I strive for callousness, if only to protect myself from my own emotional strain, but it doesn't work. I apparently care too much about what's going on in this world and with its inhabitants, and I feel the solution is so easy and yet achieving it is like building a tower in Babel. Someone's going to want to stop it. It's not that what I'm proposing is difficult, but it will be perceived as immature and probably stupid and I'll get another series of eye rolls and condescension. So, why be silent? Why let the masses dictate my thoughts when they're just going to be ignored? This isn't just my old fears creeping up that I'm not worth anything, I've already had that argument with myself this week, and I still feel downtrodden about my existence, but that too shall pass. What I'm stating is fact because I know people and I know how I interact with people and I know how my ideas are so rarely accepted. It's as if I have to ask myself why I think at all since no one wants to hear it. This isn't a catharsis for me as I had hoped, it seems the more I read and the more I write the angrier and the more solidified I become in my thoughts. It makes me sick to my stomach lately because I'm so angry about how I am viewed and what is said to me.

Am I right? Yes. I am. This goes against one of my most important principles, but not everyone has to be wrong about everything. Humility is the most important piece to my philosophical puzzle, not false humility which I have seen so many of the religious practice, I'm talking about actual humility. You don't have to flaunt knowing something or be argumentative about it. Besides, what you think you know could be totally wrong. We have to live our lives the way we see fit but if that way is wrong aren't we ultimately doing ourselves harm? Stop looking for someone else to cure you or to make all the pain go away. People of every faith and even the faithless find ways to make themselves happy that doesn't involve mind-altering medications or lifestyle choices. Start looking inward, that's really what you want anyway. Start looking at yourself and remembering that no one's perfect and that includes you. Accept some failure. Remember that even the Bible tells us to look inward and not to others. Don't compare your faith or your belief to mine, it's not an appropriate comparison. Compare your faith to someone of a different denomination if you want to, but you're still wasting your time and just living in pride. Remember. Humility. You're wrong, too.

Conclusion

I realize that this has been an angry and contrite work, but that's my mood at present and I don't see it getting any better as time goes on. I don't like to be ridiculed and I know that no one else does either... But, seriously, push the right button and all bets are off. I don't care if you're a friend or a family member or even a client. I won't stand for it any longer. I'm tired of watching the world fall apart because of fear, the ultimate enemy of existence. People need to start listening to what's going on and start making some choices and taking good hard looks at themselves. I do every day.

Farewell

I have finally done something I told myself I wouldn't do; I have stepped over a line. I have pushed extremely hard against someone I considered a friend and a part of the history of my life. I have said things and done things to attack the character of this person in ways I never believed I could stoop to. I actually said things about this person that I never would have seen before in my entire life unless other factors in my life had fallen into place to reveal the puzzle board to me so completely. Fortunately for me, they did. It wasn't that these pieces weren't there, they were just not open to me for my perceptions had been dulled by sheer existence and living in awe of the wonder of this person. They were at one time an inspiration to me for their faith and the way that they saw the world through totally rose-colored eyes, staring only to the beliefs. This showed to me great conviction at a time when I found none. This stood out to me as someone who should be looked up to as a role model of faith and someone that really lived what they believed. And they had my utmost respect for it. I have changed. So I will be taking my sandbox elsewhere so as not to offend others who actually know me. I believe this is the best course of action for everyone concerned and for those who believe I am blowing this out of proportion or in some way am overreacting... There are no words. Be well everyone.

This was the final entry in my social networking experiment. Every time I found myself at such a site, I would eventually come to realize it was the wrong place for me. I spoke only to people who knew me, with little chance of anyone else coming to see what I had. Will this be any better for me? At least it's more out there than just in a place with controls and fetters. I'm tired of being fettered by an idea or a person. The content here will be all mine and all will be meant. If there are problems, comment on them and fight me, but bring to me an argument. Don't just stand on your soapbox. Engage me in conversation, don't just yell your mantras at me. I'll not stand for mantras any longer. I'll not stand for childishness and the see no evil crowds. I'll not sit still while the world around me and people I have cared about turn their minds to dust by focusing their blinders in one area and never looking to the world around them. Too long have we looked through rose-colored stained-glass windows and I have suffered for too long because of it.

Welcome.

Freedom Isn't Free

So, the President of the United States of America, the Leader of the Free World, is threatening to veto a bill that will restrict the government's access to library records so they are not able to see what books people are checking out. What did that long sentence mean? Basically, the Patriot Act allows the government to gain access to library records in order to see who checked out what books. If a high school student were to check out books on terrorism and bomb making (not that this sort of book is available), even for the legitimate purpose of doing a research paper on the insurgency in Iraq and their methodologies, the government would need to know that, because he's a potential terrorist. However, if someone is going to the library for the purpose of learning how to be a terrorist and how to undermine the government, they're not going to find much material aside from what's already occurred.

If someone is doing honest-to-goodness research on how to take down the President, how to put a plane through a building, and how to blow themselves up, they don't need a book. If they want to learn the tactics of terrorists, they don't grab the Funk & Wagnall's 2005 and look up Al Qaeda Training Camps. They do what every other American turned Islamist extremist does; go to the source. How did they do this, you may be asking? I haven't the slightest. I imagine they used their Islamist friends or clerics or priests or whatever the representative word actually is to make contact with the necessary people.

I've been doing some serious thinking of late regarding the way in which the government is handling our situation with the Middle East, and I have to be honest when I say while I disagree with much of the policies, I fear that I would not be able to do much better, even with all the facts.

I heard on the radio that the FBI has found documents suggesting an attack on my local nuclear power station. What am I to believe? After the WMD debacle, even with all the promises that have been made regarding truth and better intelligence, what do I believe? Do I become Chicken Little? Do I pull an ostrich and stuck my head in the sand? Do I run and hide to Canada where it's frickin colder than even where I'm at now? Do I hide in Europe and wait for that situation to implode? I could become a Kiwi and head to New Zealand or some other kangaroo-infested island nation. Probably not.

These solutions are simply not feasible, for reasons I find a little too personal to bear.

The only logical solution is to hope the government can destroy those plans on a more permanent level. Still, how can I be sure that they can take down the bad guys without infringing on certain civil liberties, without effectively breaking the law? Where is the line drawn that crosses clearly separates the freedoms that we all presume we need based on the Bill of Rights and our holy Constitution, with our security and national safety on the other side? We lambaste the government for not protecting us from what happened on "September 11th", but we further berate them because this Patriot Act is just another example of big government overshadowing our "freedom" with our "protection". When does it end? When do we finally come to an agreement on protecting ourselves and letting us do what we've always done?

I'm not sure that our society today can do that. I'm not certain that we as a people are willing to go to either extreme, for the fears of what those consequences could very well mean. The problem, as I see it, may be twofold. One, and certainly the most important problem facing our nation, is the global context. No matter how we assign rights to our people, there's always the problem of those who gain entrance into our nation. Are they afforded the same rights?

If they are afforded the same rights, and if we indeed want to welcome everybody to our shores, why are we turning back on Cuban refugees who have a mostly legitimate gripe regarding political persecution? We have a problem with "illegal" immigration in this country, and there's been more news coverage recently of government organizations stepping up their arrests and deportations. We take in people from other nations when they are educated or here on a work visa or other such economic reasons, but we turn back the already poverty stricken (when we are able to find them).

Aside from people coming in, there's also the issue of how other nations handle their own laws, their own people. There's bound to be discrepancies between nations on how certain things are handled. It's clear that the Philippines has little problem with the pedophile trade that goes on, and all the tourism money that is brought in by those from many countries coming to commit such acts. Naturally, our own nation has a real issue with people who want to copulate with a child. I realize "ignorance of the law is no excuse", but is it? A simple misunderstanding is all it takes to land you in jail in certain nations, all in the name of security. All in the name of safety and keeping people happy.

The second issue is the way our society is today, the way we've become, the way we've chosen to perceive our world. Suddenly, it has become torture to force prisoners at Abu Ghraib to listen to Christina Aguilera and Metallica. It seems that we've become a blight on our world because of our "mistreatment" of these prisoners. Bullshit. This is absolutely ridiculous. We don't even know what torture is anymore. I don't even need to talk about the things that happened to the POWs in Vietnam, though I do find that those particular methods were very creative, albeit atrocious. What we constitute as reasonable amounts of pressure on a subject with the purpose of extracting information regarding a terrorist force with no reasonable types of leadership whose current mission is to kill as many Americans as possible is clearly negligible to those whining about their civil liberties. Never mind that shortly after "9/11" we were demanding Bin Laden's head without any shred of evidence. Certainly, we in America would never choose to arrest someone based upon the idea that they committed a crime but not anything to factually link them to said crime. Ask some hardcore protesters, they'll tell you.

The further problem is the matter of greed, something for which we all understand living in a nation of money. Our leadership, whether we really want to believe or not, really do have their own financial gain working as motivation for what they do. Their desire to really appease the nation as a whole is more inclined to be for the sake of keeping their jobs than for doing what we want. Provided, that's WHAT we want from them, but the President went against a good portion of the nation, and indeed the world, and he got to keep his job. What does that say about our nation?

We're indifferent to voting, but we're mad at who wins. Maybe this shouldn't be about freedom but about sociology and personal responsibility. We have a voice, but we're scared about being heard. We're scared that if we say the wrong thing the government will come down on us, for indeed they have in certain instances, whether justified or not.

...I'll have to come back to this...

"Fuck Karma"

This could be considered a quotable quote, but the source of this creative idea isn't exactly published, which is the intent of that category of mine (for those who pay that kind of attention). My understanding of karma relates directly to reincarnation. Meaning that the way in which you lived this life would influence if not determine how you lived in the next. When I watched the Matrix trilogy, which was littered with religious and philosophical ideas, we were all told it meant "What we are here to do". This later definition leans more towards a single task, or a specific path we are to take in life, with little deviation. This also makes me think of the Christian concept of predestination, or the general idea of fate; all basically ideas that no matter what we do we'll end up doing what we are supposed to and end up where we are supposed to. This idea is generally opposed by people who feel they are in control of their lives, whether they are or not.

I had not looked up the meaning of the word karma, at least not in a dictionary, until very recently. Yesterday, I think. Before I discuss that, I want to touch upon several clichés that immediately spring to my mind when I now think of karma. I really should have considered this before, as the same conversation where this phrase came out was also mentioned "Shit happens". This is a very old statement which I had first heard when I was 4. Actually, it was a rather popular bumper sticker in my trailer park. Go figure. Other clichés; "You get what you deserve", "You reap what you sow", "Rain falls on the just and the unjust", etc ad nausea.

Karma was always presented as a finality, as the end of all things. If your karma demanded your head, then you would die. If it was your karma. But, what was my karma? What *is* my karma? More importantly, how do I understand it? How do I determine what best to do with it? How do I find out what's really true in my life and how it pertains to how I live my day-to-day? Should I be concerned? Should I carry myself differently because of my karma? Should I fear it? Should I give it the same fear that I gave to God in my Christian upbringing? If that's the case, than I'm certainly afraid of karma. I'm certainly afraid of a lot of things…

God Is My Co-Defendant

I'm not sure if this is irony or just stupidity, but I'll figure that out later. There is an interesting notion here about the idea of frivolous lawsuits and that God could, in theory, be setup as a defendant in such a case. Whether these are criminal acts or not remain to be seen. After all, our laws are based upon the precept that God exists and that God's laws are ones we should follow. So, that begs the question is God guilty of crimes that were established by God in the first place? Do as I say and not as I do comes to mind as well...

All that aside, there's something else that struck me during the reading of this article. Sometimes I need to see it in print and very late in the day after I've read a gut-wrenching amount of comic books (Hellblazer, 52 books 1 AND 2), but I think it's a fair question; is God guilty of the host of things listed? What is God truly responsible for? What is it that God does on a day-to-day basis to or for our existence? I won't go to the logical endpoint: is God real?, because this isn't the time. This discussion presupposes God's existence.

I suppose questioning God's responsibility isn't the right question to ask. The context is all wrong somehow. It isn't that God is responsible for such things as earthquakes and birth defects... I used to be one of those people who thought that God DID stuff to people. Then I learned that often God just allowed stuff to happen. I started to think that people just did this shit to themselves and blaming God was just another way for us to place blame for the lies and deceits we play upon ourselves. That got me thinking tonight about something else, about the idea of God and science co-existing. It's feasible, isn't it?

A number of people, scientists I believe, have written books trying to disprove the Bible by using science as their weapon, and more often than not they find themselves converting to some form of Christianity. That's nice, God's Scientists, we can call them. Can't call them Christian Scientists because that's taken, and Scientology should be SciFiTology if you ask me. So... what, then? How do we bridge the gap that was created at least as far back as the Middle Ages, possibly further? How to eliminate the divide between faith and logic. Many people, myself included, have found that this is insurmountable. I feel that to a large extent that is still the case, but not because the premise is fouled, only that those who would need to cross this precipice are incapable of objective thought. They either worship God or they worship Science.

We have proven much of what goes on in the world is a part of nature. Is it right to blame God? God created the earth, and the earth is flawed. God created man, and man is flawed. It is fair to say that, given these two examples, that God is also flawed, but that is not our purpose here. Is it by God's design that we ravage our own bodies with toxins and feed it only the slightest form of natural food? Is it by God's design that we overpopulate and dig deep into the heart of our own planet in a vain hope to get our lazy asses to work every day? Read the Old Testament again; God was not inclined to entertain the wicked. God brought floods, right? Do we know for certain that there is evidence across the entire globe that the flood did occur? Sure, there's evidence that it did occur in sections, and that the ark may still exist on Mt Ararat (it's a bitch of a climb, you see), but who was there to say that it was global? What was "global" at that time?

We take a lot of things for granted by faith because we suspend facts. But... why? Why can't we have it both ways? Why can't we have a god who created us imperfect and that we, in turn, create imperfect things and slowly move to the entropy of our own existence? Why can't our world be flawed? Why can't our gods be flawed? Why can't we use our minds and our hearts?

Faith isn't for everyone, and science was always hard. Believe in both, trust yourself.

PS. This is a stupid lawsuit; just another knee-jerk reaction to try and prove a point and get into the limelight for re-election. The only people who have thus far defined frivolous lawsuits are those who are the most affected by them; those with the money. Our nation is quickly moving into a business state and not a political one. I have about as much faith in true democracy as I do in my not having double-vision. It's a pipe dream that we hold onto hoping that someone will smarten up and make it work. It isn't possible. Democracy, free enterprise, it's an economic structure, I don't even believe it's political in nature anymore. Read the papers, watch the news. Follow the money...

Heaven and Hell: A Response

http://www.taoism.net/living/2000/200003.htm

Wherever there is truth, there are questions.

Having a ridiculous amount of time spent in the Christian religion through the course of my life, these are two concepts that I am quite familiar with. At the very least, I've been over exposed to these concepts. I must admit to now being more torn about the opinions in the article written and what had been my own beliefs and understanding. Although, it would seem I never really had my own belief on heaven and hell, only what I was told.

One of the complaints I've always had about any concept pertaining to the future of our souls is this egotism about understanding the nature of the soul. People act as if they understand what our souls are truly intended for, and that they ultimately have a purpose that is very much what we wished our physical lives to be like. The reason heaven and hell are such tremendous tools in conversion is that it relates to people's perceptions of their own reality. The thought process is that if our souls are a part of us now, then we'll be a part of them when they move on. The soul's life will reflect the life of our physical bodies in ways only our fantasies can surmise.

While part of your argument was the way we perceive heaven and hell could be different than from others, this only furthers the problem. It isn't a matter of 'another's man trash is another man's treasure,' but a deeper lack of understanding. While it is safe to say that one's idea of heaven can be greatly different from another's idea, I think all this does is massage the layman into still accepting heaven or hell. I have friends who don't believe in heaven or hell because of staunch atheism brought on by a hatred for Christianity. I have other friends who don't believe in hell for the reason you listed; God cannot be love and send us children to Hell. That's another falsehood perpetuated by religion, which, I'm sorry to say, I've believed a different truth for many years.

God is not Love. The idea of God being love, in my mind, is a detestable untruth. Read the Old Testament. God was not Love in the Old Testament. God was something that was jealous of the people's worship and praise. I've oft referred to God as 'a 4 year old with omnipotence.' Always wanting our attentions, and damning us when it's not received. That's not Love. That's power. And, to a certain extent, God also displayed an amazing amount of justice, but based upon the rules God put into effect. Now, the argument then comes that God became Love when Christ was sent to the Earth to die for our sins. Also a fabulous joke. If God is the same yesterday, today, and forever, then how can God's attitude change from the Old to the New Testament? Especially when it's always quoted that Christ was there from the beginning. If anything, God is Merciful and Just, but not Love. That's a farce.

That having been said, let's attack this idea of heaven head on. Dogmatically, and Biblically, it is explained that our riches will be received in heaven. Yet, it is also said that we should walk by faith, that deeds are not the way to please God. Also, the prize we're supposed to keep our eyes on is eternal life in heaven, not the riches we'll receive. So, heaven, a place for our soul, will have crowns and houses and streets of gold. What does a soul need with streets of gold?

Then we have hell, a place of eternal damnation housed by the only angel with a backbone, Lucifer. The most beautiful and musical angel of them all, Lucifer gets cast down out of heaven to rule and reign over the depths of fire and brimstone. Another example of God's eternal Love. Clearly, that's Justice at work. So, now we have angels being sent to a physical place to experience eternal power. While it doesn't compare to God's ultimate power, it's still an interesting trade-off. Eternal damnation, but the power to fight against God and potentially gain souls. That's God's Mercy at work again; allowing the Enemy a certain measure of power. In my mind, Lucifer's plan worked. He got out from under God, and was even given his own kingdom. Sure, it's all bad and scary and angry all the time, but he seems to be doing fine with it.

The reason that heaven and hell, to me, couldn't exist in the way we've always assumed them to be, is because of our frail human understanding. We all have our own opinions, and no one knows the truth for certain. A belief system is, after all, a series of beliefs, and not necessarily truths. The only TRUTH is that we're still learning, and will continue to do so until we die. At that time, we will know the truth of this, and who can we tell?

And anyway, whom would listen?

Hermann Goering

"Naturally the common people don't want war. But after all, it is the leaders of a country who determine the policy, and it's always a simple matter to drag people along whether it is a democracy or a fascist dictatorship, or a parliament, or a communist dictatorship. Voice or no voice, the people can always be brought to the bidding of the leaders. This is easy. All you have to do is tell them they are being attacked, and denounce the pacifists for lack of patriotism and for exposing the country to danger. It works the same in every country." Hermann Goering, Hitler's Reich Marshall, at the Nuremberg Trials after World War II.

I must admit that I did not find this quote, but it was sent to me from a friend of mine. I believe it was around the time when the Iraq war debate was in full swing. This isn't a new concept, of course, but it's interesting to note whom would speak it out so valiantly, as though it was his duty.

This concept is true in so many areas of life and thought it's staggering. It's all about manipulation. You tell the person what they need to hear in order to do what you want of them. We do it to children all the time. Often, it is because they truly are ignorant of their situation. However, rather than explain to them the situation, we make things up in order to placate their still fragile psyche. We do it to ourselves in order to overcome fears or to accomplish certain goals. We choose the lesser of two evils in order to rule and reign over our country. We lie to ourselves. We make new year's resolutions. We join a gym and use our membership card to open that last box of Twinkies.

The secret to the Nazi War Machine was its propaganda, and here's the philosophy behind its power.

Homosexual Christian

A contradiction in terms if ever there was one. And yet, much like military intelligence, it is a concept that exists in this very day and age.

Now, you might be asking yourself why I would want to discuss such a topic given the current issues surrounding the Catholic church and homosexual marriage. Well, that's simple; the time is right. As with everything I discuss, I'd like to first say that I do not know everything there is to know about the topic. I am not a homosexual, and I cannot call myself a Christian with a clear conscious. However, I did help in converting a homosexual to Christianity. Actually, she used to say it was all my fault, but I have not talked with her in many years.

The part that seems the most distressing to me is that I did not convert her through the normal means. I did not tell her how wonderful God was and how loving Jesus was and how powerful the Holy Spirit was. Instead, I helped her to understand the reasons why her own fears were misguided and unfounded, and repeatedly stating my disapproval of Christianity for the betterment of a person's well-being.

Let's take a look at the latter argument before I discuss her fears. Christianity, by itself, does not better a person. I said it, and I meant it. Just being a part of Christianity, going to church, spending your money with Christian vendors, reading your Bible because it's the thing to do… None of these do you any good whatsoever. The real key to any religion actually working for you is desire. You don't become religious to save someone else's soul. No, you do it to save your own. By its very nature, religion is selfish. Yes, a cynical perspective, but you don't become "saved" so Christ's death meant something. You become "saved" because YOU believe Christ's death meant something.

With this in mind, let's get back to my lesbian friend. One of her biggest concerns was the continued way in which Christians, and indeed the Bible, refer to God as father. I told her several times how ridiculous this was. I understand the idea is to take the Bible word-for-word, or to at least accept it as God-inspired. Well, let it be known, yet again, that the Bible was written by man, not by God. Besides, it would seem to me that God would want us to be able to relate to something, not just an all-knowing all-powerful entity. Part of the problem is that, at the time the Bible was written, the man was the one in power. He controlled the house and all within it. A male-dominated society yields male heroes. The solution, however, was not to refer to God as father-mother, but just as God.

God is not only a title, but, in my mind, it is also a gender and a name. God is God and that's that. If God were father, who was our mother? If we're made in the image of God, why are there females?

I told her that her poor relationship with her father is not a good comparison to her possible relationship to God. For one, God has always been rumored to be love. More dogmatic lies. God is not love, not by a long shot. Ask the Jews. God is just and jealous and powerful and angry. Frankly, God would probably be a worse father than her real dad, but at least God's consistent. You know to fear God, right? I told her that God wouldn't be there one day and gone the next. God would be there always. The same yesterday, today, and forever, right?

The other problem that she had was, of course, the fact that she's gay. Well, there's some contention over her true sexual orientation, as she was previously in an interracial marriage for many years, and even has a child who should be in high school by now. In fact, there had been several occasions where she thought she wanted to spend some time with other men, after her divorce mind you, but those options never came to fruition. Actually, the problem wasn't that she was gay, but that Christians would know she was gay and would not accept her.

Well, this got my blood going. I asked her who it was she was trying to impress? I said that she's going to have a problem with Christians and her homosexuality because of their own beliefs. For a long time I had been taking a verse out of context to fuel my argument that homosexuality wasn't necessarily a sin. I found out much later it actually is a sin, even in the New Testament. Be that as it may, who was she going to worship? Was she going to be a social Christian, those people that I despise the most? Why did she want to be a Christian? When she told me because she wanted to worship Christ, I just said 'exactly'.

With these two major barriers torn down, she went to a religious outing with speaker Joyce Meyer. This, of course, is another clear contradiction of Biblical teaching, as women are not supposed to be ordained ministers. In fact, they're not supposed to talk in church. Naturally, this is a cultural issue more than a religious one, but none can ever tell me they are a full Bible believer if they allow a female pastor into their hearts or to be their leader, I don't care what you think God told you. If God's the same forever, and God's Word is infallible, then Joyce Meyer is committing a grievous sin at the expense of her own soul. Anyway, she came back from her extended weekend invigorated, excited, but above all else, a Christian.

Later, when I was discussing this little tale with my mother and some of her friends, one of them spoke up. Now, this woman likes me because I tend to get fired up about certain topics. I get fired up because I feel she is misguided and often a terrible nuisance, and others agree with me. Her comment is what got me, though.

"What kind of Christian does she think she is?"

This would imply that she is a lesser Christian because of her choice to remain homosexual, knowing full well how disallowed that truly is. Provided, God the Father and the Son do speak against those who continue to commit sins when they know full well their folly. Still, that's between the homosexual and God, and not between this emotionally inept religious zealot and the lesbian. So, with my veins exposed and my head glowing red, I responded to her.

"One who worships Christ, what kind of Christian are you?"

"Um. One who worships Christ."

That was the end of the discussion. I never took my eyes off of her during this brief exchange, which I think made her uncomfortable. The truth is, people need to really step back and let others worship who and how they want. If it works for them, who am I to judge? In fact, who are YOU to judge? If it works, more power to em. It only becomes a problem when their religious beliefs breaks the laws that we, as man and woman, have created.

If a sacrifice is called for, there better be a damned good reason…

Inconsistencies and Ironies

So, I sit in my leather chair thinking to Moby's vicious hatred of all things animal-killed and I wonder when I'm going to get a new chair with faux animal skin dried and dyed and placed beneath my rump. I think of L's staunch vegan stance and I feel remorse, but I do need a new chair that much is for certain. I think of how A and L have known each other forever as far as I know and yet how A likes bloody roast beast but red, curly hair. I think of all the books around me and how a tiny portion of them are from L and how the rest are from the comic store or Barnes and Noble. How I love the comic store. I think of my wife liking guys with big arms and yet how flimsy mine seem to be. I think of how much weight I've put on since being with her and how much weight she's taken off. I think of how I knew Tori Amos before but didn't really get her until K played it for me again. I think of how my very first ex called me after almost 7 years of not speaking to each other just to catch up and how it was about 2 weeks after I started listening to Bjork again (she had loved Bjork). I think of how my closest friends are Christian and yet how I couldn't wait to stop being one. I think of my career in computers and how I'd rather be sitting in a big, deep leather chair clackety clacking about some deep thought that I'll pretend was my original concept but I'll know in my mind someone else has said it but I haven't found the time to read about it yet. I think of all the dreams I had about being single forever and yet couldn't imagine my life not being married.

Then, I listen to the news or my talk radio shows and I think about the things in the world that matter to more than just me; they matter for the good of all or at least all those around me. I think about the persecution of race and gender and religion and I wonder if anyone's read their history. I know this country's more ready to see a black man in office than a woman, for the "hatred" of the black race really stems from the over-slaving and the European sense of entitlement that came across the pond. Slavery was as much a saleable item as livestock or vegetation, but the wholesale theft and later abuse of those commodities is what tore it down and turned it into something horrendous. Christians denounce slavery but it's well within the sacred book. Ephesians, to be specific. I think about the religious zealotry and how we're not allowed to say certain things if they pertain to the Judeo-Christian faith (not Catholicism, for Catholicism is pagan in origin). We're not allowed to question the Islamic faith because we think if we're afraid of them they'll take pity on us and back down. Bullies don't back away from the afraid; they pound on them in the schoolyard for all the world to see so the bullied can be embarrassed as well as perpetuating the fear within.

I think about all this friggin talk about choice and yet the way in which our government tears away our ability to choose with every breath. We permit abortion but prevent smoking. If it's our right to choose to end a life, because it's our body, then why can't we choose to end our own life? Murder is illegal, abortion is just good timing, and suicide's hard to punish if you succeed. We allow people to vote for someone who gives up… Why do we vote for anyone the media isn't telling us to vote for? We make our leaders disclose their earnings but then we're not allowed to talk about it. We want to have a strong leader but the first female to be close to the Presidency cries and wins primaries.

I think about religion and about science and about history and how without religion our history would look very different, which includes the formation and evolution of science. I think of how science was formed as a tool for the religious and yet today we treat science as a weapon against religion. We talk about everyone being equal but we continue with labels and more labels and still more labels, separating us out to the very DNA that makes us up. Even on a genetic level we're being labeled differently depending on the full extent of the breeding process that went on before us. Was there inbreeding in our lineage? Do certain ailments affect us greater because we're white or because we have red, curly hair, or can a cigar really be a cigar? I think about the creation of mathematics and about the evolution to advanced mathematics and how trig was created to calculate Mecca from anywhere on the globe. I think of how the Mayans had a calendaring system far more accurate than anything we've put out there and yet the religious, out of fear or superior pretense, destroyed mile after mile of thought just to protect the ways of the Godly. The Godly who wiped out entire nations in the name of progress, not because God told them to.

I think about the entertainment industry and how we scrimp and save and dream of being movie stars and entertainers but we despise them for existing and drawing our attention away from the things that matter. I think of the value of gold, which has no value when it relates to survivalism. I can't eat gold. I can only trade away gold and silver and paper and things that others say have value to get things that I say has value: food, clothes, housing, knowledge, transportation. We think of new ways to screw ourselves financially but we can't wait for it. We can't wait for the almighty buck to reach up and put itself into our pockets. I think of people who have a terrible reputation yet no one knows or cares about the truth. I think of heroes and wonder if anyone realizes what a terrible person they could be? I think of the dichotomy of courage and the luck of ignorant determination.

I sit here and I wonder if life is what we make of it or it chosen for us?

Is American Idol Aptly Named?

So, I'm sitting here in my nice leather chair feeling it against my soft, supple skin... That's not entirely true, but I am soft and the nice leather chair is really my old leather chair that needs replacing. But, I sit within it just the same. And I think about American Idol the past couple of weeks, this whole season, in fact. A great array of talent onboard for another several mind-numbing weeks of pitch problems and "dog" and "hated it" and "you're uniquely you and is Ryan gay or not? Personally, I don't think Seacrest gives a damn; long as he's making money and keeping people interested in him. Happy? Sure, but interested first and foremost. He's a product who knows how to commodify himself. Not sure that's a word.

Anyway, so there's this weekly obsession later on about how many votes there are. Week to week, how many tens of millions of votes they got. I never asked if that was individual votes or individual phones or if that's just a total count. It could be a million tweens running up their parents phone bill voting for Archuleta because he sings like he's Barry Manilow but he acts like he's in Junior High School Musical and looks like he's in a Noxzema commercial.

So, last week and this week were Beatles weeks, but they called them "Lennon & McCartney" weeks. Clearly they're forgetting George Harrison wrote some songs, too. I don't recall if Ringo did, but let's face it, he was there, dammit. Now, to be fair, they didn't let him sing for a reason, but he did keep the beat. Nothing fancy. I have drummer friends who complain about Ringo's contribution, but the Beatles weren't into grandstanding musically, they wanted their songs and their music to mean something and to feel a certain way and the sort of solo performances we get from the wanna-be Satrianis is little more than gutter noise in comparison to these artists who revolutionized music and really did usher in a new era of change for our society, most of it I don't even like but there you have it.

Last week was a pretty decent foray into Strawberry Fields in the Yellow Submarine, but Polythene Pam grabbed Maxwell's Silver Hammer this week and Ob-La-Smacked my Gently Weeping Rickenbacker Across the Universe... Everyone botched whatever they were trying to do, from little things like consistently being flat to totally butchering one of the greatest song of not only the era, I would argue of all time (Kristy

Lee Cook you need to go home). I watched with disgust and agreed with the angry Limey that a second week of Beatles was a BAD IDEA. Who's doing this anyway? Is it Ringo? Is it Michael Jackson hoping for residuals? Is it the legless model who spent 4 years of her life to get $50m? I still say that was planned extortion and someone should break her leg. The fake one, of course. She can afford a new one, calm down.

This week. Shudder. It got me thinking about why we do it? I've never voted in all the seasons I've watched, but my wife has. Usually about 3 times over the course of the season, but it still happens. We have more votes on Idol than on the Presidential Election(s). Not that there isn't more interest this year than in any other year that I can think of in my lifetime, but that just generates ratings, not necessarily actions. Do we worship these people for what they can do or are we jealous that we're not up there for the tweens and teenie boppers and yuppies and elderkins to vote us into fame and maybe fortune (sorry to everyone who isn't Kelly Clarkson, Carrie Underwood, or apparently DAUGHTRY).

Or are we really happy and excited to see people come from nothing or even something but have as much of a chance to succeed as anyone else? Is it our outlet for people of equal skill if unequal appearance? Is this really the only place that we play fair anymore? These other reality shows at the peak of the ratings tend to have the beautiful people or the trashy who aren't really in love with the former celebrity with more headbands than hair (which isn't saying much from what I've seen) that generates ratings more than it generates fans. That's yet another careful distinction. Look at Serenity or Family Guy or Jericho or any other cult show. They don't have the ratings but they have the fans.

Are we violating several of the Ten Commandments by watching this show with the obsession of a child stalker (I'm looking at you, Macaulay Culkin - what? he's weird)? Is it an example of our desire to have everyone succeed no matter what they look like as long as they have the talent and determination? Is it our lust for something on TV that requires very little thought and makes us feel part of the action? CSI doesn't bring the bodies into our house, that's for sure. We can live vicariously through these people because they're real and not on a soap opera. But I hear one was a stripper. A male stripper. For guys. The picture was grainy, though.

- Perception Is Truth -

Hmm. I had a point but I grow tired. Do we worship the regular guy for "making it"? I think they deserve what they get, frankly. I hope the best for em for getting up on stage and looking like a big dope in front of millions.

Is It Worth It?

The title of this piece is generally a question you hear from someone who is morbidly depressed and on the brink of making a decision that will seriously affect them and everyone around them. This is a question that most people don't want to hear. It's something we avoid thinking about except in the bad times, when the chips are down, the going gets tough, when we just don't have the strength to go on. Why is that? Why doesn't anyone ever ask this question in the up times? At least the plateaued times. It's a valid question. Isn't it? After all, we're only assuming that we know what the topic is, the nature of the question itself. By itself, this is an illogical question that cannot be answered in the expected context of our minds. There are carefree uses of this phrase, or that which relates dynamically to expenditure and material purchase. Obviously, that is not my intent here.

So, why am I asking this question? Am I referring to life? Cheez Doodles? Being an adult? Doing good? Bombarding people of the world with my thoughts and feelings and fears and nuances and philosophies and truths and facts and just a hint of reality...? Is this all just propagandizing for a puerile mind? Am I bored with my supposed brilliance but too lazy to do anything with it but mumble under my breath or pound on the keys here so hard that a replacement keyboard has to be purchased every few weeks to keep up with my own inane blog? Is my brilliance truly supposed or is it something that's viable and verifiable? Is it not that I am brilliant but merely more observant than others? The only thing I truly take pride in about myself is my ability to pick apart a topic as viciously as any rabid pit bull during recess. I will antagonize and instigate in order to get a reaction of someone who cares about the topic. If you don't care about what you believe in, then it's my contention you don't believe in it in the first place. Don't get angry, just don't let go. I respond to answers.

This brings me back to my point, from differing directions. Is it worth it for me to bother people? Is it worth it for them to answer me?

Is it worth it for us to have any beliefs at all?

Life and Death In The Golden State

I've been listening to the media reports here and there regarding two of the most popular cases to come out of California in some time: Scott Peterson and Robert Blake.

Honestly, the outcome of the cases are not what I'm interested in, but how the country has perceived the goings-on. While I admit to not being the most attentive on these cases, I have seen how the media has created careful differences in how we were supposed to think about these things. For example, even though there was much credence given to Scott and Amber Frey, the media was hell bent on being FOR Laci Peterson. On the other side of the coin, the media was pretty much AGAINST Robert Blake.

I realize that some of you out there think this observation is irrelevant, but let's take a better look at this. The Peterson trial was the first to really bring forward this idea that husbands murder their wives, even without a prior history of abuse. This is obviously not the first time that particular instance has occurred, but this one captured America with Scott's repeated pleas for help in finding her. He brought us into his heart and then ripped us from it when it was decided that he killed her. Overnight this man went from a hero to a murdering, lying bastard.

Am I convinced he actually did it? Why should that matter, he's been convicted and sentenced to death. What I am convinced of is that he was convicted in the American eye as soon as he was charged. Hell, America could have found him guilty as soon as the rumors came to light that he was the primary suspect. At any rate, those of us on the outside looking in thought this was a brave husband who turned out that he didn't want to be a father or a husband any longer.

Then we have Robert Blake, a man who won the hearts of Americans in Our Gang, though I forget his character name, I do recognize him. Aside from the wrinkling face and the white hair, however, it's the same Robert Blake I remember from his show Beretta. A short guy with an attitude problem, there was very little coverage on his wife Bonnie Lee Blakely. In fact, all that I am even AWARE of is that Robert fathered her child, so they were wed. Marriage of convenience, if you ask me, which no one ever does...

The whole story in the news and all the pictures I ever saw was Blake being a hard guy, someone who looks like he could have killed his wife. It's a small miracle he wasn't convicted.

Then, we have the final outcome. Scott Peterson was judged guilty and has been sentenced to death with little more than circumstantial evidence. Provided, the DNA from the boat proves Laci has been on the boat, but the rest of his activities only appeared to be that of a guilty man. On the other side of town we have Robert Blake being acquitted because the prosecution wasn't able to put the gun in his hands at the time of Bonnie's death. Never mind the fact that Scott's alibi was far more believable than Blake's "I left my gun in the restaurant and when I came back they were dead."

What's my point? Better to kill your wife in California when you've been a star. Whether intentional or not, the jurors seem to side with someone who in their subconscious really was the good guy... Is Maria Shriver next? Does this go all the way up to the top of the state...?

Who would we want to win in that case? The immigrant who made a name for himself by being as American as he could be? Or the cousin to the family that was rumored to be involved in the mafia, having adulterous relations with a movie star, and who ultimately became a hero after his death by a confused man? Who would we 'vote' for then?

Lifeboat Or Executive Decision?

This is a story about the grim facts of life and death, that no one really wants to discuss because it isn't politically correct or it's deemed insensitive. So we just sit on our hands and let everything just happen and do our best to keep the entire population alive. It's a noble gesture, but will ultimately lead to total failure. Without people triaging we would be expending many resources to help people that cannot be helped with the medicines and the techniques we have. This isn't a "playing God" decision, this is a matter of pure numbers and to a large extent, money.

This puts me in a difficult position, though, because if we learn to devalue human life well enough, we could end up with a Logan's Run situation where everyone over a certain age is euthanized... I can see where this would lead me at the very least to other conclusions but I won't go into them. I should read Logan's Run but I haven't the time. Anyway, it is important that we accept that some people will not survive a particular pandemic should such a thing overtake us unknowingly and that it would be irresponsible both financially and I would say medically or efficiently to use up valuable resources on those who are less likely to survive.

This breaks into the whole I, Robot movie nonsense but it made an interesting point. The value of life is based upon numbers; if a person is less likely to survive than someone else, then the numbers says that you should save the someone else. To a human it's not that simple. In that case we, as humans, may also waste valuable time deciding who should and should not die no matter how noble it may seem.

Ugh. All in all, I'm in favor of such guidelines if only for the fact that we have a limited amount of qualified people to care for the needs of everyone who requires medical attention, and should a huge pandemic break we will be pushed to the brink of our resources and if we use them up on those least likely to make it... that means the people who are more likely to make it will not have what they need to survive. It's an ugly decision that must be made in certain circumstances and we should not treat this subject lightly, but we shouldn't just fight against it because it refers to our own mortality as much as we hate the idea of dying.

Materiali$m

Here's a topic that seems universally accepted as a bad thing in terms of religious observation. I'm still looking up all the references, but I'll try to cram them in here with a mention of their relevancy as I can.

General Quotes Non-religious (I am currently using these quotes as my signature at work)

"The things you own end up owning you... Its not until you lose everything that you are free to do anything." -Chuck Palahniuk

"It is preoccupation with possessions, more than anything else, that prevents men from living freely and nobly." -Bertrand Russell

"Most people seek after what they do not possess and are thus enslaved by the very things they want to acquire." -Anwar El-Sadat

Bible

Ecclesiastes 5:10 (KJV) "He that loveth silver shall not be satisfied with silver; nor he that loveth abundance with increase: this is also vanity."

Matthew 6:24 (KJV) "No man can serve two masters: for either he will hate the one, and love the other; or else he will hold to the one, and despise the other. Ye cannot serve God and mammon [money]."

I Timothy 6:10 (KJV) "For the love of money is a root of all kinds of evil."

Hebrews 13:5 (NIV) "Keep your lives free from the love of money and be content with what you have."

Koran

Curiously enough, I'm having a rough time with this one...

The only references to money I can find involve killing or marrying more than one wife. I'll have to look at my other translations and get back to this.

Sura An-Nisaa 4:20-20 (Pickthall) "And if ye wish to exchange one wife for another and ye have given unto one of them a sum of money (however great), take nothing from it. Would ye take it by the way of calumny and open wrong?"

Sura An-Nisaa 4:92-92 (Yusuf Ali) "Never should a believer kill a believer; but (If it so happens) by mistake, (Compensation is due): If one (so) kills a believer, it is ordained that he should free a believing slave, and pay compensation to the deceased's family, unless they remit it freely. If the deceased belonged to a people at war with you, and he was a believer, the freeing of a believing slave (Is enough). If he belonged to a people with whom ye have treaty of Mutual alliance, compensation should be paid to his family, and a believing slave be freed. For those who find this beyond their means, (is prescribed) a fast for two months running: by way of repentance to God: for God hath all knowledge and all wisdom."

Sura Yusuf 12:88 (Shakir) "So when they came in to him, they said: O chief! distress has afflicted us and our family and we have brought scanty money, so give us full measure and be charitable to us; surely Allah rewards the charitable."

Tao

I have other translations of this I'll have to go through, for I have seen contextually the appropriate sections in other places.

3 (McDonald) "If you overvalue possessions, people will begin to steal. Do not display your treasures or people will become envious. The Master leads by... preferring simplicity and freedom from desires."

53 (McDonald) "To wear fancy clothes and ornaments, to have your fill of food and drink and to waste all of your money buying possessions is called the crime of excess."

I know there's more, but I'll find it as time permits.

I'm sure I could make a number of reasons why greed and material goods are bad, but there needs to be a balance. Shouldn't there be? It's nice to have new things; I can't find anyone that I've ever met who would disagree with that statement. It is nice to have new clothes, a new car, a new house, new love, almost everything new is fun having. Is it necessary? Obviously, new food is good and necessary, as old food tends to make people sick. Naturally, so does some new food, but that isn't the point. Having new things cause you to have other new things: bills. Those aren't so much fun, but they are necessary. Curious that balance, eh?

Modern Society will tell you that having things isn't bad in that it proves your worth. It proves you work hard and can afford nice things. This isn't greed, just prosperity. Moral Society, or the religious, would argue that having too many things means you're taking your eyes off of that which is most important, for to have such fine things one often has to work very hard and neglect friends and family in their climb to the top. What's ironic about this is often those who are the most outspoken about things not being necessary already have nice things. Ironic is the wrong term, let's touch more on hypocritical.

Part of the problem with prosperity based upon product is means. If one does not have the means, one does not prosper. By the same token, using the old meaning of prosperity, where having family meant being prosperous, than the poor of this country who earn a living on welfare by having more children would equally be prosperous. I'll explain this with a little more clarity.

Prosperity is defined by an abundance of stuff or children. In the olden days, having a house and children meant you were prosperous. Today, having more stuff and newer things and more expensive product makes you prosperous. In the past, family meant something. Today, it's an afterthought. With abortion and homosexuality running rampant in our society, it's a miracle people are having children, never mind letting it get in the way of their career. Family has taken a backseat, while money is our driving force.

We work so hard all our lives to purchase things that we merely want others to see. We have so little use for the massive amounts of crap that gets purchased in the name of prosperity. I cannot tell you how annoyed I am by yard decorations. Before, it was about your yard being cut and bright and green. Now, it's about how you decorate the damn thing for the seasons. We spend our lives waiting to retire and enjoy that which we've purchased, but then all we want to do is something else. We train our minds and bodies to expect to work everyday, and yet when the time comes to reap what we've earned, how many have a hard time passing the day by?

Take a look at irony, then take a gander at insanity. There's a certain similarity to them that fits in nicely with this topic. Irony is getting what you don't expect, while insanity is expecting what you're not getting. That's a simplistic viewpoint, but I feel it works.

Is there a way to balance it out? Is there a way to work, play, and feel like we're doing something with our lives? Are we all fine and content working day to day in places we hate for stuff we don't need so we can grow old and die and rot when our things live on for generations? Does it seem fair that those things we buy have a far greater potential of lasting longer than we possibly could?

Take a look at the first quote, and remember the word moderation.

We're not long for this world... So why not have the most toys? Why not kill ourselves every day so we can retire young and enjoy life and play and play and play?

...why not...?

Mistakes Vs Regret

This is a topic I've been meaning to discuss for sometime, but while I thought I wrote about this in school, I think that was actually a paper about cause and effect... Have to find that one sometime, too. This is also a topic that's been heavy on my heart of late. Weighing me down...

In everyone's life there are mistakes and regrets; at least that's what people tell you. The facts are a bit blurry and the truths are impossible to predict, but it's safe to say that everyone has experienced both of these in numerous ways throughout their existence. Few people I've come across truly accept the fact that mistakes are to be learned from while regrets are something you can't take back. It's not to say that my readership (which I think is just M... again...) doesn't understand this, but I find myself voicing things that everyone seems to get but I have to learn about it the hard way. Nice.

I've also come to a conclusion or eighteen in my life that I have few regrets. In fact, I think there's only one thing I regret in my entire life; everything else was just a mistake. Something to learn from. Did I learn from my regrets? Sure, but that doesn't make them any less a regret.

I find myself separating terms in an effort to better label my thoughts and to present as cohesive and consistent a philosophy as possible. A mistake can be anything you've done to anyone including yourself. I toyed with that notion for a bit but I've come back to this every single time I talk about it. To myself. A regret is most often something that affects others, but it can affect yourself. It's really how important it was to the perpetuation of your emotional existence. Making a fool of yourself in front of people is most often a mistake; avoiding them altogether is a regret. At least it is for me.

Hitting the wrong note during a show is embarrassing, but it shouldn't be something you regret; it was merely a mistake. Hitting the wrong note and flipping out then walking off the stage should be something you regret but you're just too damn self-centered to know any better...

A regret can take you down the wrong path in your life, and sometimes you find you just can't find your way back no matter how hard you try. You find that you lose friends, you lose faith, you lose sight of what mattered in your life and you lost connection with that which really brought you life. A regret can eat away at your being, etching away at the essence of what you are, leaving behind something else. A mistake is leaving the chili sauce where the dog can get it.

Don't have regrets...

Over the Rhine: Greatest Band Ever

This is about the 43rd time I've written this. It still won't be right :p

I had handwritten a long letter that every single time I would try to type it I would edit it and edit it and never send it. I tried re-writing it every time I got a new Over the Rhine album I would expand upon the initial offering but, just as much of my work, it never truly recaptured the fullness of what I feel for this little quartet from Ohio. Things have changed and they've grown and shrunk and really the heart of them are the married lyricist and vocalist, but they're still awesome.

It all began round about 1996? I was just a lump at my church trying to find a way to fit in with people, after having left a school I was hopelessly in love with. I was in desperate need of something, some connection to the outside world to keep me from going completely and utterly f'ing insane. Well, I knew this older guy who seemed kind of foppish to me... Wavy blonde hair, had to look good all the time, there was something about the way he was that made me realize he was terribly into himself but he had some great musical tastes. At least he had tastes that appealed to me in that way. He had introduced me to Harrod & Funck and most recently to Vigilantes of Love. Thus began my love affair with the acoustic, furthering my passion for Mark Heard (who produced the VoL album I had just picked up). Yeah, Jon was good for music. Knowing him was about to pay off in a big way.

Jon had followed around artists like a regional Dead Head. He would tromp from Maine to Jersey to see a band, often chasing them from state to state. He would stay late and often hang out with them and their crew. He was on guest lists all over the Northeast. That night was no exception. Jon was heading down to Gordon to see Vigilantes of Love. He was going with another guy popular in the Christian music scene, Christian. Christian and his girlfriend Star owned/owns The Eclipse Cafe in Concord some years later, where I'd see Harrod and Funck for the first and last time. How sad... Anyway, the two guys were on the guest list, while Star and I were tagging along.

Well, as I had been recently infatuated with the VoL album "The Killing Floor", this was a no-brainer. Off we went. We talked about music but mostly I listened. Their knowledge of the less-than-CCM bands was astounding to me, and the topics they covered were pretty expansive in general. Right in my element. Star and Christian fought some; he had a fairly excitable temper once he got going. He would calm down, but steer clear just the same. Give him his space. There were some tense times, but all in all the trip there and back was a great time.

Once we arrived I realized that I didn't have a ticket. I then realized I was on the guest list with Jon and Christian. This worked out well for me as my minimal means permitted me to buy more music than I would have otherwise been able to. Well, the venue had changed from the auditorium to one of the smaller cafes at the school. The turnout was light and Gordon didn't want to spare the space. So things were going to be a little cramped. At least they were till serving pizza by the slice when we got there.

On my way back out I heard the most melodious of voices, it actually brought me back to my short summer stint at camp. Camp was a great time for me, the start of a whole new existence, which memories to this day are a blessing to me. Another story perhaps. First kiss at camp, in fact. Anyway, there were two girls who sang together everywhere they went. To this day I'm convinced they learned how to sing from angels. Ivy and Heather were amazing. We would be working in the kitchen listening to them sing in the next room. All of us, the guys in the back washing pots in boiling hot water and the ladies trying not to scald themselves from the giant dishwasher, all of us could hear their voices echo through the place. It was like being in God's kitchen. Even the boiling water I was always putting my hands in felt like home as long their notes reached my ears. All was well with the world...

This voice was exactly that to me, except it was from one woman. I looked over to see her standing there, blonde, guitar strung over her shoulder, doing a sound check. I was in love with them from the sound check, and I didn't even know who they were or what they believed. At the time being a Christian musician was important to me. I distinctly remember saying to myself "I don't care what they believe. I'm buying their CD." Verbatim. I found out they were the second act. A local band, who's name was something about being red or magenta or maroon or something... They were opening, then Over the Rhine, then Vigilantes of Love. The opening band had a similar setup as the second; female lead singer who was really good, but even she couldn't compare to the dulcid tunes of Karin.

Over the Rhine set up and I was mesmerized from the moment they opened their act to the very end. I didn't know what to do, but I knew I had to get their autographs. Still got em, too. I remember being so nervous and forgetting everyone's names. Well, I really only forgot Linford's name because, well... It's Linford. It's not a name you don't remember and when you do you never forget it. I met Ric and Brian, the guitarist and drummer at the time and had been so from the beginning. Ric would leave that year to start being Monk, which is music I still need to get... Both of them would have guest spots on several track of Harrod and Funck's self-titled sophomore release, too. I met Karin and thought how beautiful she was (she's hot stuff). And I met Linford who was this gangly character who looked almost geekier than me. He was something of a hero to me after that...

VoL got me into Altoids, and it was a damn good show besides. The best part was the venue, so tight and cramped it was just us and the music. Everyone there was there for the music. It was very different from the shows I'd been to before and had staffed. It was just... The whole experience was so memorable to me and so meaningful I hold onto it tighter than my kitten over there. It warms me at night when I'm sad or angry or depressed. Over the Rhine soothes me to sleep as I dream of a better world and a life that can never be mine.

There are some bands that get under your skin. For me it's always been Over the Rhine. I picked up Good Dog, Bad Dog at that concert. They've since released a different version from their national label with a new song on it. While I have yet to purchase said second printing, I've bought every other CD they've produced, including the 3 instrumental CDs of Linford's. It's some of the most wonderful and poetic I've allowed to wave into my ears. That last perfect meal for me would be Over the Rhine... Probably "Suitcase" would be the song played at my funeral. It's so simple and it hurts so much... The sheer loss in it is just excruciating. I'll delve into the albums/songs another time.

This band has more history with me than most of my friends, and certainly more than my wife and everyone I've met from her influence. This band is a part of my very being, it's part of who I am. I hope one day to meet them again to tell them that. It's just so hard to surmise the best way to tell someone how much they changed your life in a way that's meaningful, in a way that truly represents precisely what you feel. So, I'll continue sing their praises and purchase their music and beg them to keep putting it out.

"I know a love that will not let me go. My heart is bound and happy to be so…"

Perception Is Truth: An Introduction

This is not one more category, this is simply the title of an ongoing series for which I will be putting together what I consider to be my greatest thesis to date. It should be known that, for some reason, while I think that what I'll be presenting here will be some kind of brilliance, I also don't believe for a second that I'm the first one to think this way, nor do I expect that much of what I'll be presenting here to be brilliant in itself. What I do hope to achieve through this is a clearer understanding of myself and the world in which we live and why that our society and our very lifestyle is going to implode in upon itself and the reasons why that's just the way it is or the way it has to be. Also be warned that the possibility exists that I'm wholly full of crap, but I don't think so. I think that through the readings presented you'll get a better appreciation for why my mind works the way it does and why there are so few absolutes in this world. The only absolute is that the perception of a person determines the truth by which they live their lives. Nothing more, nothing less. Each topic, which I hope will be focused to the topic at hand, will better detail what it is we're up against as people in this day and age and why I am loathe to breed for the future does not look bright to me. I have always been a pessimist and learned to be a cynic but I don't think I'm wrong, either. I also hope to present this in a very balanced manner.

Please, please, if you read nothing else, read this series. If you comment on nothing else, comment on this series. This is the reason I get up in the morning and the reason my wife and I have discussions constantly about having children and why I have bouts of "yeah, let's have kids" for a week or two at a time, but for the most part the sheer idea of procreating seems a dangerous and problematic idea to me. What kind of a world would I be passing to my offspring? I don't want to bring fear to people, just an understanding. Expect to be insulted by much of what I have to offer, but please bear with me and read the whole thoughts. Ask questions. I'm not in a position anymore where I want to destroy what people believe. I only want them to think about what they believe and why they live their lives the way they do.

Question everything.

Perception Is Truth: Opinions (Your Ideas Are Wrong)

I struggled over where was the best place to start when I came up with this topic. I have worked with these three little words for a handful of years now, and it's been part of my search to really find some focus and some clarity and to build an appropriate foundation in order to solidify myself not only as an intellectual, but hopefully that the ideas wherein I present are cohesive and strong enough so that I am not labeled a kook or a whack job or any of the things I refer often of other intellectuals. Like myself.

You'll find as you read on that each topic should build upwards like a pyramid or a house or any other structure that is built properly. There should always be a good foundation, for if there is not a good foundation, there are only problems. I should also point out that I believe a good foundation also accounts for what land you are placing said structure within, so a home with a strong cement foundation that is placed on the beach is still no good if the beach is eroding or if the tide just hasn't come in yet. You need to not only build a good foundation, but it has to start in the right place. This is what brings us here tonight.

An opinion is something that may be verifiable, but it is still nothing more than truth. The opinion may also be fact, such as "I believe the sky is blue", and it may be wrong such as "I believe the sky is orange", but it is how someone sees the sky that is important to them. This is a very careful distinction that we need to make before moving forward to any more focused topics. This should be the broadest conversation that we have, for indeed we're plotting out a large piece of land to build our structure upon and it must have the right features and suit our needs appropriately.

One of the things that we need to realize, if we haven't already, is that everyone has their own opinions on life, love, and the pursuit of happiness. We all go about our days living in the same places, doing the same jobs, being told the same things, but we think differently. Why? Opinion. We read the same books from the same language in the same class with the same teacher and yet we discuss what the author meant whether we really knew what they meant or not. We exercise our mind by interpreting often a given fact as to what really happened. We interpret fact and turn them into truths for which our minds climb the ladder of imagination and ride down it with intellectual glee. The problem with opinions has been stated above; some of them are right or can be proven, some of them are wrong or can be disproven. The real conundrum is some of these opinions cannot be properly understood by our frail minds anyway and all we're doing is making a molehill out of a mountain so our pea brains can understand it; this isn't truly understanding, but a label does make things seem simpler to us, and gives us a sense of peace. Even if it's a lie we tell ourselves to be happy.

"Ignorance is bliss, and knowledge is NOT power". How many different interpretations can I surmise on my own from that single statement? How about just the last half? I could sit here all night giving examples of why opinions are difficult, but I'll try to keep this as simple and easy to understand as possible. The one thing I don't want to do is write myself into a circle that no one can get out of. That would defeat half the point of what I'm trying to accomplish here.

Let's look at an example my father had given me many years ago. In my mind, it's a perfect example of interpretation on a small scale and why it's so important that we grasp this concept fully.

A lawyer asks the question, "Who has a watch?" Someone responds quickly by stating, "It's ten-thirteen." The lawyer says "No. That is NOT what I asked. I will ask it again. Who has a watch?" The man who had responded before did not respond. Someone else looked around and said, "Uh. Do you want to know the time?" The lawyer said again, "No. That is NOT what I asked. I will ask it again. Who has a watch?" Finally, someone else in the room said, "I do." There was a brief pause. "Thank you. Pay attention to the question being asked. Do not volunteer information. When you are asked a question; answer it. That's it."

It seems like a silly story. In an effort to be polite it was assumed that the lawyer wanted to know what time it was. At the very least, people anticipated a follow-up question regarding the time. What if this was not going to be asked? What if the answer to that question could be the last answer needed to have you sent away to prison for life or even have you put to death? What if that question determined whether or not you would enjoy eternity in bliss or damnation? This all sounds very trivial I know, but we live in a society where it seems that nothing is trivial and almost anything goes and goes with the full protection of our laws. Does that mean it's the right way to go?

I'll not trouble you with too many examples, for I fear I will lose my readers and my point if I did. What I will burden you with is the notion that the many things we believe and fight and die over are based solely upon someone's opinion on a topic. We have public schools because the Greek philosophers idealized such a construct. The same goes for politics, which amounted to philosophers discussing nothing and doing it all day and never coming to a conclusion. We laud these people for the act of accomplishing nothing because they do what we on the whole no longer do for ourselves: think.

We live our lives in ignorant bliss because it's easier that way. We complain about people giving cliché answers and "copping out" of something but at the same time we're on our judgmental high horse we're not voting because there's "no one to choose from" or we're not watching our children properly because "I worked hard all day and my wife should be taking care of them". We live in a society that's built upon lust of whatever we want; money, sex, etc. It's all about me. It's not about you and it's certainly not about us. It's just about me. And me often wants to be coddled to sleep by feeling safe but we don't want to give up any liberties. Me wants the bad guy captured but don't let anyone suspect anyone who's not a criminal. Which makes sense. Everyone who's a criminal has already been born and developed a pattern of behavior to be a criminal. Yeah. That works.

To say knowledge is power is a crock for a couple reasons. The biggest problem is we have so much knowledge and so much information now we don't even know how to handle it. We learn more and more about our world and about how our universe works but we interpret the information based upon what we know now. It's clearly impossible to base that information on what we'll know in the future, but the more we learn the more we know. Unfortunately, we're in such a place societally that we have to know everything now now now and someone's always pushing an agenda that we don't try to prove something is or is not for solely scientific reasons or for the edification of our species; we merely try to prove something to push a specific agenda or an idea or an opinion because it's popular and the numbers can be massaged to make it viable to the layman.

Let's discuss global warming. We're being told right now, and have been for some time, that we're poisoning our world with greenhouse gases and other emissions. We're killing the very planet we're living in one car ride at a time. I won't argue that we as humans do have an impact on our world since the industrial revolution, but the point I would argue is that we don't really know the temperature impact we're having because we really don't know how old the planet is and we can only guess as to what the temperature was like all those years ago, however long ago they were. Most people don't consider this, they only believe what they're told. It's the same argument I've had with my mother about church and about what's said from the pulpit, it's the same argument I have about soap box speeches; what are the facts? I want the whole picture.

If we assume the world is millions and millions of years old, how do we know what the temperature was like all those years ago? We don't. Even the scientists have stated that it's purely conjecture on our part as to how the dinosaurs lived all those years ago and how temperate the world was. We find new information on that constantly, but the accepted truths which are stated facts are changed when that happens. So, are we right now or will we be right in the future? How will we know? Our digging into our past and our search for fact and knowledge just brings up more questions. It's the same in my own life with my own research; that's where these writings come in.

We haven't even been keeping track of the weather for more than, what, 150 years? 200 years? And even then, the records weren't kept on a global weather report, they were localized to a given region or even a specific town. We have much better methods to determine the weather today, but we can't rely solely upon the data provided us, especially when for thousands of years of recorded history the weather was not tracked by every culture. We're basing the idea of global warming on information we don't even have; we can only guess. The methods of guessing are phenomenal, but who's to say it's right? Who's to say that something drastic didn't cause a major change in how the world moves? Who's to say that the world is truly only tens of thousands of years old and not millions of years old?

We live in a time when our insipid little human minds are infallible and we can explain anything that we want to with the sciences that we constructed to answer the questions that cannot be explained. We've made amazing strides in technology and general thought that we wouldn't have made if we hadn't asked some basic questions and built from there. The knowledge that we have is impressive but it's all we have to go on.

- Perception Is Truth -

Science has brought us both possible truths and certain facts, but it will never bring us the reality. It can't, for reality is the final phase in our existence. Even that is a lot of conjecture and opinion.

Is there an afterlife? That's the biggest question that no one seems to ask when they accept their religious ideals. They never stop to ask the question of whether or not they will in some form or other actually live forever. I don't even want to talk about heaven and hell or any of the iterations of the same; I'm referring to eternity. Is there such a thing? Is there such a thing as life after death? When pressed, I do often receive the preface of "I believe". This should be an admission of an opinion and therefore fallible, but often it's the admission of a truth that cannot be argued. It is accepted as fact, but it cannot be labeled as a fact as I have defined the terms. Even my terminology listed beforehand is purely my opinion, my truth, but for the basis of these discussions, for them to make any sense at all, they must be treated as fact.

Even for a word to have any meaning there must be an opposite or something else to use as a reference point otherwise our words mean nothing. Apparently this was not understood by the Romans when they determined how to count, but this is another perfect example of truth. The Roman method of counting presumes there is no zero; that there is not nothing. There must always be something. We have since determined that is not true. Which is right?

We could not have the idea of nothing without the idea of something; the inverse may not be true, of course, and indeed I've just proven that it is not or at least was not. However, why would we have nothing if we didn't have something? How would we know what nothing was, what zero was, without one. To lack you must first understand what it means to have.

Everyone has an opinion and most of us believe that our opinion is right. Many of the facts we now have like colors and ideas of gravity and math and lofty and simple ideals all across the intellectual spectrum are truly facts based upon the rules that we established. We have colors because we gave them names. We needed to be able to call something by something because the name of nothing is nothing and there are more somethings than there are nothings.

Everyone has something to say, but not everyone will ever be right.

Perception Is Truth: The Beginning

For some, this will be a recap. I tend to repeat ideas but not on purpose, more for clarification or because they apply to this conversation as much as they did to the last one.

I'm here to work out what I hope to be my philosophy, or at least a collection of the thoughts and feelings I have about the direction society should go or I would like to see it go. I've recently started digging through the mall of Philosophy and while I'm still at the "You Are Here" sign I have been reading at least the names of all the stores. Some interesting points put out there that I hope to get through while I work on this. Being that I've already found several places where I'm in agreement with certain philosophers and I know some of you know how to read and have perused such materials it may be another refresher.

I'm not here to repeat the thoughts of Plato and Socrates (though I wonder if Socrates ever existed - what philosopher doesn't write anything down?), I'm not here to disprove teleology (which has already been done) or get into the idea that metaphysics didn't mean what it means now when it was first assembled as a word. What I'm here to do is try to redefine logic and reason and emotion and personage through carefully selected and maybe one day edited words. I sit or stand or walk or work and day in and day out I see atrocity after atrocity that could be easily resolved if we just had a little willpower. If we just grew a spine and did what needed to be done. Part of the problem is knowing what needs to be done. I'm still in the situation where I have no spine and I don't know what needs to be done. I'm a firm disbeliever in the "do as I say not as I do" mentality but giving people suggestions for their lives is something I've done for years. Half the time I get ignored so I don't suspect much different now. My goal is to educate and open minds and hope and pray that one day some of what I say might actually work for people. I think I can be of help in at least changing your minds.

This is where the title of my thesis comes in: perception is truth. There are some facts that should be explained before going any further. For most this is a refresher course, but as I've opened a new section to be used strictly for this ideologue of mine it bears repeating. First, there are three facets of understanding that amount to semantics but it will prove quite useful to know this upfront. Three words to keep in mind: truth,

- Perception Is Truth -

fact, reality. Truth is not truth but it's our opinion or how we see things; she's pretty. Facts are things that are insurmountable or have been proven by our own realms of science or logic; she is short for her age. Reality is the opposite of both, it is what really is; she's a man, baby! Truth is opinion. Facts are above suspicion. Reality we don't have the knowledge of. This will come in handy later on.

With that said, we should then go into a couple of Rules that I would like to define. This is by no means a complete list at this time, but it's a good place to start.

1. Everyone has their own truths.

2. You might be wrong.

This seems an oversimplification, but Ockham was right. The simplest answer... I should clarify here that this doesn't make everyone right or everyone wrong, this is just to point out that I think the most important emotion or activity a human can undertake is that of humility. Pride comes before a fall is a fact, though the timing of "before" is never set in stone. If you understand and truly remember these two points it will make life much easier. I don't always remember them but I'm working on it and have done a fare job better at this idea than most people I know. Everyone has reasons for why they do things, but most don't care about the whys. Most only care about what happened and how it affected them. Well, how it affects you also comes into play in how you react to it and if you were right or not. I've blown my stack needlessly before and found out what an ass I was to have responded that way. I do it a couple times a week. This is as much for me as it is for you.

I could go on for days and days about why these two rules are factual and may be part of reality, but by my definition we wouldn't know about them, because we really don't know exactly what's going on out there. So, we make it up as we go along to try and live our lives as best and as happily as we can. That doesn't always work, and I blame greed for that but I'll come to that later.

This is the foundation of where I want to take us in future commentaries. The rules may get added to but I may just spend some time detailing those rules and offering specific examples. Indeed, the best arguments I've had is by taking what other people said and turn it back on them. In many ways in the Socratic method of just asking questions, but some things needed to be pointed out specifically in order to make my points. I'll spend a lot of time discussing religion and human emotions, the society of a people and why culture is defined by more than what tourists bring home from the gift shop. I hope to educate and to entertain and push as many buttons as I can. It's the only thing that'll get peoples' attentions.

This is important to me in ways I don't even understand. I feel compelled to put these words to whatever medium I have available to me and develop them and spread them far and wide. Do I think I can change lives? Honestly? Yes. It'll take time to put this all together and I hope some of you will join me on this ride and work with me. I'll want people to respond to this and help me develop this but understand I may argue specific points but I'll give more than specific reasons for such. I really do want to tear down everything we know and rebuild our own minds and our society. I don't see any other way to get out of the pit of despair we're all falling into.

I just want people to be free of the fears I've lived with for so long.

Petra

It should be noted here that no matter what may have transpired in my past or present or future, and no matter how much I like Rich Mullins and Mark Heard and even Steve Taylor, there isn't a Christian band out there that can hold a candle to the one and only truly Christian rock band who started it all, Petra. Without Petra I doubt very seriously such Christian crossovers would have been possible. Never mind the fact that the words that Petra said and the music they said it with have yet to be properly copied, at least in my opinion.

Now, with all that said, let's begin. For those of you who don't know... Uh... Dr Steel... I was raised as a Born Again Christian. Jesus Freaks. Bible Thumpers. Holy Rollers. The kind of Christians you see on Jerry Springer? That was me. Raised in a trailer park, just without the twang and the incest, we believed everything that the Bible had to offer. I decided of my own volition to be Saved at the age of 4. Then, the odyssey of music began. I remember nothing of music other than Mylon LeFevre, Russ Taff, and Petra.

The lyrics were hard-hitting and Biblically-based and they weren't shy about their faith. They weren't Stryper and certainly the black-and-yellow striped glam rockers weren't anything like the grandfathers of the Christian rock movement. From their humble beginnings as a more Southern rock or borderline country band without a legit lead singer to the heart-felt pitches of Greg X Volz, even to the handoff to John Schlitt and the eventual departure of one of the founding members, Bob Hartman, all the way to their retirement in 2005... Best Christian Band Ever.

Yeah, I listened to a lot of Christian music and still do, but I had 95% of their albums from 1979 to 1993 memorized. That's 14 years of music in this brain. I still remember a lot of it. Naturally, I'm about an octave or two too low to keep up with Greg, but the lyrics are still there. I've started recollecting the music via MP3 since it's such a nightmare to record it from tape. Though I was, for a while, recording each individual song onto my computer as a WAV file then converting them to MP3. A time-consuming process that required to listen to the songs that I may have never liked. Still, well worth it.

However, I have recently managed to get my hands on some of the band's earlier releases and I hope to get more in the coming days, just to fill out my collection. I would have to say that my favorite album, and the only one for which I owned a real record, is More Power To Ya. Between Judas' Kiss, Rose Colored Stained Glass Windows, All Over Me, and Road To Zion... Gives me shivers just to think about how long I've listened to that album and how many times I've had to replace it from wear and tear. Although... Never Say Die has some kick-ass tunes, too... The Coloring Song, Angel of Light, For Annie... Such good stuff.

Always focused on the music and the message, they were preachy but not too preachy, nor were they compromising their faith to sell a few albums, or using their faith as other previously-mentioned bands have been blamed for. If you can, get your hands on some of this music. If you already have it, dig it out and turn it up. Oddly enough, I am right now .

"Why are you looking for the Devil when you oughta be looking for the Lord?"

Reincarnation and Skeptics: A Response

http://www.taoism.net/living/2000/200004.htm

I chose this article to comment on because of it's... How do I word this... Lack of argument? I cannot find a 'nicer' way of putting this. I found myself opposing reincarnation even more after reading this piece; clearly not your intention. However, I felt I had to bring certain points to light before passing off the skeptics completely.

The first thing that I took notice of was the choice of skeptics you used to base your talk upon. There was nothing objective about your initial refute: 'Can you feel the arrogance oozing out of these words?' While I cannot argue a certain ignorance in their discussion, it seemed the only logical solution to the superficial knowledge they have of Buddhism. While I, in truth, have almost no knowledge of the subject, I know a good argument when I see one. I also do my best to recognize a bad one, or one lacking foundation. What I felt here was more hostility than understanding, or even an appreciation for their ability to think about things from their own perspective. Yes, it's a poorly put together argument on their part, but I felt no arrogance. Perhaps it was their tone, I do not know.

The reasons reincarnation could not be true were always explained to me in terms of Biblical doctrine and Christian dogma. Since it goes outside of the aspects the Bible covers pertaining to death, the afterlife, and heaven and hell, reincarnation could not be real. It goes against God. If reincarnation goes against God, then explain to me the Risen Christ. That, in a sense, is reincarnation. Christ's mortal body had died, but His soul had indeed left to begin a spiritual journey. Three days later, the body was, in essence, reborn, and Christ rose to heaven with a deeper understanding and explanation of the afterlife and the power Christians all are capable of. Reincarnation could parallel resurrection in this context, if my small knowledge of reincarnation is correct. Surely, I would be insulting my fellow Christians by promoting such an idea, but I only want some better understanding of truth. I can't walk around accepting concepts blindly. I need more.

The next point that got to me was the 'mountain of evidence' that Dr Ian Stevenson's study supposedly prove reincarnation. While I am an American, born and bred, and grew up a Christian, I have a hard time accepting this evidence as proof. While I cannot argue the findings, I can argue your conclusion. It may seem a logical conclusion, but it also seems somehow suited to fit your argument more than a deeper understanding of the inner workings of the human soul.

The boy who knew the specifics of an auto mechanic's life doesn't prove to me the mechanic was reincarnated. There is a belief amongst Christians, and indeed others of many cultures, that we can talk to the spirits. I'm not talking 'The Sixth Sense,' but something along that idea. Whose to say this boy isn't hearing the voice of this mechanic, who is wandering around, trying to find someone to hear him? Within that idea, there's a host of other possibilities relating to this wandering spirit; is he wandering because he has something to do before he can rest in eternal peace? Is it a different spirit trying to sway people into believing in reincarnation or that this child can channel the dead? I won't for a second say this sort of thing is a hoax, unless it's provable that it is, but the truth behind it seems to me to be bigger than simply citing reincarnation or channeling or whatever other term can be thrown out to explain it.

This other idea that the skeptics have a hard time accepting the findings because of the culture of the people also seems weak to me. That's not a valid reason for not accepting documented and proven results. That's the West pretending to know everything and be smarter than peoples who have lived for many millennia longer than us. The cultural acceptance of reincarnation aside, the Eastern world, as far as I know, have a deeper acceptance of the spiritual. While we're over here telling ghost stories, the East is really trying to understand the ways of the spirits, in terms of their ancestors, the past lives they believe to have lived, etc. We in America are only concerned with our health and wealth, and while we have several beliefs about the afterlife, they are academic at best. Our existence is based upon greed and materialism; pleasing our own bodies, not our souls. The idea that a child can know deep family truths based upon their own imagination is equally ludicrous. If a child can know the specifics of a person's existence whom they've never met and has no connection with their family is an example of why we should be studying this sort of phenomena further, not passing it off as unscientific hogwash. It's happening; let's find out why. Let's at least try, even though we probably can't answer that question with our current techniques. Maybe one day we can…

I also wanted to answer the questions you posed. The one about children not relaying stories of past lives in an environment that doesn't readily accept reincarnation is curious to me. If the child is unfamiliar with the idea of reincarnation in the first place, then all they're doing is telling stories. The parents may or may not accept them as past lives, or a voice in the child's head relaying such information, out of fear. I have a hard time accepting culture as a reason not to accept certain facts that are in front of your face. It's an arrogant perspective. Culture does not make a spirit more or less receptive to the things involving the spirit. Culture only affects the mind and body. The spirit is touched by these other two forces, but it exists on a different playing field altogether. If it didn't, we'd already know the truth about the afterlife, wouldn't we?

Religion

Why must it always be religion that I focus my thoughts upon? I suppose it works well in the fantasy environment with which I seem to want to write. Yet, for a subject that I try so hard to ignore, I let myself talk about it and argue about it every chance I get. I suppose I'm trying to ignore religion, but I'm trying to ignore the nagging within my soul to make some sort of decision about it. Even though I'm convinced I've decided against any classical Western religion, it seems that I only have an uphill climb when discussing it with others. Realistically, I wholly understand that those with whom I have spent most of my time are either Christian or atheist/agnostic/apathetic in their religious inklings. I'm certain that I would have people call me some sort of hypocrite for listening to Christian music but not following its precepts. Irrelevant. The music is a big part of my life, and I cannot turn my back upon that which I had grown to love so intensely. That which kept me alive was faith in music, but fear of Christianity.

Well, I suppose it's fear of God, but I think it was more the dogma that I was pressured to believe so emphatically. Every decision I made, I had to be concerned about the future of my soul. Nothing was ever a simple choice; everything evolved around my eternal salvation. Even as a child, I committed the only unforgiveable sin during playtime, and I feared for my soul... I cried, I was terrified. Mother, of course, told me that God knows our hearts and would know that I was merely playing and not being honest or true. I have seen what power wielded in the name of the Holy Spirit can do, and it scares me to ever truly blaspheme it.

Christianity is not a religion wielded in the name of the greater good, but a power wielded and enforced through fear. Western civilization is considered civilized for our beliefs, but it's mostly considered civilized because we're not a tribal society as the Indians were. Yet, something that bothers me, if we're truly so civilized, why is abortion legal, and stoning a harlot no longer...? Slavery is a God-given right, but we consider it an insult to one's human rights... Sacrifice is no longer allowed, but an eye for an eye still holds sway amongst the truly religious... Murder is wrong, but killing a killer is a debated practice. Hunting with an AK-47 is legal again, but what difference does it make if they shoot you with a .45 or a .223 automatic...? You're still dead.

How can I not let the religion that bore me take the full brunt of my anger about decisions in my life? True, my parents created much of my issues before my birth, before Christianity, before their two lives ever staggered across each others' paths. Still, I have much to blame religion for. The failure of my family is one of those reasons. It is difficult to get people to understand why this is the case when my parents are together and things seem happy and healthy. However, for those who are unaware, there is such a debate over Christianity versus Messianic Judaism between my parents that it seems medication has been prescribed to both.

More to come...

Religious Claim Jumping

Before I get too much further into my continuing thoughts, I felt now was a good time to explain where I'm ultimately coming from and where my mind is headed. I realize I have minimal readers and certainly a singular commentator (at present), but this blog is as much about me putting my thoughts out there as it is others partaking in those thoughts. With that in mind I'm going to lay a foundation that I hope can be built upon in the coming... uh... whenever. The first thing we should discuss is the foundation of religion and history. Please be warned: I expect this to go across many points and cover many tangent trails. Try to keep up. And can someone send me a map?

Who Owns God?

I realize this appears a loaded question, but it's something I've been asking myself over the course of the past many years and I think it's one that's hugely important. Never mind the specific aspects of God or how religions worship a singular deity referred to as God. This includes Allah, which is just Arabic for God. Let us consider the very notion of God, for God did start as a concept to man, and not the Creator. Like any deity or worshipped being, the idea of doing such was brought upon by man. The last time God was really revealed and directly observed by man was Moses. This is part of why many people believe that Moses, who brought down the Ten Commandments, started Judaism. I'm finding out this may not actually have been so, but let's move on.

Judaism was the first religion to suggest a single deity over everything. Before then, ancestor worship, animal worship and shamanism, and pantheistic faiths were the norm. The idea of a single god, including one of such fire and jealousy as this Jewish god, was terribly unusual and often resented. Greater detail can be found in Karen Armstrong's A History of God. Good stuff. Still going through that. Expansive.

Today the perception is that God is not "owned" by anyone. I realize my question to be a difficult one, but we need to consider some historical implications. I am of the mindset that other religions who claim God as their deity to be worshipping the same god. So, Jews, Christians, Muslims, Catholics, et al, are worshipping the same deity, but their religion portrays this in different ways. I realize that by lumping Muslims with the rest I'm making myself something of a target of nothing more than ignorance. You must read your history. Mohammed got the idea of God from the Jews. It was Mohammed who decided he was the Prophet of Allah. The Quran refers to those in the Old Testament as also being Prophets, such as Moses and David, even Jesus is considered a Prophet of Allah. So while some do not adhere to the same belief as I do, it doesn't make any less a fact.

So, the question still remains, but I'll alter it slightly for the sake of conversation; Who owns the idea of God? I realize this is not some simple question of copyright or who came first, but there are deep philosophical nuances that should be massaged when it comes to idea of ownership and intellectual property.

In this day and age, an idea is bought and sold like any other commodity and is enforced as though it is of Biblical proportions. Someone's ideas are often all they have (me) and those people don't want them to be stolen or used without giving the appropriate credit. Is this not also true of history? It seems that it is not. Who wrote the Bible? Who put the books together? God-inspired or not, man was the one who assembled it and printed it and passed it and translated it and taught it and used it and created dogma around it and lie about it every single day...

So, who owns God? Historically speaking, I have to go with the Jews. The ideas of Hell and Satan and eternity and Christ and martyrdom and immaculate conception and limbo and purgatory and golden streets and what we get when we die... Most of these are not what came with the Torah; they did not come with God when God first started kicking our asses and showing us a new way with a single mindset instead of having to make sure the rock god was okay with us sitting our butt down and that karma didn't smite us for squishing the bug which was attached to our clothing that was colored specifically not to insult Vishnu...

Am I saying that Christianity is a farce and all those already mentioned are as well? Hmm. That's a tough one. I know why Catholicism bears no semblance to a Christian faith, but that's a different series altogether. I'll get to that. Islam comes from the same God of the Jews, some of the teachings of the Iranian Zoroastrians crept into both Islam and Judaism in later years. There's so much that no one really knows or wants to know about their faith.

...Faith... The evidence of things not seen. Doesn't mean you are blinded to the evidence.

God's Word?

Here's where, if I haven't already lost you, I'll either lose you by interest or by anger. Typically, when I start attacking anything involving faith, I get chastised and fights start because of it. That's not to say I know what buttons to push, but there has to be a reason God gave us free will and the capacity to think, right? Not that I buy into Free Will... God's way or damnation isn't a choice; it's a sentence. Anyway, I was always raised under the belief that the Bible was God's written word. I was later taught that, well, God spoke to those who wrote it. Then it became God inspired them to write. Soon it became something else; man wrote the Bible and man chose what would be contained within the Bible. Huh. So where's God?

I realize the DaVinci Coders out there will love this, but there is still fact to that fiction. God didn't put pen to paper and I will never be convinced otherwise. The only instance where this was not the case was the Ten Commandments (a movie I have not seen in its entirety in my entire life). It can be argued that Moses carved the stones himself, but there is a clear indicator within the Bible that God put them into effect. Based on some of what was said within it could also be argued that God did indeed write the Torah, but this is probably not factual.

The Bible has a rich and vast history of survival and change that only humanity itself can boast. It has survived destruction by many hands, but I would argue that the Bible itself is still missing. People are finding new and exciting texts constantly that are seemingly linked to the Bible by time and by theme. The Gospel of Q, of Thomas, for example. It's theorized the first three Gospels are taken from this one supposed writing from a place called Nag Hammadi. The Bible has survived censorship and has increasingly grown in popularity over the millennia. The books of the Bible were not, however, always together, so the question in my mind had been for some time that if this was God's Word and God wanted to tell us something from it, then was it God who assembled and put it together?

The answer has always been no. I further expect that the largest argument I will receive is that God can do anything. God wanted these given books in the Bible and allowed man to make that choice. Well, then if God wanted the books that we have here, then that would mean man did not have the free will to put together the Bible canon. Hmm... I see a circular argument forming: If we have free will then man put the Bible together but if it is God's Word then God put it together which means man doesn't have free will. A conundrum in my mind, but many things are.

My concern is that we put such faith into a book that has stood the test of time in concept, but not in physical form. The Bible has clearly had to have been added to and changed, otherwise there would only ever have been one version of the Bible and only one religion to worship by it. This is not the case, not by a long shot. We have so many translations and so many different variations that it is impossible to predict who is right and who will, ultimately, be punished by God.

The Bible is full of great stories and amazing ideas that may or may not be complete. So, are we content with learning half the truth or perhaps half the lie? The answer is not to just be satisfied with what you have and make the most of it. I'm sorry, that's not good enough. If we're supposed to find God and be of God and to learn about God... Shouldn't we learn to dig a little deeper?

Religious Claim Jumping Pt2

I realized I missed something back there. I forgot about Christ. Christ is the unbalancing factor. What Christ offers us is something more than even Buddha, and certainly more than Allah and his Prophet. What Christ offers us is a glimpse into divinity from a human perspective. Buddha was enlightened, but was not divine. Buddha's immortality could be seen more as a gift than a birthright, but there's some philosophical questions about fate that I just don't have the energy to ask at present.

This is all dependent upon the Gospels telling of the immaculate conception to be accurate. What's unusual here is that the only question that can be asked is if Christ was truly Messiah. We know Christ existed at this time or close enough to this time (carbon dating is such a bitch). What we don't really is if Christ was the son of God. This is where faith comes in. This is where you step back and give up on all sense of logic and reason and a growing societal hatred for all things spiritual that can't be proven. This is where you just believe. While I can't prove or disprove God, even though I would argue our ability to think beyond our necessities precludes the existence of at least a deity willing to share with us some logic, I have no arguments against Christ that show up with any validity.

The irony here is that people who argue Christ doesn't exist because we can't see him also argue for evolution even though we have no examples of human evolution aside from some dented skulls. Advancement of a species, metamorphosis, even the presence of defense mechanisms are not evolution. The advancement crack abounds to our ability to adapt to our surroundings. Do I argue against the evolutionary chart? Yeah. The gaps from ape to man are drastic enough to disprove the whole notion, but people still have faith in it. People without faith have faith in evolution... Irony is all around me. ...Maybe that's just dumbasses :D...

In terms of who would own Christ that's a tough one. The Prophets discussed the coming of the Messiah a long time ago. This would cause the Jews to likewise have a claim upon the idea of Christ as being Messiah. Messiah is their term and their chosen one. Christianity stems from the coming of Christ as any decent religion should. They have their deity, who did the opposite of Buddha and gave up immortality for a chance to die, but they still hold on to the ways that brought them this far. The Torah and the

Old Testament. Hmm.

I once had an uncle who believed in only the New Testament because that's what mattered. Actually, he went further in that the Gospels were all that mattered because that's what Christ said. Never mind what God instructed in the Old Testament, but that whole "I came to fulfill the Law" has people really confused. I understand his point, though. If you're a Christian, a "Little Christ" as it were, then wouldn't it make the most sense to follow only what your chosen savior has spoke? Hmm. Some do that, some don't. Again, it's back to the religious argument over who is worshipping correctly. Yeah.

Christ also offers us miracles in larger ways than previously recorded or told. There are those who would have similar stories of healing, but their ministries would last longer than Christ's. Does that make others like Smith Wigglesworth more worthy of our praise than Christ? Hmm. This is tricky. If Christ was the Son of God, then that's an easy answer. If not… Then we have to consider that what we're really doing IS worshipping God and the power bestowed upon us by our Creator. Hmm… Power… From God.

Simply put, while I have my doubts over how we serve and worship God, I cannot argue against the existence of the Creator. There's nothing to work with, and just touting "God doesn't exist" is not an argument. I'm too smart to NOT believe in God. As far as Christ goes I'm often not so sure, but there's too much going for Jesus in the way our entire world has advanced since His coming that it's impossible to whine about the impact it has had. Was Christ Messiah? We won't know until he fulfills the rest of the prophecies. We won't know until the Orthodox Jews are satisfied… When they believe, then we should believe, too.

Reminiscent Of A Memory

I remember things in my life I find out are wrong, never happened, or I've somehow misconstrued the truth of their happenings. This is not to say this occurs all the time, for indeed there are some travesties that I recall first-hand fluently as though I were still there, or had just experienced it for the first time. Being mocked, laughed at, beat up, hated, making mistakes of menial proportions but kicking myself for it even today, a decade or more after the fact. Why is it some people remember the bad, some the good, and some actually a clear delineation of both? Is it due to our natures? Is it because some are naturally bright and chipper and others dark and morose, sometimes needlessly so on both counts? For as hard as I try to balance myself emotionally I find that all I've done is try to hide behind some facade of intelligence because I never bothered to learn how to really deal with things; having an overemotional and often oversensitive family will do that to you I've discovered, but being the only sane one in the gene pool is still an accomplishment.

I look back on those mistakes and realize that what I learned is how to be afraid. I didn't "learn" the lesson that others would have learned, I learned first and foremost to be afraid of what I could do by sheer accident, and how embarrassed I would be because of it. I have made real efforts to speak to certain people and find that the initial reaching out didn't do anything but make me look a fool and I never followed up on it. I've avoided conversations from everyone because of fear, I've avoided having fun because of fear, I've avoided living my life because of fear. I'm happily married now, don't get me wrong. I've learned in many ways to adapt to my fear and my loving wife has managed to see the real me through it all and love me for what I am. She sees everything about me and in me and I wonder how she can stand it.

I look back on my life as a series of mistakes that have, for some reason, brought me to a fairly decent existence (not everything was a mistake); far better than what was had by my family by this time in their lives that is for certain. Still, I find an emptiness because of my fears, and they're stupid fears, too. Truly. For the most part, I don't even know what I'm really afraid of. I don't fear death but I don't want to experience it either. I don't fear life necessarily but there's a lot to make you want to curl up into a ball in a corner and just wait for the end of it all. But, even that, is that a fair assessment of my fear? Am I just lazy? Is it just that I'm afraid to finish something? Am I just afraid of failure and rejection even after all these years? Am I afraid I've become something that I feel will repel people just so that I can be alone and continue in my fear without having to subject people to it?

Hmm. It's funny some of the things I am afraid of, but I'll not discuss them here. I guess I'm really just afraid of being looked down upon or pitied, or just being looked at whatsoever. Oh, I know it's all in my head. My fears are my own and haven't been put there by anyone else for many, many years. Try to hide behind emotional logic but I'm not that good.

In other words, don't do drugs, wear your seatbelt, and... uh... don't drink and drive.

Response To The Abortion Discussion

Seems I write too much. I may also create this major argument or just cause people to not want to talk to me anymore. Seems I'm somewhere on the edge of sanity with this…

First, let me say I believe that people here are half-right about this issue. I do believe that earlier education is necessary to understand not what abortion is, but what human life is and why we should cherish it and why, if we don't want it, we shouldn't create it. Don't destroy it (abortion), just don't create it (abstinence). There are methods that you can undertake to prevent abortion during intercourse that don't involve the standard "birth control" methods, but for some reason people can't seem to make this work because, as already stated, we have self control problems (apparently I'm the only guy I know who can handle that). Anyway, education is vital to our survival on a number of levels, and A touched upon the fact that what we teach and who teaches it is paramount. If we offer children an incorrect worldview whereby humanity isn't valued, they're going to act on their impulses without thought of consequence. We are a nation of "convenience" with no real understanding.

People argue for science and evolution and psychology but against God without ever considering the fact that both are necessary to our survival and the perpetuation of our species. The Chinese "devalue" life because they ARE overpopulated and because the various religions which have come and stayed there value duty and honor and the passage into death as much as they value life and it's only a matter of time before a country with those standards treats the unborn with such a seemingly callous attitude. I don't believe they devalue the unborn as much as they value the currently living. We're coming into this argument from the approach that all life is worth living; I must state in my own callousness I do not believe this is true, but I will not speak any further on it. I must also warn people that by denouncing abortion and denouncing murder and by suggesting that all life is worth living we will overrun our natural resources. It will not be in our lifetime, but it will occur. It must.

Is this our way of handling overpopulation of our species? Possibly. Is it handled appropriately? No. It's funny, if we kill unborn indiscriminately we're okay, for the most part, but if we kill what we know merely because we can't handle it (i.e. Baby

Doe), we're treated as evil and heartless. I hear all these assumptions from the religious and the conservative about who deserves to live and die and who gets punished or who should go free. We complain that we're setting ourselves up for "playing God" but aren't we playing God by telling people what they can and cannot do with their lives and the lives of those who are supposed to be subservient to the heads of the household?

Does anyone remember the Old Testament? Didn't God wipe out Creation just because we were "bad"? Didn't God get really pissed when we didn't do the will of God; even with Free Will? Did God single out people because of a disability? We don't know. We do know that the disabilities that God wiped out was based upon someone's birth, but we denounce racism as unGodly. We put all this pressure on a deity that we barely understand and say we don't understand but we say things in God's name as though we are God's Voice. Abraham and Isaac, anyone? Sure, this was a test, but Abraham proved he was more concerned about what God would think than anyone else. He was willing to kill his own son for God. When we hear that people are doing this to their own children we realize they're mentally unstable and put them away for as long as we possibly can; but because of Abraham's significance (to Jews, Christians, Catholics, AND Muslims) in religious history, this sort of connection is overlooked.

As usual, I'm rambling. All I'm saying is that abortion can serve a purpose in the "right" situation (please don't ask me what that means, because by rights I should not have been born [or my mother] and probably would not have if I were leading the world at that time), but the fact it's become this wholesale tossing away of human life and a convenient way to continue to give into our impulses and turn our attentions inward... It's being abused. There's no sense of balance and I know I'm liable to lose people by stating that not everyone deserves to live. If we did there'd be chaos. If we did, if we all truly deserved to live, then we would still be able to see Adam and Eve walking around. We talk about God using people to do "His Will", but we complain when it's not something we THINK they should be doing. Again, this dichotomy of knowing God's mind by stating we don't know the Will of God but this is what God would want. Lot's wife. Pharaoh. Judas. Name me a martyr. Job...

Remember that God gave us the ability to reason, even if it was only so we would choose to serve and worship the Almighty. Why would be given choice if there was no choice? Why would we be given the opportunity to be barren if we're all supposed to procreate. Why would we be mortal if we all deserve to live? Why would there be disease?

Please. I want to know. I want to know that either I'm totally insane and I can be easily dissuaded… Or that I'm not alone.

Sci Fi vs. Fantasy

Alright, I've had this little conversation recently and one of the things that's been said to me about it has been said to me about a lot of the things that I think about and feel are important on a number of levels; "Who cares? It's a stupid thing to argue about." That may be true in this particular instance, but what I'm still trying to do is get people to a deeper level of understanding of not only the world around them, but the language that we utilize on a daily basis.

Now, I'm no English major, though I do know some. However, I have a dictionary or two and I find the Internet is littered with dictionaries. I've also seen where words meant one thing in 1972 and something else today (my folks have a 36 year old dictionary, it's GREAT). However, what bothers me about topics like this, seemingly trivial, and larger topics, like religion and interpretation, are not taken seriously. People think and believe what they want to believe and no one can change that. Well, part of the problem is no one is willing to accept if they're wrong about something. Part of it really is that people just don't care, and I find that trite and childish to a point. We should care if we're using bad information to tailor our thoughts or discussions. We should care if what we're basing our existence on or even our concept of over salting your fries is actually been a lie. Hell, there's scientists who were of the Liberal leaning who are starting to claim that global warming may not actually be happening because of Man; maybe it's actually just a part of the ebb and flow of nature. NO KIDDING!

As usual, I digress and depart from my main point, but that's the beauty of a blog; you can talk about whatever you like when it comes to you.

So, here we are, the end of Star Wars already behind us, but the start of a television show within the next year or two. Star Trek's making a strange comeback, complete with a new movie. Billions of dollars were made by both franchises, but a humble amount of speculation and hatred remains between them. One of which is who is more powerful, the Star Trek universe or the Star Wars universe.

Aside from being a Star Wars fan, I still have to side with Star Wars. For one thing there's a host more space faring civilizations than in Star Trek. For two, nothing in the mythos of Star Trek that I'm aware of has weapons capable of destroying a planet, a star, a star system, launch star destroying missiles through hyperspace from almost any point in the galaxy... Yeah, nothing like that. The Force plays a pretty handy role in this argument, too. But, this isn't my primary purpose either.

What we're here to talk about is the difference between science fiction and fantasy. The crux of the argument is that Star Trek is Sci-Fi and Star Wars is Fantasy. Now, writing this for the first time I see how ridiculous this argument is, but it ventures to a deeper point as mentioned earlier: no one cares.

Okay, it's a fair statement to make that both Star Trek and Star Wars are BOTH Science Fiction and Fantasy. Both of them have ships that fly through space, but where Star Wars doesn't really discuss it, just treats it as something normal and part of their history, Star Trek has gone to great lengths over the years to discuss their propulsion systems and how they do things and why things are what they are. And in all of it, there's a certain factual scientific-ness to the Trek way of doing things. Sure, a lot of it ends up as theory, some of which was spawned from Roddenberry's genius, but that's why Star Trek is sci-fi. Star Wars, they travel through hyperspace and there's still discussions about what hyperspace really is. Are they just traveling at the speed of light or are they entering an alternate, parallel dimension wherein time slows down or where objects with mass when propelled within it move at unreal speeds. It's a bit of magic from a scientific perspective. This is more fantasy than fiction.

Then there's the aliens, but this is moot as they both HAVE aliens and they all have their own sociology, psychology, terminology... This is where Star Trek is like Lord of the Rings in that languages have been created and people of the "geek" variety use them in everyday conversation. I am not one of them I must profess. I prefer languages of this world, but that's just me. I do not wish to dispell the time and patience and effort to create these languages, merely that I have a hard enough time with anything I've already learned in another tongue... Why add to my frustration? This is another point for both in the science-fiction category in my opinion, for the possibility exists scientifically that there is other life, but it also crests upon fantasy in how they are presented and treated.

Hrm... My primary argument for the separation of Trek & Wars is timeframe and location. Star Wars professes to take place a long time ago and far far away, right? Trek is supposed to take place in our future, OUR future. This is the clearest distinction in my mind between all things sci-fi and fantasy. If it takes place with our world, Earth, as a primary focus or subject matter, it's science-fiction. If it takes place in a world completely made up, it's fantasy. In the case of Lucas, it's a universe of fantasy.

I realize now that I've narrowed down my whole complaint to a single separation, but I feel it's an important one and an important victory for the language I was born with. Distinction and opposite is why we have language. If words didn't have opposites we'd have very little to talk about. Think about it sometime. Think about it hard. Take 2 Advil and let me know if you think I'm right…

Scientology

Well, I was listening to Stern this morning (I do that sometimes, except when there's gross stuff or nudity. Aural nudity is pointless.), and they were discussing Katie Holmes and her recent entry into Scientology. There is apparently someone who has been assigned to Katie from the Church of Scientology that is at the same level in the religion as her boyfriend, Tom Cruise. Well, it seems that this particular lady has a vast array of knowledge and power, not the least of which is a knack for knowing whomever is against Scientology, be it the media, friends, or family. Yay. That's a skill. Anyway, other abilities include manipulation of space and time, which is why I'm now researching this fascinating concept. The other thing that was mentioned was the knowledge of some six-figure something of Xenu, who's an evil goddess that implanted (basically) alien spirits into volcanoes 75 million years ago, but the spirits escaped and inhabited humans. Interesting? Sort of.

I think it's great that a man who wrote science fiction novels in the beginning can also create a religion. Not for nothing, but his initial book <u>Dianetics</u> is still one of the most popular books sold today. This book was published in the 1950s! That's longevity for any book, especially one that is really a self-help book, so the stories go. It, much like marijuana, was Hubbard's gateway drug to what would later become Scientology. Fabulous stuff. I'll come back with more.

The Test

I found a page from the Scientology home page, and it's a "free" personality test. All I have to do is provide them with personal information, which I'm not about to do. Nor am I willing to have said information sent to me at work, for sundry reasons, the third reason being that I don't think work would appreciate it. SO, I did the next best thing. I downloaded the free PDF copy which I can print and fill out and send to them. This also entails personal information and someone actually contacting me from the Church of Scientology (CoS) to go over the answers. Again, not an option.

The next best thing was to do a little online research. Naturally, I found some sites. The first hit sums up the ridiculousness of the test, but gives more detail as to how the test is actually determined. Turns out the whole domain is about blowing the Scientology "religion" apart. I'll have to spend some time here

The Religion

This is a rather simplistic religion to research with the onset of the Internet (thank you, Al Gore). I had always heard that the idea of the religion was to spend money. You put money into the religion, you get to advance up the ladder. Truth? Partially. In order to attain new levels of understanding, thus gaining something akin to a rank, you have to take courses and learn how the religion works. The courses are where the money comes in. They seem to increase as you go further down the line, so that each course is equivalent to a full semester at a state community college. Fascinating idea.

What is Operating Thetan or OT?

Operating Thetan is a spiritual state of being above Clear. Thetan refers to the spiritual being, and operating means here ?able to operate without dependency on things.? An Operating Thetan (OT) is able to control matter, energy, space and time rather than being controlled by these things. As a result, an OT is able to be at cause over life. -From the website

What is Clear?

The goal and end result of Dianetics is the state of Clear, attained through many hours of Dianetics auditing. One who has achieved the state of Clear no longer has his own reactive mind and therefore suffers none of the ill effects the reactive mind can cause. Clear is a new state for man. -From the website

So. Let me see if I have this correct. The "goal and end result... is the state of Clear", but "Operating Thetan is a spiritual state of being above Clear." That seems about right. I have to wonder how much of this was actually planned by L. Ron Hubbard, whose death is something of a mystery, before certain levels of the religion were ever made available. Reincarnation? Is his thetan still speaking to others?

Separation Of Church and State

I have a question for the masses who think with a Western mind. Rather, I have a question for us Americans under a President who often speaks of being a Christian. Just any good Texan should. Of course, the Bushes are from Connecticut and Dubya managed to run an oil company out of business, put people out of work, and made a fortune doing it.

Now, the point of this is let's consider the decisions of this President. Not only that, but let's consider the actions of our country in general. Our country is considered a Christian country, much like Britain and other sundry nations whose government falls under the pretense that God is all powerful and dictates how man should live. Beyond that, let's even go so far as to say that the United States of America was indeed founded by Christians under the Christian Bible with Christian ideals. That, my friends, is undisputed fact. If it were not the case, we would not be having a discussion in the Supreme Court over the constitutionality of having the Ten Commandments so prominently displayed amongst our government buildings, etc.

Before we tackle our current administration, of which many people are fed up because of the war mongering, let's take a look at what our country was supposed to stand for.

First, let's take a look at slavery, which we decided to abolish a century after our forefather put this country into place. Well, slavery is a Biblical principle, as indeed written by Paul, the man who once killed Christians, only to be turned into one as God chose to use him. So, if the Bible is indeed God-inspired, then God allows for slavery. Of course, we abolished slavery, and therefore decided amongst ourselves to no longer adhere to one of God's principles. Oh, and to those of you who study the Bible, prove me wrong... Honestly. If you can prove to me in the Bible that slavery is NOT a God-given right, and was mandated by God that slaves should obey their masters as the church obeys Christ, then I shall discontinue this little spat of "nonsense".

Second, let's look at this whole deal with stem cell research. Where in the Bible does it say that the slaying of an unborn child is murder? Tell me. Let's see for ourselves what IS said in the Book of God. In the Old Testament, one of the plagues was the plague of the Firstborn. In this, all the Firstborn of those who did not sacrifice a lamb and put blood upon their door were killed by a Godly power. If the people did not show their penance to God by slaughtering an animal, as was their religious custom, they would lose their child. This included Moses, the man that God used to free the slaves. Of course, most of them died having spent 40 years wandering around the desert because they were too stupid to accept their freedom. No, they had to anger God, who just let them go, by complaining that they weren't living the high life anymore. Man's pride killed them in the desert, just as it is today...

To continue this, my second point, let's take a look at the New Testament. In my heart, I believe that we, as a Christian nation, do not approve of abortion because of how close we came to not having Christ. If Herod had succeeded, there would have been no Christ, no Christianity, and possibly no us. Of course, this was not allowed, as God had a different plan.

So, we have taken it upon ourselves to decide who should live and who should die. Not just from an abortion standpoint, but from an anti-abortion standpoint. There's this argument over a woman who's been a vegetable for 14 years. FOURTEEN YEARS! Her parents insist her daughter would want to continue to stay alive, and have often argued that there is treatment available to help her. Her husband has decided different, and he would be the one who has to live with the decision. Now, it's up the courts to decide what to do with this woman. The courts decided many years ago that life was not "precious" in the way that we all decided it to be. Why do we continue to fight? The laws are there, laws that WE as MEN put into place for the betterment of our peoples. Thanks to the legalization of abortion, death sentences (also Biblical), and preemptive warfare, we've proven to the world that life has no sanctimony in our country.

Let's see... I know there's a Third observation I had...

Oh, gay marriage. I may have discussed this previously, but not in this context. Now, the President has decided to make it a constitutional ban on gay marriage. This, of course, has to be the worst idea that has come from this administration since "nuculer" became an appropriate term. The Constitution was created by our forefathers, Christians in case I haven't mentioned it yet, so that we would have rights. Not our slaves, mind you, because they couldn't have been considered men. Now we want to throw all that freedom away by turning the Constitution into a dictionary. Now we want to set a precedent by setting limits on our people using a document designed to set our liberty.

Why does the President, whose election was won in the courts and not the streets, want to do this? Because he feels it is God's Will that this should happen. Why? What business is it of ours? What's happened to this world that we have decided that we know what's best for a person sexually? In some older cultures, sex with children was not looked down upon the way it is now. In fact, some children did this sort of pleasuring as a vocation, and not out of slavery. I, of course, do not condone such acts. Then again, I come from a 20th Century mindset about sex, and have no real intention on changing. Homosexuality was the norm, orgies were quite popular, and breasts were considered far too risqué to be seen. It's curious to me that children are allowed to be naked in front of other people, because it's considered cute. Yet, when adults do it, it's considered in bad taste. Still, when children are performing sex acts, it's a crime. When adults do it, it's a multi-billion dollar industry. It's considered a different thing, but is it?

We talk about the sanctity of marriage when we talk about the homosexuals and their desires to have the same rights as everyone else. Sure, what the hell, let them have those rights. Let them have the taxes and the paperwork and the hassle and the ceremony and the expectations. My other question is, if marriage is so sanctimonious, why is divorce legal? God hates divorce, it says so in the Bible. If we're a nation trying to adhere to religious principles because of moral superiority, why do we allow one of God's least favorite sins to continue?

Let's talk about morality, quickly becoming one of my more favored topics. Morality is determined by those in power, not by any sort of genetic code. Anyone who tells you we have this sense of morality built in is lying to you. If we all felt the same way, if we all were born with the same moral code, then the terrorists would "know" that what they were doing is wrong. If they knew that, why would they continue to do it? It's simple; their morals state that what they are doing is right. They believe so strongly in their Bible that they are willing to give their lives, and indeed take the lives of others. Where's our commitment to our own Bible? We have none. That is why the church will die.

Again, the morality of another nation in another time stated that copulation with an underage person was not the worst thing someone could do. Concubines were expected, and often continued a royal bloodline. Slaves were bought and sold, killed on a whim. Human sacrifices are made in the name of religion, of morals. Of fear.

I have a hard time accepting anyone telling me they are truly a Christian. Well, I suppose not, because they believe in their religion. Of course, if they really believed in the Bible in its fullest, we'd have Christians martyring themselves left and right to prove their point, much like the psychotic Islamists are doing. We'd have people willing to sacrifice their families, their children, just to prove their faith in God. A Christian who thinks that slavery is wrong does not believe in the full truth of the Bible. That's only one example, but I digress.

We're not a nation of Christians, atheists, Jews, or Hindus. We're a nation of greed, power, pride, and we're going to fall just as the Roman Empire did. It's historically inevitable. So, I would say that everyone who has some sort of faith should pray, or whatever the equivalent in their religion would be. We're confused, we're emotional, and we have no idea what we're doing.

Do I have the answers? No. I just like to think that I'm asking more of the right questions…

Sexual Harassment/Discrimination/Deviance

I am by no means a sociologist or a psychologist, but I do like to think of myself as an observer of the human condition. I also think of myself as a rabid cynic with little better to do in my free time than bitch and moan about that which tickles my ever-increasing fancy at the moment it strikes me. This week, I came across a concept for which I had taken advantage of in my day-to-day, but I realize that an issue that wasn't related to this one annoyed me so intensely, that it brought to my attention a problem with our society that I would like to see remedied, though I know it won't even be addressed. That is, of course, sexual discrimination in the workplace. Not that my particular conversation will stick to just that area, but it's what pissed me off first.

It came to my attention that the male of the species is horribly discriminated against in the American workplace. It does not center around the words we say or the way in which we stare at our female co-workers. Well, to an extent it is those things, but it's for ridiculously different reasons. There's a certain amount of entrapment in what the female co-worker is allowed to wear to work, in what is considered "business attire."

Let's start with the most obvious difference in the human genders, the mammaries, breasts, boobs, etc. Now, I'm into em as much as the next guy. Good stuff. God's gift to man, in my opinion. Sure, the whole girl is nice, but a guy generally notices only a couple things at a time, and for me it's these. The eyes are great, too. Eyes knock me off my feet. At any rate, there's a certain amount of cleavage that is available to the "weaker sex" by virtue of this being a man's world. Yes, I said it, boo f'in hoo. At my current employ, we have a casual Friday, as do many other places. Well, on this day, I am allowed to wear jeans, but not a tee shirt. I still have to wear something with a collar as I do every other day of the week. Polo shirt, button down, Hawaiian, etc, as long as there's an actual collar. Further, we're allowed to wear sweaters without a collar sticking through it, but we're not allowed to wear a sweatshirt in a similar manner. I'm not about to go out and get a v-neck sleeveless shirt that shows my chest, but that isn't the point. Isn't it still harassment if I find myself in a compromising position based upon my own lack of self-discipline? Have we not learned in our society of late that we're not actually responsible for our actions? So, this sort of flagrant seduction should be disallowed in the workplace.

However, a tighter than normal shirt is still within, what I would consider, the bounds of good taste. Some ladies are more buxom than average, or they have waists that are far smaller than their chest, and they feel the need to wear something that accentuates their figures in such a way as they aren't construed as "fat" or whatever goes through the female mind. Yes, I'm a guy, but I have a vague idea what women think about based on what they tell me. Are they lying to me? Possibly, but I wouldn't know.

To move the conversation even lower than I've probably already gone, the legs. I like legs, sure, but they don't grab me. Usually. Anyway, men are pretty much forced to wear slacks on a day-to-day. Provided, no one really wants to see our hairy legs, but it isn't fair that while we're covered up during all sorts of weather, the ladies are allowed to wear skirts that allow more of a breeze to some of the warmest areas of the human anatomy. I'm not after wearing my sundress into the office, but I'm not allowed to wear shorts. Shorts, mind you. Not hip huggers, but some nice, presentable khakis like I've seen some upscale well-to-dos wearing during their golf extravaganza.

Sandals, too. Ladies get to wear pumps and stilettos and other shoes that show off their feet, allowing them to breath better and show off their painted toes. I don't paint my toes, I don't paint my fingers, I just tire of wearing socks and shoes in 75+-degree weather.

All I'm getting at is it's a matter of principle to me, a matter of consistent thought. If the ladies want "equal treatment" or "equal respect", then don't flaunt what you got and then expect me not to stare. Furthermore, don't tell me I'm not allowed to show a little skin, which is not my intent, when half of the female staff have left nothing to my imagination. I merely want to be able to wear shorts to breath a little better, get a decent draft from the A/C, and be able to grab some sort of tan when I eat outside.

Is this too much to ask...?

Straight Talk On D&D?: A Response

Well, I suppose I'm in just the right mood to tackle something head-on, if only for my own benefit. I don't know who's actually reading this beyond M and I think my wife... But, ever since high school I have loved a decent argument. If it's not too terribly emotional. I know that people get emotional and while I admitted earlier that I get angry about nothing sometimes, I do my best to keep my cool. There are some things about debating and arguing that I absolutely thrive on, not the least of which is the changing of a mind or the learning of a new concept. I also do my best to take someone's perspective into consideration when having the argument, for often the ways that I win my arguments are by turning someone's words against them. Yeah, the snake did that in the Garden of Eden, most argue that Satan does that, but I have my doubts about Lucifer on the whole... Different topic. Anyway, during the previous topic I did some sniffing around the Net about D&D. I was looking for a specific video/mp3 that talks about the "evils" of D&D, but it's really just a recording of geeks trying to play a game. It's hilarious stuff, especially for us gamers, because it's EXACTLY what gaming is like much of the time. Always someone wanting more food or some soda (RPing really did help ruin my teeth though. Mountain Dew eats through enamel like fire through tissue paper... Or something... It's REALLY REALLY BAD), trying to play or "metagame" even when they're not at the table or their character isn't in the room where stuff's going on. But, I came across another interesting article that I, for some reason at damn near tomorrow, feel needs to have some lessons taught to it.

The Article

http://www.chick.com/articles/dnd.asp

The Response

I find it difficult to properly respond point-by-point to any given argument, often because it's not a readily simplistic task, but I do feel that major points of a given article needs to be rendered appropriately. I will here place various specific quotes from the document (correct credit has been placed so I should not have any copyright violations here), along with my given rebuttal(s). There is a follow-up article but that can come later.

- Perception Is Truth -

Introduction

The author, William Schnoebelen (WS), makes his first mistake in the opening paragraph. "It is essentially a feeding program for occultism and witchcraft." This just isn't true. He later details that TSR had actually sent out representatives from the company to learn more about the occult and witchcraft to make the game "more authentic", but this doesn't indicate that those employees were in any way associated with the occult or in the recruiting of other potential witches. He further advises that much of what goes on in D&D "certainly appears evil". I realize he will later detail why it IS evil, but it's the manner in which he represents himself in the beginning as hard on D&D then to say it appears evil for the sake of a Bible verse… It's only condemning in the context he gave it, because the appearance of evil is, thus far, objective. I just don't like it :p

Yes, expect me to be nitpicky about this. Any decent argument has its holes and I intend to find them. Find holes in mine so I can close them up. Please. Seriously.

I do enjoy the fact that TSR, the originator of D&D, wanted their game to be so authentically magical that they learned the rituals of witches and Satanists. This gives you the "feel" that you're really doing something. However, this is also assuming that the spells in which they learned have any power at all anyway. The author gives far too much credence to the power of witches and warlocks and Satanists and the summoning of demons and casting spells. What's interesting to note is that the spells in D&D are not so ritualistic in nature and are often merely an "in-game effect". They may have real names and some groups may even bother to make you go through actual spell casting, in terms of making up a phrase or a little poem to cast your spells, but this is not mandatory and does negate the purpose of his argument. The spells you cast in D&D are by no means real in their application and I wonder how much D&D this guy has actually played. Yes, there are material components required and other effects that make it seem realistic, but seriously… I want to wipe out the enemy with a giant ball of fire; find me a Satanist that can actually summon fire. As I recall, only God does that. I seem to recall Elijah (or was it Elisha) proving a point to the so-called god of fire… C'mon, where's the real power?

One of the things I hate most about any argument is the drastic comparison. There's just no realism to it, it is used merely to express their point in the worst light possible and convince all those people who are ignorant of the topic that he is right. If I had less of an objective viewpoint on things I would just compare the nudity ban passed in Brattleboro, VT, to gang rapes in the streets. I would just state that without the banning of public nudity it would lead to public acts of immorality including gang rapes and was therefore necessary. This just isn't true. In fact, I'm all for public nudity. If you're willing to see some of those people naked, it's you who will ultimately suffer in the end... Ugh... Some people should just stay dressed forever. Back to my point.

The author makes a very openly ridiculous statement with the following:

"Now, the question becomes—if a person "innocently" works an authentic ritual that conjures up a demon, or curses someone; thinking that they are only playing a game -might not the ritual still have efficacy? I think we know the answer to that question. If you play at shooting your friend in the head with what you think is an unloaded pistol and don't know a shell is in the chamber, is your friend any less dead because you were playing?"

His point is made, but at the cost of my better judgment. Obviously, connecting the rolling of dice and laying a curse on a character who isn't real to shooting my friend in the head makes absolutely perfect sense. This makes me want to run right out and play Russian roulette as soon as possible. I'm a horrible shot so I won't hit myself anyway. The problem with this is that he's stating that we're honestly laying a curse upon someone that we're playing the game with. This isn't accurate, either. To play D&D you need to have a group of people with a common goal. Sure, there's in-fighting and people have a different opinion, but to say we're ever laying a curse upon them intentionally or otherwise is as erroneous as anything I'm liable to get from this guy. Conjuring up a demon may happen, it's part of the game. Often the demon is disagreeable and tries to kill you for thinking you can control him... Man, that sucked... Or you do run into demons for they are a race in this game.

That's the other thing; D&D isn't played by the same rules as Earth. That's part of what makes it fun. I realize some of the spells can be construed or even stated factually as "real" spells from Earth, but the idea that D&D has any authenticity is comical. It gives you a comparison place to play your game wherein certain things evolved in a similar fashion to how things evolved in Earth. To give D&D any real or physical credibility is another hoax. Show me where elves live on Earth? I want to see a stone giant. I want to know how to get to the Plane of Negative Energy so I can push my most hated foes into it... Yeah, D&D authentic? Authentic to what? There are specific aspects such as the medieval and certain pre-industrial nature of the game that is comparable to our world, but that doesn't mean it's "real" or "authentic". It's merely a reference to help fuel your imagination with some facts that you can account for because you took history in school or you learned about King Arthur or you wondered how skewering a pig could muster Beelzebub into your living room. I'll admit that my plan for my own world is to use many MANY facts from ours, but it's in such a way as to suggest that people over the course of history may evolve fairly similarly if given different circumstances. I have gone so far as to suggest that what writers actually write are glimpses into other realities, other possible alternate dimensions of things that really happened. This is, of course, absurd, but the philosophical implications still exist...

To further the point, or perhaps redirect, look at the audacity of that middle statement. "I think we know the answer to that question." Where does his pompous attitude come from? Does he know from experience that pretending to curse someone will actually curse them? Does he believe everyone has this experience or does he expect us all to follow him blindly like lemmings? When was the last time you really tried to "innocently" conjure a demon? Curse your friends? I know when we're kids we may do certain things in anger; does that mean when I want someone to drop dead he's going to? It hasn't worked yet, and I've been asking for certain people to die for MANY years. I'm not really bitter, it'll just make things simpler not to have them around. So, I think the answer to his question is "Maybe."

It's arguable that the Ouija board is a perfect example of his question, more so than D&D. Even I am offended at the idea that such an item is listed as a "toy" and is on the lower shelves at Toys R Us for all the toddlers to see. I used to know kids who read Narnia and played with the aforementioned board. We also had one girl who went to séances at her aunt's house... SO glad I go out of public school. Yes, while the Ouija board is considered a game, it's only considered a game now... But it was intended originally to contact the spirit world. By Pythagoras of all people... Does this mean we should stop learning his theorems because he wanted to tap into the spirit world?

Maybe… Not sure I want to get onto that topic. Ever. "Why Math Is Evil!" D&D was not intended to recruit demon worshippers but to entertain people who had vivid imaginations and needed a way to focus it. This should be a closing argument but it will probably be repeated later, so let's keep going. God, this makes me feel alive… More so than anything else I do…

Deadly Games?

Only the first paragraph of this section I can accept as even worthy of my time. That's right, I've brought a little pompous to the table. The possibility exists that if you are actively doing something to invite demons into your life whether a game or otherwise, it will work. Yes, I will not say that it is out of the realm of possibility that pretending to call forth a demon could actually work. What I am saying is D&D doesn't properly equip you for this task, nor are you likely to have the necessary ingredients that are often required of the stereotypical ritual. If someone brings feet of newt and blood from a baby chick, I would be less concerned about the game and more concerned about where the nearest bullet-proof vest is. That guy's clearly tweaked and about to do something dangerous. Yes, there are elements who play this game who take it seriously. Those are the ones to watch out for not because they're going to summon a demon but because they're so dissociated from reality that at any point they could snap and blow something up. Though if they DO summon a demon just be sure you can tell the difference from saying you're drawing a pentagram on the floor and actually drawing it out. This stuff doesn't happen in the game. Seriously. If you want to go home and summon demons, that's fine. Don't bring it to my table, summonings take too long and my character has some SERIOUS drinking to get to.

Here's where I feel the need to bop this guy in the head with as little reason and logic as possible. Ever see Rowan and Martin's Laugh-In? It's where Goldie Hawn got her start as a tattooed go-go dancer. Well, "It's Sock It To Me Time". The ignorance of the remaining three paragraphs just hurts me. I'm surprised he could get out full sentences while writing this drivel.

I'll start with the beginning paragraph but take it from somewhere in the middle.

"In fact, the Dungeon Master's Guide gives the celebrated Adolph Hitler as an example of a real historical person that exhibited D&D charisma!"

- Perception Is Truth -

Is this guy off his rocker? He is insinuating here that the game lauds the acts of Hitler on the whole instead of making the specific point that it is making. If you know anything about history was that Hitler was a brilliant orator. He knew how to get people fired up and do what he wanted. He had charisma to spare. He would meet people in a cramped room where it was already too hot and then show up late so they were already in a fervor. He would then push them to their limits and by the end he had them eating out of his hand. Politicians would do well to learn from Hitler's methodology if not his ultimate outcome. He had manipulated himself to power from being basically nothing. That is the height of charisma if you ask me. Am I saying I condone his slaughtering needlessly of Jews and others in his homeland? I think we all know the answer to that question... Jackass... "celebrated"... wtf. Hello out of context!

He then goes on or continues to go on to talk about the sexual overtones of the game, including torture and rape as part of the game. Never have I read or seen anyone or any material referencing rape or sexual depravity. Vampires, the most sexually overt and depraved of any I'd read, even they are understood to be deeply sexual in nature but truly they're just out for a light snack. The S&M people may play with rape and torture, but it's because their own sexual fantasies meet a logical end at "snuff"... This goes back to bringing chalk to the game and drawing a pentagram while I'm trying to get my high-level fighter drunk off his gourd so the little waitress will go rumpy pumpy with me upstairs. Yeah. That's right, my dude's horny. I rolled my dice and I got a really good roll on my pryopism check. Please. Do you think we actually have games like that? Obviously you want your character to have a good time and you're really just writing a story so you would want your character to do what your character would want to do, but if your character wants to rape someone or torture someone... Perhaps it is YOU who wants to rape and torture someone. I admit I'm a bit of a deviant when it comes to such things, but the idea that even pretending to rape someone is fun is just disturbing to me. The arson thing in the game is fun, but who doesn't like to set little fires?

. ...the cover of one D&D supplement, called Eldrich Wizardry, shows a naked woman reclining on an obviously satanic ritual altar. This tragic scene is compelling because it is really what is done in genuine satanic groups all over the nation. It is extremely sado-masochistic because the fate of such a woman is to be either raped, gang-raped, tortured or sacrificed to a demon god.

Uh. This is probably true, but this is another example of "authenticity". This was not an unpopular activity in certain ritualistic or tribal cultures. Even the more learned sacrificed people to the gods. This is what was called for to appease their deities. Should we have not slaughtered sheep or cattle to offer up to God because today we have different feelings towards animals? I wonder how a vegan would have survived in the Old Testament if they weren't willing to sacrifice… Yes, I'm offering a comparison, but doesn't it seem a tad more consistent with the thought? I thought so.

Additionally, male characters in the game often try to seduce female characters; and references abound to things like venereal disease and satyriasis (a male condition of permanent sexual arousal).

What? What kind of games was this guy playing…? In the act of seduction this is often to get additional information or trick a character into getting killed. Just like any decent episode of 24 or Alias or other similarly-themed television shows or movies. Look at history, this isn't all that uncommon to use sex to get what we want, whether it's perceived sex or penetrative. Besides, we're rolling dice we're not rolling around in the hay with each other. Geez. Again, never have I ever heard of anyone playing a character with a venereal disease. Often, if anything "untoward" was used to define a character, it was seen as a weakness that we would expect to have exploited through the course of the game. It made things interesting if your character had a problem holding his drink and pinching the behind of the barkeep and not his attractive young redheaded daughter. Often that would go better than actually getting the right ass between your imagined fingertips, as the barkeep wasn't too keen on drunks getting their hands on his pride and joy. That he flaunted about the place because he didn't have any sons…

There are sexual aspects to everything we do in life. None of us live in a society above the presence of temptation, and none of us ever will. The key is what do we choose to do with it? I admit that I have a host of deviance listed for my series of stories, but it's with a purpose. This doesn't mean that I am of such a level of deviance, it means that I understand there are those that are and that there are reasons for such activity; doesn't mean I agree it just means I recognize… If you're playing this game with a mature outlook or even the willingness to accept some maturity you're going to be just fine. If you're playing to learn how to summon demons and gang rape chicks you've got something wrong with you in the first place that D&D isn't going to exacerbate. Hopefully it keeps you indoors long enough that your teeth grow as fuzzy as your face and the closest you get to a girl is the online porn you watch in the basement of your mom's house and not out eating cats or flashing yourself to children. Weirdoes...

Do-It-Yourself Brainwashing

Wow. This is going to be point-by-point. I don't have the stomach to argue this as a whole thought of its connection to brainwashing is staggering. It returns to the maturity and authenticity of the game. I will point out that nowhere here does he really specify what the brainwashing is supposed to accomplish. At least, it's not right there in your face. I think I understand what he's getting at through more reading, but it just doesn't fit.

1. Fear generation: I don't understand this at all. If you're talking about this creates fear because of the fear-related spells and the fact that your character could die, I heartily disagree. Doesn't anyone understand facing your fears? Am I supposed to just hide in a corner and pray that God will take my fear away? Doesn't God give us opportunities to face our fears and our problems head on so we learn how to handle things? I don't think God wants us to do anything outside of God, but I've been under the impression that God isn't our puppeteer either.

2. Isolation: If your "traditional support structure" isn't nurturing, whatever you choose to do outside of that which doesn't involve that structure isn't going to be any less isolating than D&D. Drugs. Violence. There's other things to focus your time on. Hey, at least this is, in a way, constructive. Unless you think you're really conjuring a demon or going to get some illicit sex from the hotness bringing you that giant mug of mead... Mmm. Chewy...

3. Physical torture and killings: This dude loves to bring up torture, I wonder how much leather he has in his house. The focus of the game is really that you're the good guys. if the good guys are torturing and killing for wealth and power than maybe you aren't really good and you should rethink your campaign. Oh, and "survival of characters" is a nice touch. Is it morally wrong to fight evil or protect yourself by killing your opponent who's trying to kill you? Should I compare this argument to that of us wanting

to be all touchy-feely with the Islamist who just want to kill us? HELLO! WAKE UP! They don't want our pity or out friendship, they want us to convert or die. What about our own survival...?

4. Erosion of family values-the Dungeon Master (DM) demands an all-encompassing and total loyalty, control and allegiance.

This one deserves to be set apart, which is the definition of righteousness as I recall. Forgive the vernacular, but what the fuck is this guy smoking? The DM is the one running the game, he's the one bringing focus to chaos, clarity to nonsense. He's the one making sure that your little game of make believe stays on point. It's like having a project manager or a boss. The DM, it can be argued, is the one writing the story and you are merely playing as characters in his world. This by no means erode family values by telling you not to listen to your parents. Where does he get off making such a claim and stating such a blatant lie? This alone is powerful enough for me to say that everything the author says here is moot because he is asinine enough to make this statement... Asinine. This one actually makes me mad because it preys upon the ignorant like nothing else he states. There's no explanation as to how he came to this conclusion, but I'd like to conclude my boot in his ass... I love Red Foreman...

5. Situational Ethics: I love how he links two totally abstract thoughts under a single heading. I'm guilty of it, but I at least have a trail. This guy jumps logic like a woman being gang raped before her sacrifice... It just doesn't make sense in the real world, though it clearly does happen. The point morality he refers to is a bit sketchy. He is partially right, unfortunately, with this comment. Situational ethics do exist in the game, but it goes back often to sheer survival. Sure, there are times when we would venture out to start trouble or slay a dragon, but some of those dragons are evil. Not all of them. But some of them. The final line about win-win situation and good not triumphing over evil isn't accurate. The game's about being the good guys. If you decide that your game is about being the bad guys, then this statement is true. Also, if your DM doesn't really want you to win because he's a control hungry prick who can't control anything in his life so he makes the game impossible to "win"... Yeah, then that's true.

6. Religion: You'd think this one would be my favorite topic, but really it's not. The guy lost me after 4 so the rest of this is just to say I completed something. First, he

starts off with "traditional Judeo-Christian ethics (which most people in Western culture adhere to) to belief in multiple gods and deities". Yeah? And? Not everyone in the world follows the traditional Judeo-Christian ethos, and this is an argument I won't have here, but this moves to realm of who has the right religion in the first place. Yes, this whole argument is taken from a Christian, but the point he's making here about Western culture, again, has no bearing on his argument. He is correct about the pantheistic nature of the game and that it is occult gods only. I admit this is something I have had a problem with, but this provides a check to the game that our real religions do not have. Pantheistic faiths do have deities of different levels of power and what it is they rule over, but to implement a God character to the game wouldn't work because God would have power over all of them. This isn't game friendly. This is also something that does bother me in that it doesn't properly represent religions on the whole, but that's something else I'm working with in my own books. Not sure how many Christians will like what I'm doing, though. I digress. Or is it advertise? The defilement comment is another something he's pulling out of thin air. If you want to get a god's attention or the attention of those that worship said god, then yeah, piss on a statue or crap on the altar. Set fire to a holy place and watch as someone else's beliefs burn. Sounds like something you do to start a fight, or end it...

7. Loss of Self-control: "authority over self is surrendered to the DM". If you're playing in a game where the DM has total control over you, then you're playing with a bad DM. The point is to have fun and to try and do things with your character that you in your real life could never do. The DM merely knows the rules of the game and allows you to bend them as necessary, often with the roll of a die or two. Watch the whole kung-fu segment of The Matrix; same thing. Exactly the same thing. Of course, I won't play where characters become as powerful as Neo, that's just too unreal for me. Am I a principled geek? Back to the maturation of the person, if you never learn how to handle your character you must then never learn how to handle yourself. If you're someone who gets walked over in a game you probably get walked over in life. Pay attention to how you are when you're gaming, you could learn something about yourself. Like if you enjoy the idea of gang raping and summonings. Yes, I suspect I'll keep bringing this up...

8. Degradation: I think I've responded to this guy's interest in sadism, sexual situations, and porn more than I'd like to count.

A Clash of World Views!

I started off believing and agreeing with everything this guy has to say here, making it actually refreshing to think that we would agree upon something. He let me down, and I don't think it's the last time. He does make some excellent points here that I've already listed above. I think people, if at all still interested by this point, should read this section, even though at the end of it I'm just shaking my head...

His discussion about the differing world views is dead on. Magic is a moral ambiguity in D&D on the whole (though its application can be considered good or evil). It is the reason that there are not more machinations in the world for why do people need machines if they can just conjure up a solution? Obviously, this is not the world view held by traditional Western cultures. I have to say here that I find that whole terminology a tad ridiculous. Before there were "traditional Western" anything there were Indians who believed in spirituality and sacrifice. The values he's referring to comes from the same place where today's death and destruction are coming from, The Middle East. There's nothing Western about the birth of Judaism or Christianity. To call it a Western ideal of any kind is an insult to those who bore it from their own blood. Christ wasn't white... Damn Europeans.

He then starts to make this comparison that is absolutely accurate in that the monotheistic god worldview is different from the one that pervades in D&D, but he must be careful here in that in our own world people have the worldview that magic is real and the worldview that it is not. Using this argument in a gaming world, while still viable, doesn't go far enough. This goes back to authenticity so I won't go back into it too much further, but he's right in that the worldviews cannot coexist and that is a factor as to why God is not part of the game. I still think my definition is more accurate from above, where God is just too powerful to have in the game. It's unbalancing. Or it would be unbalancing if they were to add in God appropriately. Another advertisement for what I intend to accomplish differently...

What's interesting is he proves a point about something that I've thought about for a long time. Miracles are this world's magic. What I have found so interesting is that I

- Perception Is Truth -

have seen miracles and been a part of miracles only to find that they weren't of God that they were pure emotion. Well, that begs the question of where do miracles then come from? Obviously the right answer would be God, but if God didn't perform some of those miracles (I think emotional healing is also a miracle), if those were merely the suggestive nature of faith like we were hypnotized into thinking and doing certain things, then where do miracles come from? I'd had a discussion with my mother about this. Psychics. Aren't they merely prophets without God? Diviners, something you can be in D&D by the way, true diviners are able to perform similar tasks to a prophet of God. The fact was that if they gave credit to God they were okay and were prophetic (which wasn't always true either; again, a person creates their own miracle apparently), but if they didn't give credit to God, they were clearly the pawn of Satan or some other demon. Why? Why would who you give credit to matter? Doesn't all things come from God? Previous arguments I've already made elude to the fact that Satan couldn't have created evil and to suggest that the corruption of good is evil still isn't accurate. I think that, if anything, Satan corrupted evil and pushed it beyond what God had intended when permitting free will. That's right, good and evil are part of free will, but Satan has us thinking that gang rapes are just okay. So, the possibility exists that magic, miracles, are something we can all perform, not like a trick, because God gave us the capacity to do so. What are we going to do with it? Summon a demon or heal the sick? Ever heard of Smith Wigglesworth? How about a Calling? There's prophecy for ya...

In the course of playing a game or watching a movie or reading a book you have to accept the worldview of the subject and the characters or it won't make any sense. Further, I would argue that you have to at least be aware of others' worldviews if you expect to get anywhere in life. God doesn't want us to segregate ourselves because of faith; if that's so then it's a faith I don't want. People are what make the world interesting. If we're not to associate with people because of their faith, let's just setup a class society right now. We're already heading in that direction, let's just complete the puzzle. Ignore blind faith, learn to think and interact...

Interlude

Ugh... This guy bothers me. I'm also weak with hunger... Brb.

- Electronic Revolution -
A D&D "Hall of Shame"

"This provides us with a spiritual explanation of why the following tragic litany of evil keeps growing around players of Dungeons and Dragons." The hell it does. Pun intended. This doesn't prove anything. What's funny is he does recognize the argument I'm about to give:

Of course, just like everything else, some people (young or otherwise) will say, "Those people were just weird or losers to begin with. I'm too together to fall into stuff like that. It's just a game!" Yeah, and an H-bomb is just a firecracker! Like the people who think they can play around with crack or pre-marital sex and not get burned by death, AIDS or pregnancy, the person who thinks they can mess with D&D without getting burnt is whistling in the dark.

This guy... The problem with all this is that just because they played D&D doesn't mean that's the only thing going on in their life. He does admit there are psychological reasons, but clearly he's too convinced about the spiritual reasons to quantify anything against his argument. At least he has that part right. The people who conducted these acts clearly do have problems. Yes, D&D could be a factor which I will not dispute, but to suggest it is the only reason for these actions is just ignorant and dangerous. I've already mentioned if someone's willing to try and summon a demon for real or if they believe they can truly be raised from the dead because of the game... Say, don't Christians believe they, too, will rise from the dead? Or that Christ caused Lazarus to rise from the dead or he himself rose after being nailed to the cross? There's as much resurrection in religion as there is in D&D. No, I'm not suggesting that suicide because of your faith is smart, and it's certainly not martyrdom by any stretch. These people were never properly trained to control themselves or understand how to grow and mature and act. They chose a path of destruction and D&D was just one of the stops. Some of them appeared to need hope in their life but all they got was some dice and apparently a shotgun. Oh, does D&D teach you how to shoot yourself in the head? Does it teach you to take a gun your parents clearly can't keep away from you and kill yourself? No. The game does not teach suicide or death pacts or that you can be raised from the dead especially if you kill yourself and certainly not without a cleric of the appropriate level (yes, you can be raised from the dead in the game).

This is just more fear-mongering which he has already suggested you get from D&D. And married people gets AIDS, too, you crackpot.

Conclusions

This is always my favorite part, and it should be yours, too. At least by now...

Clearly those of you who profess to be Christians should have nothing to do with me, for it is apparently God's notion that we shouldn't try to convert or teach or understand anything and that if someone is evil we should shun them so they can perpetuate their evil. Do you know why good doesn't win and why Christians are scorned and laughed at? Because there's no fight in em. Just hide away in your little conclaves learning about your faith and ignore the world around you. If you can, find Petra's "Rose Colored Stained Glass Windows." It has always ALWAYS been one of my ABSOLUTE favorite songs, even when I was a Christian and was told I had the same gifts as Smith Wigglesworth. Even when I lived in fear every day of God and Christ and that when I was playing a game while very young and pretended a character was blaspheming the Holy Spirit I thought that it was I who was going to go Hell for even uttering such a thing not in jest, for I was very serious about it during the game, but I was trying to voice what I knew about being a Christian and I feared for my very soul.

I will state that I have seen more fear and hurt and separation in Christianity than all my years living in the world as merely someone who didn't go to church. Most didn't know I was raised born again or that I'd seen miracles or that I still had faith that God existed. It never entered the discussion. My entire life changed when I lost my sense of morality and started getting laid. Funny, D&D didn't help me get into premarital sex, it was just something that came naturally. I found myself meeting more people and being a much more adapted person by not being "saved". I found that I was someone worth spending time with and all the years of self-induced angst and isolation was just me crying out for acceptance from a world who just didn't want to hear it or just thought that God could heal anything if I just believed hard enough. I was suicidal as a child not because of D&D but because I thought that was the only way out. Of course, fear that I wouldn't be able to enter heaven and of pain stayed my hand. I was 10. I didn't even know what D&D was until at least 15.

I have wondered as to the dichotomy of Christianity in that people are taught to basically ignore those who won't turn to God, but yet to preach to people and try and convert them. How does that make sense? Shouldn't you try and convert everyone? Isn't that what Jesus said in Matthew? Instead, all I've seen is that people are people whatever their faith is. I know I'm singling out Christians but I was raised by one since I was 2, I became one myself when I was 4, and basically that didn't change till I moved out of my parents house while they were away visiting relatives. It's all I know. Catholics don't try and convert, they're merely Catholic and it's just that simple. Islamists don't try and convert, you either agree or are killed. That's the way the Koran teaches it and the way Mohammed preached it at the very beginning. Hindu is a caste societal religion if my understanding is accurate, so you are born into your station anyway. Religion is just a part of their life.

Christianity offers various things that other religions don't and causes it to be one of the most vocal of all the worldviews. For as many problems as I have with it, I also must say that I feel that its importance to the future of our society cannot be undermined. We need Christianity. We need God. If nothing else, we need something to set our morality and to set what really is right and wrong, for moral ambiguity is something that's become the expectation in our society because God clearly doesn't factor in to anyone's thinking. This doesn't mean that I'm going to stop playing D&D or that my arguments have in any way changed. The fact is God gave us free will to be ignorant or to be creative. God gave us good and evil to choose from and God gave us the ability to be redeemed. God doesn't want us to be purveyors of our faith ignorantly, God wants us to make the conscious decision. I don't believe that the ignorant believer is of any use to God…

Yes, I strayed just a bit from the topic, but I feel that people need to really understand where I'm coming from. D&D is as responsible for death as video games and television. Our society does not permit us much time to care for our young as we should and often the emotional needs are put on hold so we can ourselves find wealth and power and survival. We are emotionally empty as a people and it saddens me every day to see just how wretched we are. My cynicism and pessimism doesn't permit me to be of any greater stock on this regard, but I see it and I recognize this weakness and I hope one day that God's Judgment is really real and that it falls heavily on us all.

Suicide Is Painless

[Authors Note: Initially this story listed links to several articles from CNN, MSN, etc, regarding Terri Schiavo, The Bloomington Baby, and Jack Kevorkian]

These three issues are connected, in my opinion, for the simple fact that life has a weird lack of importance in our society. We execute murderers, which is typically unheard of in the more 'civilized' countries around the globe. We endorse abortion, but only by the hands of trained professionals because the back alley abortion can hurt the mother; never mind the child inside.

So, that being said, I would also like to give mention to Dr Death Jack Kevorkian and others that endorse and perform assisted suicides. I do not want them to be left out of this particular topic, but they truly do not belong within it either. What they do is generally endorsed by the party involved, whether morally correct or not. What we're discussing here is the party's inability to decide for themselves what they would rather do.

To continue, let's take a look at each case separately. First, we have Baby Doe, a child who was given no name, and his parents names were left out of the impending lawsuit, thus even a fake name with a real last name is impossible. At any rate, in 1982 Bloomington, Indiana, these parents decided that their child, who was born with Down's syndrome and a digestive disorder (which I read is easily corrected), was not at all what they expected when they decided to bring forth new life into this world. It seems the old adage that begins, "I brought you into this world..." holds some weight.

In a startling decision, the judge motioned that the parents had the legal responsibility for the child, in effect, and that the child's handicap gave them the right to determine how best to care for the child. So, the parents chose to starve the child, and the hospital and the few who were able and willing to complain meant nothing. The child was died a short time after the judge's decision. The parents were heralded for their brave decision, while many others consider what they did to be infanticide. In this instance, the child, though he did have a voice, it was one that none understood, or cared to.

Move ahead many years later to Terri Schiavo, the Floridian with brain damage who has lived like a vegetable for 14 years. Her husband has been fighting an equally valiant fight to watch his wife starve, while her parents fight back for the life that cannot be lived. Even before the severe brain damage took its hold, there was apparently nothing in existence that stated how she would rather be handled were such an incident occur, so there's been lots of legal room to continue this fight. Now, there are even politicians trying to alter laws and create bills in order to let this woman live. As a vegetable who cannot even feed herself.

We're in a place that's designed for freedom, but when we make our decisions, we're told we're wrong and we should do things differently. We complain about the government taking our children away, but we then complain when a child is killed and not saved by the government. We allow abortions to continue unabated, but we're still discussing the moral tenets of the issue. We demand our young people have sex by endorsing things like MTV and condoms in our schools, then scold them for the side effect of pregnancy.

Life is no longer determined by the ability to breath or even think. Life is determined by those who are in charge of our care, be it family or guardian, doctor or lawyer. For the record, the cheapening of humanity is no big thing to me. I say let the parents starve their child. Think about this, though, if they had done it in their home they would have been charged for murder. With Terri Schiavo... That is more an issue of who is responsible for her life than whether she would want to die. A person who hasn't made a decision in over a decade cannot be claimed to "want" anything, let alone death. But who, in that instance, should the judge listen to? And is it the right of politicians to make laws that say she should live? In that case, we may as well give the courts and the government the rights to say who should die, too.

If one day it's decided that people who wear glasses should be executed because their lack of vision is a hindrance to the perpetuation of the species... Don't say I didn't warn you.

"We should investigate every avenue before we take the life of a living human being," said House Majority Leader Tom DeLay, a Texas Republican.

Taken out of context or not, this is a loaded statement from a man who helped send our country into war.

Just in case some of you wonder why I put up this most recent link. A lot of times I will post links for my own benefit, because the topic interests me and I won't remember why. The idea of assisted suicide is fascinating to me in the sense that regular suicide fascinates me. I don't mean to sound morbid, but I had my own suicidal tendencies at the age of 10. I never followed through with it because of general fear and my irritation with pain. Then again, perhaps I wasn't really suicidal, I was just trying to think of some way to better my situation, who knows. Either way, I take a hard line on people who ARE suicidal. I don't believe that any tries suicide, they either succeed or fail. If you jump from a building and merely handicap yourself, at least you took the first step. If you stand at the building's edge and get talked down, you weren't suicidal in the first place. Is it factually a valid point? Perhaps not, I don't study much on people who think their lives ending would be better for everyone.

Diverging from my point, this guy helped a few people meet death in a way that was sufficient for them. Their will was not strong enough that they could truly die, so they required help. Their bodies were often falling apart, and indeed they were going to die anyway. So, the question remains, who determines who has the right to live and to die. You could take the Hunter S Thompson approach and take a self-inflicted shotgun wound to the head while on the phone with your wife, but that seems awful messy.

In all three cases, it seems that the courts decide who lives and who dies, not ourselves. Are we therefore taking the place of God in such matters? I'm sure the overwhelming argument would be no, simply because overall it's felt that would be the right thing to do. Naturally, I must then postulate that we're denying people their free will to take their life into their own hands, or to relent and deny themselves breath. It's perfectly fine to kill a child when it's in the womb, or apparently starve the child if they're not everything we hoped they would be, but there's issues with people who have actually seen the world and tried to live their life.

I expect some sort of wrongful death civil suit or perhaps trying to convince a judge it was intentional or at the very least an attempt to make up a new law representing Terri's situation, whether the husband ends up being right or not. The tactic will change when she has passed on, but it's the same battle.

This battle will end when her life is at an end. No sooner.

So... People die every day from this sort of thing, but for some reason the brain-dead parents of the 'brain-dead' person have managed to get the public behind them on this foray into legal conundrums. The husband is the legal guardian, whether she truly wanted to be kept alive or not. If she were to get better, she'd be a 3 year old for physical and mental acuity. How's that living...?

I felt that it would be best to end this particular tale of death, murder, suicide, love, and pain, with something that reminded you of everything you just read. Because, realistically, there are no happy endings in this, our physical lives. Whether there's an afterlife is not mine to answer or ponder in this situation, as this is not what we were here to discuss.

No, we were here to answer the question about what life really is, about what it means to be alive, about whether or not we have the right to ask that question at all. I think, in the end, we've learned that life has no solid definition. That we live in a land where killing the unborn is legal, and where a woman who has lived a tenth of her life in no better a situation than a child recently escaped form the womb is not worthy of life. That no matter how you look at the Bloomington Baby or the woman from Florida who had a face, and no matter how I really feel about the viability that either of those two represented in "living a full life".

We, as a nation, as a people, as fellow humans, watched two beings starve to death because it was "humane"...

Telepathy

I was at a medieval fair this weekend, where I was impressed by the sheer amount of cleavage I was exposed to. Very few complaints in that area, but that's not why I went. Entirely.

At any rate, one of the shows involved a man reading people minds. Naturally, this was with a deck of cards and some admitted tricks of the trade. Towards the end, which is when I ventured over to the mini-stage that held his act, he did speak of various statistics that gave him a certain edge when it came to the sort of guessing game he was portraying. This was to prepare us for his final trick. He grabbed people at random and told them to find a word in a small paperback book of his. He chose 5 or 6 different people. He was able to name the world that every single person had chosen. This was pretty impressive, even to me, but I'll get to that in a minute.

One of the people I went with asked how he was able to do this. I actually didn't answer her. I said I would tell her later, but then later seemingly didn't come. So, I thought I'd prep this little explainer on my own take regarding these tricks. As always, it's minimally researched, but it pertains to the beliefs I was raised with coupled with some of my own interpretations or thoughts.

One of the areas which must be considered is that of prophecy. If you believe in prophesying, specifically from a religious standpoint, then it isn't much of a jump to get to this guessing game. While it seems that he is reading minds, it's possible that he is merely prophesying the correct response and speaking it forth. The other term for this particular activity is divination. Divination is covered in the New Testament as a thing of witchcraft, but indeed certain things are divined by Christ and the disciples and others who can perform such miracles. There's a rather significant difference: responsibility. Who is responsible for the power? If they are a religious person, then God would be the correct answer, or Christ or the Holy Spirit, depending on what denomination. If they are not, then most times it is their own gift, or some other such explanation. The simple fact is that if they don't thank and praise God for this, then it's evil and of Satan. Well, that seems strange to me since it's the exact same thing. It just means that Satan has the same abilities as God in certain areas.

The next possibility is something called familiar spirits. I don't know how many people know of this term, but I was practically raised on the concept. Familiar spirits amounts to voices or impressions that one hears regarding certain questions, and the ability to interpret that correctly and use it to their advantage. Psychics, mediums, those who have lived in past lives, all of these are often linked to the idea of the familiar spirit. It's possible that something was reading their mind and telling the man what card or what word they chose. It's also possible that their own spirit was talking to his spirit or some other such incarnation of this idea. A spirit talking to the man is the point.

I firmly believe in this kind of activity, whether it is mindreading or not. I also am no slouch and think that magicians or your garden-variety psychic have such powers. I am well aware that often it is swindlers and charlatans who are smarter than most of the populace that is interested in them and are able to use their gullibility to be famous or at least well paid. Again, however, it's a fascinating topic, one that bears some further research.

I'm sure more will come to mind regarding this, including the idea that the general use of magic is somehow linked to dark arts. It's possible these people are performing miracles, or it's further possible that they really are tricks that we, as the audience, are never privy to.

The Greatest Power

I realize that the title of this topic will generate much criticism from those of you of a religious perspective, but bear with me. In no way is what I am about to lay down constitute a power greater than the Creator of all that is or was or ever will be. Indeed, it is merely a specific facet of power that was used to give to everything an understanding of all that is and was and ever will be.

The greatest power ever granted to Creation is not life or death, money or political power, but comparison. This simplistic term is often overlooked as nothing more than an idea, but its power is near limitless in its application. If we didn't have reason, if we had no ability to communicate how we felt or what we needed to survive, we'd still be animals.

After all, what need does a monkey have to know whether something is brown or purple? Is it interesting? Is it fun? Will it attack me? Can I eat it? These are the sorts of instinctive responses necessary for survival, not for dominating the food chain. Forget the opposable thumb idea; monkeys have 4 thumbs, we only have 2: why are we in charge? Because we have a reason to compare colors to each other.

I could give countless examples of why comparison is so powerful, but just pick up some Sartre. He goes into extensive detail about how touching his arm with his finger is actually two specific acts: touching and feeling. It's a bit tedious, but the comparison between the two types of physical contact is amazing.

The next question that may be going through your mind is how important is this? My feeling is that the more we know or perceive or compare with our minds, the more basic we're able to take concepts that we often take for granted, the more likely we are to understand who we really are as people, and where we're headed...

The Love Letter

Love, a many splendored thing, comes to many but once in a lifetime. To others, it comes many times, for many different reasons. For all, though, there comes a certain apprehension in regards to the knowing if the one they are with IS the one for them.

But, I feel that I have truly found love. Yet, I can't help but wonder if it's a new love, or if I have fallen in love for truly the first time. All I am capable of understanding is that I have the feeling of wanting to be with someone. To be with this one girl, this one that makes me happy and alive, and makes me feel capable. A person with such heart and emotion that I may never have to feel alone again.

A touch, a feel, a kiss, to steal

My heart is better though chained in fetter

And lo, I have perched upon high to search

Love has the bound, from above were it found

Cause of divine sort

Brought us together in retort

To those who do not believe,

To thoughts no one could conceive

Of happiness that is honest and true

I love you dearly…

The Source Of Biblical Confusion

There's no way this is going to be complete, but I feel compelled to explain myself in ways I haven't really done yet (surprise, I have more to say).

Let's start off by stating simply the biggest problem I've developed with religion or Christianity or any of them have been the people. In one way or another I've been let down or confused or thrown for a loop and it's left me doubting whatever faith I had. Yes, I know that the whole point to being a Christian is to look to Christ and ultimately to God for guidance and not rely on people, but if that were the case there'd have been no need for disciples and the more classical Sith variation of one master and one teacher would have been sufficient. We look to people to be our example, to lead us. I was a follower for a long time, now I'm back to being a wallflower, but for once I'm asking questions instead of shooting spitballs at the people at the party...

I realize that most of my problem is really just me getting too involved in so many other things and other thoughts that it makes me question everything, but that's healthy, isn't it? When I realized there was a world beyond the borders of the Bible I started to see things differently, but I never let go of what I learned and what I grew up being taught. It totally colors your worldview, even though things may come along to change it. The only way to keep the questions away really would be to focus wholly on the Bible and whatever happens to be thrown at me from the pulpit, but I've spent too much time watching to just accept things blindly. It's funny, J actually gave me another angle on questioning everything and I've never forgotten it. I like the irony of where things are at now; it amuses me.

Most of it started out as a feeling, a "that doesn't feel right to me". I'm not one to wholly trust my feelings instinctually, but I do well enough to start questioning. I don't think I have a good instinct for saving my own hide unless I'm preparing to have to save my own hide. If I had to react to something quickly, all my questioning would probably get me killed quick, so there's a good and a bad side to all this nonsense.

I grew up totally believing in God and Jesus and everything that went with it. I believed for a long time that my old man was deceived by Satan and that he drank because Satan made him. I later realized that it was his choice to drink rather than choosing something else to be addicted to, but he's since turned to Torah and chocolate so he's refocused and it's better now than ever before. But I really saw that people actually did make their own choices. We have Free Will, right? Works both ways. God doesn't make us do stuff, neither does Satan. Okay... So that means people really CAN screw up their own lives, it's not always spiritual.

My mother has tried her damndest to live by the Bible for almost thirty years and all I see in her life is struggle and pain. Is she being deceived? Does she need more faith? I don't think so. There are barely any people in this world with whom I respect their walk with God more than my own mother. I challenge her and argue with her, but she makes good points and I make good points and we walk away pleased with the whole thing. The only reason she's changed her whole viewpoint on Christianity is because history has led her to that point, and my old man showing her the history and the facts about it. I'm not in any way prepared to talk about it here, but needless to say it was devastating to mom to find out the culture she had tried to live her life by was flawed and needed correcting. So now she's walking a new path even closer to God and I don't see anything getting any better. She has turned away friends and family for years because of her faith and walk with God that I think at certain points even I have suffered because of it. Well, I haven't suffered consciously because I understand why mom did what she did through her life and where she's at now and while I can be a little bitter that I didn't have a better start to life, I wouldn't be who I am today if those things didn't happen to me or around me, so I'm grateful because I actually think I'm pretty nifty all things considered. I'm still lazy and overweight but I'm working on it. Kind of...

Anyway, my entire life was about the Bible and God and Jesus and Satan... My entire life is putting it lightly... When I was, let's say 9, I was playing with my toys and I actually had one of them be the bad guy and say he was blaspheming the Holy Spirit; the only unforgiveable sin. Well, for some reason, it didn't hit me till after I said it what I said and I got really really scared that I was destined for Hell because of it. That's when mom assured me that God sees the heart and that I was just playing a game and the guy making that choice was a bad guy anyway who was probably deceived by Satan, too. Made it all go away for me. But I never forgot that experience either. It gave me a different perspective on God and how God sees us; one I didn't have before.

Obviously things changed and I met most of you who can read this in high school and there were great times and not so great times and I really stuck my foot in my mouth and my heart into a well and my head up my butt, and while I'm still really embarrassed about a lot of what I did and I'm sure some of you have picked up on that, I'm still much better than I was in high school. I think. But I still have doubts.

When I was in the 8th Grade, I had just started to go to our church's youth group (this was Faith Christian Center back in the day), and the first night I was at Pastor Phil's house and they prophesied over me. That was the thing you did when you first went to that youth group, you got put in the hot seat and the elders of the group would enter into a Holy Spirit trance and start prophesying over you. It was overwhelming to me, the kid who wanted to be in the background all the time. Well, it was an exciting experience, too, one that my mother will never forget. I was the last kid to be prophesied over, and about this time she showed up to pick me up (it was a late night).

Anyway, there were some powerful things said about me and about my future but the one that really clicked with her was the name Smith Wigglesworth. For those who don't know, Smith had a powerful healing anointing and a really close walk with God; some would argue he spent every waking and sleeping moment thinking or talking to God. Turn of the last century, too. Wiki him sometime, it's a good read. Anyway, I was told that the anointing of Smith Wigglesworth was upon me. Now, I didn't know who this was until mom told me, I could hear her crying in glee when the words were uttered. Keep in mind the only thing I'd really been doing was going to church, listening to what I was being taught, and repeating the same prayer every morning with my mother. We had a whole routine set down that had some variations over the years, starting in the 5th Grade. But, by now it was just something I did in the morning when mom was around.

So, mom and I went out to Canada for some serious healing and deliverance. Didn't work but we did learn new ways to pray and I was actually prayed over and experienced a real-life miracle. It's a little embarrassing to say in such a public forum but for those who believe in miracles this was one of them, and for those that don't believe in miracles you're fools to not even be open to the possibility. I was healed of a life-long affliction that weekend and it's not been a problem since. We also came away with the method for that healing, and it seemed I had the magic touch. It went so far as to a friend of ours who didn't believe in faith healing and certainly not the whole "falling under the power" experience; that was all bunk to her. So, we started praying for her and just before I laid my hands on her (see Hebrews you pervs), she fell over. I had just gotten my hands out there and was about to connect when she went down. She was a believer then and to her that was a miracle. I was 13. Seems I was destined for something bigger than myself. So this went on but I was still terrified of telling anyone about it. I had to rely on having mom around to embolden me. I think the old guy was back at this point, too, my memory's sketchy, but I recall him being there and being into it at the time. Life continued but my faith healing really didn't. We eventually fell out of practice and other things happened and it stopped being something we did. Funny how fickle faith is.

So, moving on, I was in high school and we were going to Grace Tabernacle a lot as a school and just because. I was infatuated with various women at the time because they actually talked to me and I thought they were cute. Boy, are you all glad you didn't take a turn on the Mc Coaster... What a dope us guys are. Sheesh. But it's important to mention that because I still lived by the rule of fear. Metus Lex or something... I could barely breath I was so fearful but I tried and I tried but I couldn't let go. I still have fears don't get me wrong, I'm just trying to care less about them. So, various persons at Grace had gone through real intense deliverance training and wanted to offer it up to the teenagers. We were already half in the bag with God and the Holy Spirit, having healings and prayers and falling under the power of the Spirit, all the stuff that made being a Holy Roller... uh... a Holy Roller. Naturally, I signed up, and mom was so into it she couldn't wait to give me what little money we had to go ahead and do this (deliverance isn't cheap), because we both knew I needed it. Well, I went through it and it was really intense and I felt so much better, I was almost free of my fears. Almost. It stuck and didn't stick all at the same time. I was affected by those around me as things started to fall apart.

It became clear that those who were at Grace were not everything they said they were or led us to believe they were, and that became abundantly clear as time dragged on. People left the church, left their marriages, left the school... Other things were affecting me at this time but I won't discuss those now. My not being able to return to school for my senior year did not help my situation. I wasn't about to go to public school either. That was the last time I can remember actually crying. I've shed a tear here and there but I haven't had a good cry since then; I'm really good at locking that stuff up. I learned yet again at how temporary everything is and that God really was the only thing I could rely upon because everything passes away, even the Word of God itself will pass away before the very end. We won't need it if God comes back, right? Well, as life continued that all became a mystery to me, too...

I started to learn about history and about how things were greatly affected by history and how the Bible has been proven to accurately depict historical events but that isn't enough to base an entire belief system on. I've read about people who started out their careers trying to disprove the Bible through science and end up coming around and becoming head over heels for the whole thing. I've since learned that science really was started to prove God, not to disprove; this is important for everyone, even those who haven't read this far. I learned more and the more I learned and the more I lived my life the less faith I had. Ultimately, it would be destroyed by experience and not be any singular event. I didn't look at the Holocaust and say it was a tragedy that God should have prevented or starvation or disease or any of the things we believe God can fix but doesn't. That's part of a larger whole but that also makes the assumption that God doesn't want us to work for our rewards in Heaven; that's just not true. "Faith without works is dead" and all that. I just, lost faith the more I was around people of different variants of Christian belief and saw how a lot of them felt superior to everyone around them, including other Christians. I saw the fallacy in their voices and the words they tried to teach had subtle overtones of why they're better than everyone else. It was becoming a growing concern for me. We bounced from church to church to get away from the pride but we would always see it, it would come out everywhere. This isn't to lambaste anyone who's churches I may have visited in my youth, this is only for those churches that we spent months at. My faith was etched away at me day by day as we prayed for my protection and I got beat up anyway, as we prayed for my healing and I remained with certain ailments (others were healed but I hadn't experienced a healing like that in years and was losing faith that I would ever be healed), as I trusted people with my heart and I got it ripped from me in one way or another. I've been hated and lied about. There's a situation in my life that I'm still really upset about even though I'm also super pissed at the one who it also affected. I made a mistake, sure, but I was made to look like a predator and a jerk when it wasn't physically possible for such things to go on and there was no way I was psychologically capable of such things. Hell, I still can't plan that far ahead; I can't even budget week to week yet. So, others took away my faith for me by just existing. And I met other people who had other ideas about Christ and history that has other ideas about Christ.

I took off my holy blinders and I haven't put them back on since. I realize that many people have faith because they want to have faith but they only believe they have faith without looking deeper at it. This is what I want people to really think about; why do you have faith? I should also point out that I'm also the worst kind of Christian as far as my mother was concerned; I knew the truth and I turned my back on it. Yup. That's true. Not a day goes by that I feel bad about it, either.

I still believe in faith and prayer, which for my money are the same thing, but who am I praying to? No one specific at this point. It's just out loud and aimed upward. I presume God is up there looking down on me just shaking that omnipotent head, but I still feel blessed where my life is. And I did it while turning my back on the faith I grew up in. So… Did I make the right choice for me? Will my choices only affect me in this life but I'll be screwed in the next? I don't know, and neither does anyone else. Not until we're dead, but then who are we going to tell?

…I really could write a book about my life, but who'd read it?

V.A.S.T. – Jon Crosby Is My Hero

So, I know that Over the Rhine's my favorite band, but there's another band that I think everyone should know about. VAST. That's V A S T. Visual Audio Sensory Theater. While Over the Rhine meets me melodically and spiritually, VAST meets me everywhere else. They're a great rock band from the brainchild of one classically-trained Jon Crosby. Great story about how they started, check out the website. I'm hoping to make both VAST and Jon my MySpace friends soooooon. Of course, there's a story behind VAST.

Admittedly, I don't remember the whole thing. At least not how it started. I picked up VAST I think on a fluke. "Touched" was big on the radio and the haunting sounds of the Gregorian Chants (or which chants they are I honestly don't remember) in the background really got my attention. There was something deeply religious about the track that perked my better judgment. So, I picked it up. At the time I was living with a roommate (first and last) and playing a lot - a lot - of a computer game known otherwise as "Diablo". Well, I was doubly hooked. For a while. Diablo waned in interest around Diablo II. I never really got into the Hellfire expansion.

But, VAST... That was completely different. The raw emotion poured into the music was more intense than even OtR could surmise. Jon had put it all out there for anyone and everyone to hear and experience and feel. It was such a moving time for me. I learned every song as best I could (a couple of them I'd skip), but I was set as far as being a fan. The self-titled (acronym-defining) "Visual Audio Sensory Theater" was a treat for the mind and the soul with such songs as "I'm Dying" and "Dirty Hole" (it seems like an AIDS song but others are trying to complicate it). The opening "Here" grabs your attention from the build-up intro to the controlled screams of Jon's voice. An instrumental track, we'll just call Track 11, also shows off some of Jon's training to be a composer of classical music. The Beatles and the desire to get some would change the course of his history, and I'm glad for it.

The sophomore release, "Music for People", would introduce us to new band members (VAST was done completely by Jon as memory serves). It also had a different feel to it. It wasn't as brooding but was still accessible musically and lyrically. Another musical track at the end would soothe me to sleep. Overall a great follow-up but it's hard to capture that same sound and feel, but Jon still kept my attention. The lyrics were rich and the music kept on coming.

Then, he all but disappeared. This was several years ago. Several. I wanna say 2000-ish.

It wasn't until this very year, 2007, that I would find VAST again. By accident. Again. I was at a local Circuit City buying… Something… When I passed the CD line. Well, there it was, plain as day, VAST had a new album. Not to be topped, it was a DOUBLE ALBUM. I was elated. Like a little school girl… Except I'm not little or a school girl. Mostly.

"Turquoise & Crimson" was its name, and I was again immediately hooked on the music. I was late coming back from lunch because I wanted to sample every track and read the liner notes and find out what's been going on. Basically, Jon dropped off the national music scene and went underground, making music in his home studio, having a child, and basically giving the finger to the establishment. He makes music for his fans, and he makes money doing it so all the better.

Well, just as before, the lyrics were connected but insightful, the music was tasteful yet you knew you were listening to something Jon put together. I started to skim the website I was presented with, joining the forum to be a real fan. I then realized how out of the loop I was. VAST had been releasing albums since 2004 online! I immediately purchased the ZIPped copy of the MP3 version of the CDs that were not released in print (en masse, anyway), but online. This was fine. It fit into my iTunes library with everything else I had. I bought every other album put out that same day. I haven't yet joined the fan club, but that's coming.

VAST is the only band for which I have a fan site at my real web space. I have to put other material at said web space, but meanwhile warm yourselves in VAST. It's AWESOME!

Violence

I find it humorous that what once passed for actual entertainment is now considered in poor taste and we are censored from it. The execution of Christ brought a lot of people to see the King of the Jews, the Christians that were martyred brought capacity crowds, and history's example of William Wallace was also brutality in public. What's happened?

We've decided that it's much more civilized to protect our children from seeing the truth of violence and showing it to them on film. That way they have little real understanding that their favorite movie star dies in a movie and is then perfectly fine in his next flick.

I'm not saying every child feels this way, or that every parent is that inept that they cannot explain to their child the difference, or at least set the building blocks for later understanding. What I'm saying is that we focus all this attention on protecting our children and their minds and their 'growth', when we're really raising spoiled brats with no understanding of respect, no concept of what their forebears had to go through to give them the freedoms that in so many other nations and even parts of the US they would be haplessly denied.

No, all they understand is that people die on the news and in movies it's just pretend...

What happens when the real war begins? What happens when it's right on their doorstep and there's no Vin Diesel to protect them? What about Barney, will he still be laughing when one of those terrorists we're all taught to be so afraid of comes onto the set and puts a bullet through his purple head? Hell, what will *I* do? I've helped my brother with his martial arts training for a time, and I've seen lots of kung fu movies. That doesn't prepare me for war. Hell, that doesn't prepare me for anything.

What am I suggesting? Be realistic. People die every day under horrible circumstances. People are tortured, shot, starved, dragged naked through the streets, eaten, burned, mutilated, raped, beheaded, destroyed in ways too foul for even my mind to concoct. Do not allow yourself to be one of those people who are offended by what you see on the news, what you read in the papers. Be annoyed that it's all they talk about; for indeed, I am.

Do not allow your 'delicate sensibilities' to be tainted every time you hear about another death: we're one of the few countries in the world where warfare truly doesn't even begin to touch us. Don't blame video games for killing innocent children in schools. Poor parenting and emotional stress and this American idea that we don't have it as good as everyone else says we do brought that on. We allow bullies to perpetuate our school systems, but we don't let our children watch certain cartoons because of the violence. Violence is everywhere in our lives, and has been for most of time. 'The Lord of the Flies' isn't too far off from our true natures, in my own opinion.

What separates this violent mentality of humans from the animals? Our understanding or at least belief of necessity. Then again, the reasons for the many wars we fight are often ludicrous by today's standards, but it seems to be constantly and forever about someone rebelling against someone else' ideals. War isn't bred in the media, it's bred in the heart.

Being subjected to guns doesn't make you a killer, it just makes you a better shot. Playing violent video games gives you better hand-eye coordination, it doesn't drive you insane enough to thinking that you carry around a BFG 5000 and blow away all your co-workers. Listening to Judas Priest won't cause you to commit suicide, neither will Nirvana. People need a reason to do harmful things, society needs someplace to put the blame…

War Of The Words

http://dictionary.reference.com/search?q=propaganda

There is one word in the language of men that proves, at the very least in my mind, that my theory that perception is truth is absolutely correct. That word is *propaganda*. I'll say it again. Propaganda. It's a word we all know and may sneer at, but it's a word and a force of such great political power that it seems almost comical to me what little attention we pay to it.

While etymology isn't one of my more studied subjects, it is quickly becoming one of my favorite hobbies. Let's go back all the way to the root of propaganda, *propagation*. This word is first recorded in the middle 15th century, and stems from the Latin for "offspring" or "forth". So, breeding, procreation, planting, these are all examples of propagating.

Furthermore, the word *propaganda* is first used in reference to the missionary work of the Catholic church. It wasn't used in a political sense until World War I, and I'm not certain that it was properly understood as a viable weapon until a short man with a short mustache found it as a means to a brilliant political end, until megalomania set in, of course. The church used the word, in a sense, in that they were propagating their own ideas, breeding new converts, and bringing forth a larger and growing church body. The Nazis used it to breed their own ideas of hatred and intolerance while they cashed in and threatened to take over the globe. Our own country has used this, in effect, against its own people to achieve a political goal.

2005.04.12

For now, let's take a look at the most recent example of government-sponsored propaganda: the War Against Terror. It is true that we were attacked on 11 September 2001, and it is true that I do believe those responsible should be brought to justice. However, I have the same serious doubts about the Iraq action that much of America also felt. This isn't to say that Saddam Hussein should have been left in control of his people, but to what end was it truly our business? Even with all the time necessary to hide whatever WMDs he may or may not have possessed, the fact is he did not attack us, neither directly or indirectly, at least not with immutable proof. Ere go, while it's fine and dandy that we were able to take down a nation that is mostly made up of third world tribes, there was very little in the way of national security that was an immediate threat to us. It can be argued that he was supplying our enemies with weapons or moneys to purchase what was needed to fight us, it seems more than likely that the radicals were able to achieve their own ends through their own sort of propaganda. It doesn't hurt that their 'leader' is a rather wealthy Saudi national, but that's rarely mentioned in the mainstream press.

What's more interesting to me is that no matter what our current and former administration says about the subject, it was not the overwhelming will of the People to enact this war. In a Democracy, after all, who is it that makes the decisions? That's a different matter altogether, however, wherein many people would consider that the beginning of a dictatorship. Again, that's another discussion...

So, we were told we needed to go to this war, and that we should 'support our troops'. I find Noam Chomsky's discussion on this to be a major factor in what I'm trying to get across here, and his point regarding the sheer ambiguity of that phrase to be mind-blowing.

Mobilizing community opinion in favor of vapid, empty concepts like Americanism. Who can be against that? Or, to bring it up to date, "Support our troops." Who can be against that? Or yellow ribbons. Who can be against that?... The point of public relations slogans like "Support our troops" is that they don't mean anything. They mean as much as whether you support the people in Iowa. Media Control, Massachusetts Institute of Technology, March 17, 1991. Excerpted from the Alternative Press Review, Fall 1993

Very simply, if you were to continue reading his article, if you are able to distract the common man from the real issue, that is war, and give them something else to focus on, everyone is content with the situation. Likewise, they're also very confused about the situation. What purpose do we really have to fight this war? Who knows, just support the troops and the war effort and war against terror, another ambivalent and empty concept if I've ever heard one. You cannot fight against a leaderless rebellion, which is really what the Muslim extremists are. We look at Bin Laden being the answer to all of our problems: if we kill him, we stop the terror. I seriously doubt anything will end when he's captured. In fact, I expect it to increase. I also expect much of these attacks to go unreported, but that's my own personal opine.

2005.04.13

Let's take a quick look at a current event to give a comparison of what propaganda really means. According to various news sources, including the British Columbia paper that I'm thumbing through this week during my work trip to Vancouver, are reporting that the Japanese are putting out new textbooks which all but ignore atrocities in that nation's past. This has specifically incensed the Chinese, who were the victims of the Japanese military's actions during World War II. Even though the Japanese have apologized and paid, in a sense, reparations for those actions, the Chinese are still opposed to this move that would "whitewash" the historical facts.

"Only a country that respects history, takes responsibility for past history and wins over the trust of the people in Asia and the world at large can take greater responsibility in the international community." -Chinese Premier Wen Jiabao.

What is interesting is that it's become such a huge deal with the international community, but how do the local Japanese feel? How do the children who will be learning from these textbooks feel? Do they even know what's being discussed regarding these facts that they will NOT be learning about? Are they even aware that there's a problem with forgetting history? I'll have to dig a little deeper, but I'm curious if anyone from our own Administration is concerned about this activity, even though we Americans have done it for years... That would be ironic, don't you think?

2005.04.14

Let's shift gears for a second and take a look at the United Nations Secretary General, Kofi Annan. Recently, he put out a document wherein he defines terrorism, as well as 63 pages total of his report "towards development, security and human rights for all".

Affirm that no cause or grievance, no matter how legitimate, justifies the targeting and deliberate killing of civilians and non-combatants; and declare that any action that is intended to cause death or serious bodily harm to civilians or noncombatants, when the purpose of such an act, by its nature or context, is to intimidate a population or to compel a Government or an international organization to do or to abstain from doing any act, constitutes an act of terrorism.

I found online an article which specifies various Middle Eastern states taking issue with this definition, and rightly so in my opinion. This very simply defines precisely what is going on in Israel at this day and time. Take the Palestinian side, a nomadic people without a home where history is not on their side in this regard. At least, that's my understanding. They conduct daily acts of terrorism against the ruling Israeli people, those that would hinder them from their 'homeland'.

On the other side of that coin, we have the Israelis. Now, many argue that the Israelis are defending themselves. Yet, they conduct pre-emptive strikes, assassinations of enemy leadership, and have managed to section off the Palestinians from Gaza proper, even while giving up part of the land. It isn't considered 'terrorism' because they are merely defending themselves, but it isn't possible to call it anything BUT terrorism, especially given the definition presented by the UN Secretary General. If this definition is adopted as one of the General Assembly's decisions, then Israel and the US should be labeled as terrorist nations.

Who can forget those clips from the first Iraq war of the US bombing facilities in the middle of Baghdad. Undoubtedly there were civilian casualties. We invaded Iraq, overthrew its government, and plunged the country into currently worse situations than they were in before. Starvation, lack of education, power struggles, and insurgency has exploded in a nation that was otherwise afraid of a despot who took over that country 20 years ago. My biggest gripe about this second war is why wasn't it dealt with in this fashion during the first Gulf War, when we were 'in the right' to go and save tiny Kuwait from the invading forces of Hussein.

That aside... There are many other fine examples of the United States disregarding world opinion, even when we were blatantly incorrect in our actions. Even when we conducted the same sort of insurgencies in other nations, helped to create military coups and see to it that those in power were nothing short of American puppets, even when we were denounced by the World Court for our belligerent actions... We showed no signs that we would stop. Indeed, there's still little signs that we can or will be stopped through simple diplomacy. We bend or break the rules that we helped to establish, so why would we bother to let a little thing like the World Court get in our way?

2005.06.15

I realize I haven't touched this subject in just over two months, but I'm abruptly annoyed with myself for missing the most obvious form of daily propaganda in our lives: the daily news. If you subject people to the same idea across the board, then you can, in most situations, convince a people that what you're telling them is truth.

All you have to do is twist a headline to make people think like you, to manipulate a situation to your advantage. I heard that a radio program had convicted Michael Jackson based on the way the judge's face looked. Ridiculous. The original War of the Worlds experience convinced a nation they were being invaded by aliens. This was not done purposely, but it still achieved comical results.

I've heard that the media is biased, or that it's liberal or conservative or run by the government. What I see the news as is an elite organization run by the powerful businessmen who ultimately own the news agencies. It's a mean of twisting the truth so it fits with whatever has been decided that Americans should think. If you read the news from around the world, you'll often see that our press may not only distort the truth, but may leave it out completely. That's propaganda, too, hiding the truth.

Warfare On The Religious Front

I tried writing an expansive concept mere moments ago, and indeed was up to several impressive paragraphs involving big words and ideas. Ultimately, I felt it sucked. Hardcore. Not in a good way, either. So, I'm here to try to redeem myself. This is, of course, for myself as I seem to be the only person reading this particular blog, but it's my way of editing my material.

We're living in a time when God has become more pop culture oriented than perhaps ever before. This is certainly true of American culture, as there wasn't really "pop" anything during the time of the Founding Fathers. Mel Gibson, President Bush, the Rev. Jesse Jackson, and then some, have all come forward with some belief in the Almighty God. We also have a huge Hollywood following Scientology. We have Jews, Orthodox and Messianic, we have Islamists, we have Buddhists, we have a religious explosion going on all around us, and it's finally being talked about on a larger scale. What we don't have are any answers, but I'll come to that.

We're also living in a world of extreme ignorance in many areas of life. We seem to be filled with people who know just enough to survive, to get by on a day-to-day basis, and that's really all they need. There's no concept of truth, or an understanding of the religion they so quickly attach themselves to, or seemingly any understanding of history.

Let's talk first about a major religious controversy brought on by "pop" culture. The movie Dogma, which I felt was a great film and correctly satirized the dangers of dogmatic faith, was considered an insult to all religions. I was dating a Jehovah's Witness at the time who refused to see this film on the basis it would insult her. My own parents refused to see it because of the way in which it mocks the Catholic faith. My parents are not Catholic, mind you, but it mocks many other beliefs about God and Jesus and the Bible that were, in my opinion, necessary for the film's success. There was an uproar in the religious community as a whole, and protests abound. Naturally, this drove throngs of people to see this movie.

To continue, we should take a look at a movie that set records and made Mel Gibson a man of faith, The Passion. This accurately portrays the pain and torture felt by a man who was crucified for his stance. Whether you believe in Jesus being the Son of

God or not, I have heard in my time that historians and scholars of many different faiths and standpoints have agreed that Jesus Christ did exist, and was indeed crucified. No matter what you believe, the truth of crucifixion is displayed in graphic detail. Still, this movie received much controversy. For one, it showed to the world just how much faith Mel has achieved in the Bible and God. Turns out he's basically Catholic, but his particular sect of the religion has decided not to respect certain viewpoints the church voted on many years ago. They've decided to be slightly more orthodox than the Catholics of today.

Still, this is not what the controversy was all about. The largest portion of the controversy seemed to involve Mel's potential anti-Semitism. This is, and was, a ridiculous notion, but the media still wanted to portray Mel as the bad guy. Easy enough, since the story of Christ's crucifixion often lends itself to hatred of the Jews, but it's still a loaded concept that a man who is trying to display the fundamental story of the faith for which he believes in so strongly would have made a movie simply because of his anger against another people. It isn't impossible, but the devotion to the authenticity of the film seems to negate this idea. Furthermore, there were some attacks on the historical accuracies of the portrayals made in the movie, but these arguments have no weight. Mel stuck with the Biblical interpretation of Christ's crucifixion. If there's any historical accuracies, one will have to argue with those who wrote and edited the Bible itself.

In both instances, I feel controversy was created, not really found. A man who satirizes will always be criticized, so the situation with Kevin Smith should have been no surprise regarding Dogma. Likewise, Mel was attacked for no other reason than to give the media a reason to create controversy and try to put blood in the water.

Let's take a step in a different direction and discuss a bit of political and war history. I could start with the Crusades, but my basic understanding of this torrid tale will not be enough to mount a convincing argument, I can already tell. Simply put, though, the Church had decided it was needed in order to restore proper order to the Holy Cities which had been taken over by Islamists. It was their duty before God that these lands should be taken back. This was, in its pure form, a holy war. Well, that part could be debated, as the Church was ultimately behind the liberation of the cities, and the atrocities that came along the way. The Islamists wanted their holy cities back, which were indeed holy cities in the Christian faith. Fabulous. I would still argue that politics played a huge role in what ultimately went down, but I would have to get more detail before being able to back that up.

Now, to our most recent Crusade into the Middle East; the war with Iraq (both of them), and the War on Terror. This has been argued as being a holy war, and to the Islamist extremists, it is. But, it isn't a holy war or even a political war along the same bead as the Crusades. This is a fundamentalist war involving those who believe the Islamic faith to the absolute letter, and those that don't. They are portrayed as evil because they are against us. There is no other reason. If you truly believe that it is evil to kill innocent civilians or that trying to instate your own political ideals through force is evil, than our own country is evil. Nicaragua, Afghanistan, Vietnam, all are examples of our superior ideology at work. We've devastated nations with chemical warfare before that term was ever coined, we've overthrown governments in the name of Democracy, we've turned our backs on refugees, we've snubbed our noses at International Law. We do things our own way, and everyone who does things against us are the enemy, and anyone of our own who aren't behind us are "unpatriotic" and don't support the troops.

By the same token, religious perspective takes on this very basic "us and them" mentality, or "if you're not for us, you're against us" nonsense. In the Christian faith, you are taught that Satan is evil, and God is good, love, merciful, blah blah blah. This is, of course, bogus in my mind, and it grows more ridiculous as I get older and more cynical.

Do I believe my cynicism is a part of why I write on some of the topics I choose to write on? Abso-frickin-lutely.

I have not believed for a LONG time about God being good based upon what I know of the Old Testament. God creates. Simple as that. God creates man and woman. God gives them free will, but also gives them a single rule, which they do not follow. So, in their Free Will, they break a rule. Ironic? Wait. God curses them, though I begin to wonder what the importance of the cursing is. In my own way of thinking, I would have left Adam and Eve alone in their shame, for that is often worse than physical pain or enmity between a child and a parent. That's just me, though. They're kicked out of Eden, of paradise, and are forced to live and work the land.

- Perception Is Truth -

Skipping ahead, we can talk about the Flood. In man's desire to please their own flesh, again a product of the Free Will God had given them, they were ultimately executed for such acts. God found a single man with a single family worthy of being saved. So, God obliterated everything on the planet except for those species which were acceptable to procreate. God proved that jealousy was indeed part of the divine repertoire, but we were still not supposed to practice it ourselves.

I find myself needing to change my usual statement that "God is a four-year old with omnipotence", for it is not entirely accurate. Still, it's close. To say God is a jealous god is an understatement, but I digress. God is jealous, and God is just based upon the laws that were created by the Divinity, the Triune God (Father, Son, and Holy Spirit). Is God merciful? God has shown numerous times in which mercy is warranted, but I am confused as to the why. When Adam and Eve sinned, they were shunted from Paradise and made to survive instead of just live. When Cain sinned, he was marked and shunned by the world. When the Israelites were freed and were searching for the Promised Land they complained and murmured enough that God denied them the Promised Land, effectively shunting them to the desert for 40 years. When the Flood occurred, God found one family worthy of being saved. When it was decided that Christ should be born and died, God showed mercy by removing the need to slaughter animals in order to hide from the Divine Wrath that is God's touch.

Still, I cannot find where God is necessarily "good". Creating life is good, but God clearly supports slaughter and genocide. Read the Old Testament again, you'll find it. The argument is made that when Christ came, God's methodology changed. But, if God's the same yesterday, today, and forever, that's a clear violation of the rules that were established by those of the Christian faith.

Moving ahead, we have Satan, Lucifer, Beelzebub, the Angel of Light, etc, was kicked out of Heaven because of pride. I'm having difficulty even finding reference to this "fall from grace", but I'll add some stuff in here when I can put my grubby paws on it. The way it was explained to me, however, was that Satan felt he had achieved a place within the angelic hierarchy where he was more important than he was, or that he was more important than even God. His impudence, for the angels were not granted free will, at least we are not told they were, achieved him a place as God's favored enemy.

God cast Satan to the earth and out of heaven much as had been done to Adam and Eve. From that point forward, Satan became the bad guy. Satan now wants to attract as many people away from God as he possibly can. Doesn't everyone who has ever been reprimanded by their parents want to draw as many people to their belief about the situation as possible? It seems too "human" to me.

I'm also having trouble finding references to Satan whatsoever in the Old Testament, where the groundwork for Christianity is supposed to have been laid. Job is the most direct example of Satan's power or desire, but there's something of a game about it. God wanted to prove Job's faith to Satan just as much as Job's faith needed testing. So, Satan was allowed to do all sorts of nasty things BECAUSE God said he could. Interesting that. To this day, many people believe that Satan does stuff to us, but doesn't Job teach us that God ultimately decides if stuff happens to us, even if Satan's involved? ...yeah

So, Satan's the bad guy because God says so, because God allows Satan to do bad things to us, because God wants us to worship only God and nothing and no one else. Frankly, this sounds a tad like Caesar to me. Or any other totalitarian whine bag who wants to be the only thing their people look at or think about.

We're Growing Up To Be Wimps

I've been purposely trying to avoid this topic because it just makes me mad and a little depressed and I have to ask my wife why in the world, why in THIS world, would she possibly want a child? How could she do that to whatever offspring we would have? It just seems a mean thing to do. My objective here is to cover a lot of different topics but I'll try to keep it focused. I'm sure that's the biggest complaint people would have were they saying anything about my work. Or they just don't agree with it, but that's hardly a complaint to me. So, without further...

First: The clincher, the reason you're all here: Tag Banned. What the crap has this country come to where we can't play the one game that has always been associated with childhood? We can't play tag? I thought I had read somewhere other schools had banned hide and seek. I'll have to find that so, for now, disregard that comment. At any rate, people are opposed to games where people are chased and are made uncomfortable. Well, are we always supposed to be comfortable? I hope not. Embarrassment is a good thing to experience; it's what helps us grow up to be adult. Right now, we're not raising adults, just big f'ing children. Cry babies.

Now, the 3 of you subscribed to my blog might be asking yourself if I, who was tortured by my peers growing up, if I would have preferred to be part of the group, to be left alone, for things to have been different. Nope. Not a chance. I wouldn't be who I am today married to whom I am today living the life I have today. Do I wish things could have been better for me? Sure. But I wouldn't change that to change who I am now. The problem here is people don't want to accept responsibility for their actions, they want to be able to place blame on everyone else. I have several examples of that. Let's start with obesity. Hey, according to my height and my BMI, I'm morbidly obese. Couldn't tell to look at me; I just look like a fat ass right now, well, fat gut, my ass is still nice. Heh.

Alright, let's get the Google-a-going...

Excuses: Viral, Social, Genetic, Prenatal, and while I'm sure the list goes on, I think these are fine examples. Now, some of these stories may be outdated, but I haven't heard anyone retracting their thoughts on the matter. It's obvious to me we'll do anything we can to deny our own responsibilities to our body. Or any other actions. Weight is not the only topic that's been blamed on other people. The thing that kills me is while it's everyone else's fault for my being overweight, why can they not then be blamed for it?

There's this lack of personal responsibility but the group responsibility is alive and well. Don't single anyone out; let's just blame an entire group of people for my faults. Yeah, that seems fair. Don't blame WWI and the poor decision making on your part, just blame the Jews. Yeah, that makes sense. But, let's look at this deeper; it's not my fault that I'm overweight, it's my wife's fault for also being overweight or my buddy who's bigger than I am (we think; he won't tell me how much he really weighs). So, why can't I blame them? Well, it's not their fault either. They had their own reasons for being overweight, never mind the fact that, in some small part, they decided to eat poorly and avoid exercise or eat out of emotion and not exercise or eat rich foods without any balance or exercise. We all make choices here.

Hrm... I almost don't want to go because this whole concept makes me so mad I could strangle someone. Or electrocute them. In a bathtub. For not fighting well enough. I guess that's a segue way to Michael Vick. I had rather hoped not to talk about him; I realized how non-news this is, but it is interesting for the fact that this isn't the first person to be charged for dog fighting, etc. Nor is it the first time a major athlete has been so accosted by the public. What is interesting is he's getting worse treatment than those stars who beat their wives or their girlfriends, at least in the court of public opinion and their news presence. I mean, we've been hearing about this almost every day since it happened. Why? I'm totally opposed to the kind of animal abuse that this thug has perpetuated, but what about those other lives who are devastated or hurt because someone with a lot of money and nothing but pride does something that gets them off but ends up causing serious or detrimental physical or emotional pain? What about the woman who killed her husband and managed less than a year on her sentence? I realize that was a case of self-defense, but she still murdered her husband. That hasn't gotten nearly the kind of press that this life-long thug Vick got.

Oh, I was listening to talk radio and they were comparing the guys that put in the Big Dig where ... Devalya ... I can't remember her first name but I can pronounce her last name (that's a long A at the end). Anyway, they were comparing that company to Michael Vick and were trying to figure out who was the worst kind of criminal. Well, I hate these comparison things (as noted in previous blogs I might add); this one isn't even remotely fair or comparable. Let's look at the crimes perpetuated. The company that has since paid for its crimes with money (a minimal amount for them it has been suggested), will no longer be charged with a crime. In fact, now the company that made the adhesive is the only one being charged with her death. This is a matter of negligence and not intent to kill. At worst, it was intentionally covered up that the glue was not so sticky for the purpose it was given. The intention here was to protect them financially and not criminally.

Let's look at Michael Vick, who is one person where the glue factory is significantly more than that. Michael Vick purposely bought space, put the money up for making kennels and fighting rings, purchased dogs, allowed them to fight in a space under his direct control, tortured and killed through torture those dogs that weren't up to snuff in the ring. Michael Vick intentionally hurt these animals. He wasn't covering this up for his financial benefit, but to avoid being found out and sent to prison. What irks me about the comparison is that Vick intended on doing this from the beginning; Elmer's Suck Concrete Glue didn't. They didn't start that day thinking that they'd make the adhesive less adhesive-y for the sole purpose of putting in place holding these several ton concrete ceiling panels in the hope that someone would get splattered one day. At the very least, they were unaware of the mistake made in the mixture that day and, like everyone else, has been blaming someone else for what happened.

These are two completely different crimes.

Let's also look at the fact that the contracting firm who got the glue in the first place paid to get out of litigation. I didn't realize you could settle out of court for manslaughter, but I'm not as legally minded as I ought to be I suppose. So, while the glue ended up causing a vile and unfortunate accident, that's all it was. Vick meant to be that way. Purposely.

Intent. Who's got more of it?

Oh, so much more I could talk about but it's late and I'm working on work stuff and think I just killed someone's server. I'm not amused...

What's On My Mind?

Hrm. I just realized MySpace doesn't have a Category with "History" listed. Curious. A shame, too. This little section isn't about a specific book, but about my mind being opened and truly interested in the vastness of the philosophers. All of them. My mind has opened to a new understanding and appreciation for the movements of the synapses in our brains that connect and reconnect and for new connections... Should I take some melatonin and relax? Nah.

Part of this does involve The Complete Idiot's Guide To Philosophy, which I've recently picked back up after several months on my bookshelf. I really didn't read the first few chapters very well and will need to go back, but I did instead skip to where specific philosophers and philosophies were being discussed. I should point out that the only actual reading of philosophy I've ever done was a little bit of Sartre a few years back. Probably 3 or 5, hard to remember... I was with my wife but I think we were dating at the time so it was... Yeah, 3 to 5 years back. I was also reading Jung at the time now that I think about it... Anyway, that was the only, the ONLY, philosophy I've ever read. Turns out something ironic happened.

During the discourse, some ideas from sundry of philosophy's greats were mentioned and I realized that many of those ideas were ones I've had or were recently coming to, but had been influenced by my own life and observations. Fact was I had come to the same conclusions as Socrates, Plato, Aristotle, etc. Naturally, this inspired me to want to write about what I think and I realized that I already did that. I then thought about the media we have available to us in this day and age and I wonder how long the printed book will truly be worthwhile? How long will the viewing of words last and not the viewing of people just talking? Thanks to YouTube we can spread our message of hate, stupidity, thought, and genuine bliss anytime we want to (within good taste and if it doesn't upset copyright). With everyone's ability to put their thoughts out there, are we bombarded to the point no one's thoughts matter?

The more I read the more fascinated I am, and yet the more skeptical and cynical I become... And dare I say... Happy? I am starting to truly grasp why people don't want to know anything. Why life is easier without stress and without worry. Just live your lives and die when the time comes. Do the most with the physical life as you possibly can, and let those things that truly don't matter... slide. Watch Fight Club again; I think I pulled that last statement from there but I can't remember for certain. Yes I can. Thanks, Chuck P. Good stuff.

I've been watching the commercials for the Presidential election and it's really bothering me what a waste the whole thing is. We're voting the supposed leader of the free world, but is he really he leader? We have checks and balances so no one has too much power, but then we have things like "lame ducks" where the President is almost worthless because the House and Senate are just going to f with the country because they don't like the President. There are valid reasons for having a single ruler.

Consider the religious parallels to democracy. Religions don't have or print their own money. The government doesn't actually have any money; they get it from taxes. Religions get their money from donations. It isn't forced by the same measure as the government does it, but reread Malachi ... I think 2 and you'll see why tithing is still necessary. So, in a way, both demand tithes and offerings. Democracy we vote for who will ultimately make our decisions for us. It's to streamline the process that was created so many years ago where EVERYONE (the males only) was expected to participate. This way cuts down on the days of arguing over what to rename the town of Coxsackie, NY; but it doesn't represent the whole of the nation. It only represents those with the will to get off their butts and make really one of the most important decisions in our lives. Religion. You don't choose who leads you; not in the same fashion. Someone typically sends them to you or you find someone you like to follow. There's a certain parallel to that.

However, the biggest thing is that the church has a single head: God. We have a pastor or preacher or reverend or priest or cleric or whatever the title is, but there's a person in a true leadership position. One person. Yeah there may be deacons, there may not be. The preacher is the one we look to. The President is the one we look to. But, the President can, as mentioned, be stonewalled into making a decision or not being able to make one. It creates bureaucracy on a scale never intended by our Founding Fathers (I would bet money on that), and all it does is stall the growth of our nation so those in power can line their pockets. It's the philosophy of politics and greed. It's never about our future, only their future. And we're letting them lie to us so they can take away more of our money to fund programs for the lazy.

We are a society of victims where the victims are no longer the real victims but its the perpetrator who's been victimized by society and by a lack of money. Money we should be providing them, unless you're already stupidly rich in which case don't bother. It's not important for those in power to do any more than to speak and placate about what they've done; they haven't really had to DO anything. I'm not speaking to anyone's individual record, nor will I entertain such arguments. It's the ones with the means to stay in the fight who will win this battle, not those fit to serve. Our nation is leaning to a liberal perspective on everything; healthcare, marriage, finances, social programs, etc.

The motto of our justice system shouldn't be "Innocent till proven guilty", it should be… "Everyone's innocent, have a cookie…" We harbor deadbeat dads for not paying child support but we release murderers into the street because someone didn't file the necessary paperwork. Are we being protected by our government who continually spits fear in our face and tells us they're going to take care of it? I don't think so. Bureaucracy can't protect us, it only confuses us.

I hope to write more in the coming weeks about philosophy, including why religion is just a philosophy and why I can't see that any of it is fact and I find myself doubting more and more the mere existence of a singular or pantheistic deity. We have ghosts, but there could be any thousands of explanations to explain it. People can be telekinetic or psychic I suppose, but after all our own instruments only detect activity in 10ish% of our brains so who's to say we're not missing something very important to our futures… Maybe our past?

Oh, and remember, Darwin's theory was a theory, not scientific fact. He stuck his thumb up his butt and pulled it out to sniff the wind of the Galapagos and came up with this brilliant notion that random mutations determined evolutionary cycles… RANDOM MUTATIONS! How can this be? Wouldn't that be indicative of those with Down's Syndrome or dwarfism could be the next wave in the human evolutionary chain? All they have to do is survive and they could be next… I have recently come to the conclusion that Darwin was a quack and rumor has it he admitted as much on his deathbed.

The real question is… Who cares? I mean, I'm obviously not one to talk knowing how my brain functions, but seriously. What are we going to do with this information once we have it? It puts us no closer to really truly factually understanding the nature and origin of our universe or where it's going. Sorry, Dr. Hawking. If we determine God created everything… Great. What next? Which god? Does God even like us? Are we in some kid's snow globe like our whole lives are from St. Elsewhere or something. Are we just a bad television drama and are we going to end as crappy as we began?

It's funny, coming to some of these points in my life has actually made me happier about being alive. Weird, huh? Irony is one of those things that I can't seem to get enough of.

Well I think that's about as random a trail as I can lay down… Happy New Year and vote for someone you believe in; don't kowtow to advertising or the fact whoever you pick probably won't get the nomination… Primaries are where you vote to make a point. Make yours tomorrow.

Which Part Of The Bible Is Valid?

How many of you really truly deeply believe the entire Bible is accurate and should be followed? Seriously? How many of you have sat down and read or skimmed the entire Bible and honestly believes in all of it? Front to back? Find any contradictions? Let's set aside the translation argument for a minute here and just talk about how it's been translated into English. Let's face it, there's well over 100 major translations of the Bible, and let's not even get into the discussion about what books are biblical canon and what books were not included, were decimated before they were able to be considered, or were found buried in pots in the desert... Let's talk about the 66 books we have right now thanks to people who weren't God.

How many of you know people who do not accept the full of the Bible but still claim it is God's Word? I had an uncle (RIP) who was a New Testament only guy, and really he was just a Gospels guy because if Christ was truly the Son of God then only His words mattered because the Old Testament didn't apply and Paul was NOT Christ. One of my clients happens to be a Methodist organization and they have homosexual pastors all over the place, male AND female. One of the staffers is not Methodist any longer, and she's started her own church with friends of hers who basically believe the same thing and have started leaving out certain parts of the Bible; like tithing.

I enjoy the conversations and the stipulations I hear from the religious (not from everyone of course) about how to live your life or at the very least how they're going to live their lives by the Bible, and I've wondered for a damn long time which parts of the Bible still legitimately apply, but it's not a subject I've broached with many people. My parents, now of the Hebraic persuasion, are not of the Messianic movement, but they do follow the entirety of the Bible from the correct perspective that both Old and New Testaments were actually written in Hebrew and not in Hebrew/Greek. Greek was the dominating language of the biblical authors, it was Hebrew. Aramaic was the language of the high priests, so that wouldn't apply to anyone who was writing for the fledgling Christianity.

I'm also forced to bring up the fact that God did not publish this sacred work. Man did. It's a sticking point because everyone I've argued this with says that "Well, God inspired them to write it". Yeah. And? God didn't put "pen to paper" except in the instance of the Ten Commandments, and technically, with Christ. So, whether God inspired it or not, if you believe in Free Will then you have to believe that Man had a say in what was actually written down. Later on, Man would have the say over which books get listed as canon and which books don't count for one reason or another.

I'm not trying to throw out the purpose of the Bible by any means, though that purpose could be argued till the cows came home (some of the arguments listed above). I'm trying to get some discussion about this because there's a pretty handy array of beliefs just amongst my Facebook friends, not including the ones I haven't harassed yet. I think it's important to really discuss this because this is how people are basing their entire lives or at least claim they are but they're really just living their lives based on what seminary teaches or how Man re-interprets the Bible and stands on a podium spouting mostly Malachi and "give me money"...

For not having cracked a Bible open for a purpose other than looking up something terribly specific for a very long time, I still remember a great deal of what I learned growing up and in high school and a little bit beyond there. I also realize that a lot of what religion is really about is living a certain lifestyle and committing yourself to an ideal, whether your particular philosophy is a respected religion or not. However, I'm a huge fan of the idea that means matters... The ends do NOT justify the means. They may bring about the same resolution and it may be good, but it's important that you still do things right. I can't stand it when people tell me they adhere to the Bible yet they're homosexual or they knock aside the whole tithing thing or they say that Christians should love everyone because the Bible says so. Sorry, re-read Leviticus 13 and I Corinthians 6:9 and tell me to love everyone.

So. Tell me. After the diatribe above, can anyone tell me which parts of the Bible they don't like?

Why I Like Music

I decided to go with something a bit light-hearted for tonight. What is Mc's favorite music. Well, as with everything in my life, there's a story. This one actually starts with none other than AJ, our fair math teacher who introduced us to the Kansas classic, Dust In The Wind. Not sure who else was there besides AJ himself, but I'll continue.

To be honest, I forget why we were hearing this song, something to the effect of Kerry Livgren wrote this song and a year later found Christ. I had only known of Kerry from the short-lived 80s Christian Band, AD. And only one very crappy tape from my brother, Art Of The State. Anyway, this had not the opposite effect but an unexpected one from what Mr. H (Andy's Dad?) had intended: we loved the song. I had heard it shortly thereafter on one of my geeky television shows Highlander: The Series (I know, BEST TITLE EVER). It was a spiritual moment where the main character's chicky gets killed towards the end of the first season. Main character's immortal, so her dying shouldn't have been a surprise but she was murdered so it was tragic blah blah blah. I'm over it now.

Well, this opened the door to other music for me. First, however, Andrew J would solidify himself as my gateway drug to better music (I'll explain why my brother wasn't one of those people in a minute) by introducing us to the pinnacle of Christian cynicism and one of the reasons I seek out the truths and facts of religion: Steve Taylor. For those who don't know Steve's work or don't remember my infatuation with it I don't have the breath to help you out (I worked out AGAIN tonight... that's twice... in a row... a record to be sure). Needless to say Steve takes a similar perspective on much of Christianity that I do... Or I took the viewpoint Steve had and then I jumped off the edge into the abyss... (You'll find my puns are intentional, rarely do I fake a pun. I grew up on the Marx Brothers and Dick Van Dyke after all. That Morey Amsterdam...)

Well, that was it. I was hooked. Then, a little known and little liked album showed up; the first tribute album before someone died. I thought this was a sign, but it did seem to show the end of Steve's recording career... Lazy so and so... There was a tribute album to Steve Taylor by some of the least-known bands in Christian alternative music. I think at the time Sixpence was the only one really with their own little following, being on their sophomore album This Beautiful Mess (can you believe I'm doing

- Perception Is Truth -

this from memory?)... I remember when Demon Boy picked that up. J and I were so jealous standing in their kitchen... rassin-frassin...

SO, with Steve Taylor firmly in my grasp and the likes of Sixpence and Starflyer 59, I realized Christian music wasn't just Petra, Rich Mullins, and Mark Heard. Admittedly, I still listen to all of those bands. Such good music. Good stuff. Earlier Petra's the best, when Greg X Volz was still lead singer. John Schlitt was okay for the most part, but when Bob Hartman left to just produce... Forget about it.

Anyway. My brother had been into secular music for some time, being the family rebel. He liked 80s dance music, the stuff that got him to shake his moneymaker... hairball... hold on... Okay. So, I wouldn't listen to his music because they weren't Christian. I was such a good boy. Then I moved out... Hmm... Yeah... Well, I started to listen to more and more music that was less than directly uplifting to God. I mean, let's face it, most of Starflyer's music doesn't say anything about God, Sometime Sunday (also from Tooth and Nail Records who had a brief stint at being cool as such schools as Central) had some lyrics related to God, but their sound was often too hard for people to take seriously in the CCM market. Mark Heard talked about God the way he wanted to, and the love he had for his wife. Great interview with him talking about his music, I'll get some excerpts for later nonsense. For anyone still around to read all of this :p

To continue, I started listening to the euro pop like music of my brother's generation; Depeche Mode and Information Society are really the ones I latched onto and still listen to. I just played some Depeche Mode at work today in fact. Well, this also reminded me of the great music my folks had listened to years and years ago but... things happened... and such music wasn't even allowed in the house. Things have since changed for them on that, but that's a different series altogether. So, I got into The Beatles and the Doors and Zeppelin and even the occasional Zappa ditty (weren't they all ditties really?)

I found myself expanding into a whole new world of music I never imagined. Dave Matthews (even though the rumor at the time was he liked little boys) brought me into such things as Damien Rice and Willy Porter and half of my acoustic collection seems to come from Dave Matthews really getting it out there in the public. Harrod and Funck are still my all-time favorite acoustic acts, even over Simon and Garfunkel. Awesome.

I'm so angry they broke up but life doesn't always keep you on the same path you started, no matter how much you want to give it up. Sometimes it's God...

I got into Over the Rhine which opened me up to Fiona Apple and Tori Amos. I still find OtR to be a better fit for me over Tori and certainly over the whiny spoiled Fiona (saw her live; never again). Vigilantes of Love were at the same show with OtR, in fact they're who I went to see. They were part of the Mark Heard sound, southern Christian rock. Not quite as twangy as the usual country types but not the Lynyrd Skynyrd sounds either. Nice. Melodic. The kind of music you can picture friends sitting around a fire doing. Impromptu. I just changed from Better Than Ezra to Mark Heard. So nice.

Alright, now. Uh. Has anyone seen my point? Anyone?

Well, music's such a part of me I feel it and think about it more than my wife, my job, my cats, my problems... I just want music going all the time. I'm jealous of Marco's skill and talent and everyone else's ability to be in front of people and really put themselves out there. Typing is so much safer for me here. My dad's a great guitar player and used to sing in clubs and such. I can sing, kind of, mostly if I drink just water I can do alright. So I'm told. Better than my wife... SHHHH....

Yeah. I listen to music constantly. I love it. I need more. Robert Deeble's about the most depressing music I can get my hands on. Not that I'm trying to get depressed, but it helps set the mood for when I'm trying to write something dramatic. I still find that OtR works great for almost everything I'm doing, while Rage or even some Black Eyed Peas work out nicely for action sequences.

Anyway. Why do you all like music? What are your favorites? Ever given it any thought?

Why I'm Grumpy

Where to begin. I'm a little heated after an email thread I was reading got me going and my lovely wife was watching some reality television. I've decided reality television has done more to hurt our society than The Great Depression. That's purely opinion and hardly able to be backed up, but what we lost in monies then we should be losing in pride now. What shame has befallen us. I realize other countries have far "stupider" TV, but are we aspiring to be so foolish in our own representations? Must we give the happiest tales and the worst tales all in the same show? Should I want to watch celebrities or former celebs or former really crappy celebs go through rehab on a reality game show? Should I care that Britney Spears is well paid trailer park and that K-Fed's ACTUALLY a better parent? Who cares? This sort of stuff is going on where there aren't any cameras (except when COPS is in town) and nothing's being done about it. I'd love it if Dr Phil invaded a hospital in some distant Nebraska town where the mother got drunk and locked herself in her wall-boarded trailer keeping the sober father outside. Won't see that, because she's not important enough.

We worship people who have money and give them more money. They are the golden calves of our time. We need them to look up to them so we can see how the "other half" live. Well, the other half's lives suck as much as ours, and they have the one thing everyone thinks they want: money. Money can't buy happiness isn't as shallow as it looks. Sure you don't see someone frowning on a jet ski (I stole that from a comedian whose name doesn't come to mind), but you don't seem to see really rich people stay really happy. Typically there's a scandal that gets brushed under the rug but we still make jokes about it (didn't Teddy Kennedy's cousin kill someone sometime...?). It makes us feel better about ourselves. We're like schoolyard bullies wishing we had better lives but wanting everyone else's life to suck in the process.

We can't handle fame as people because people aren't meant to be famous. We're not meant to be this singular and self-important. We're supposed to be a society. When I go outside and I see people in my town who live on the streets and people walk past them and look away (I do it, too) or who walk around in gangs, I don't see society. I see a dismal end to what was supposed to be a great nation. Oh, and being a great nation meant kicking the locals off their land by force and manipulation. We started out as imperialist invaders, why should we be any different now? I see the downfall of humanity one greedy little sycophant at a time.

I don't have hope for the future because I have no basis for it. Sure, I'll work hard and make more money, but unless I can turn all this rambling into something really lucrative, I'll never be anything more than a humble taxpayer. A taxpayer under the boot of the government that's supposed to protect me by letting illegal immigrants drive poorly and hit people and do nothing about it. We let criminals knowingly walk the streets and protest that they're not legal immigrants because we haven't made them so... WE LET CRIMINALS DICTATE THE COURSE OF THIS COUNTRY!

I don't see Christian ideals working out either because there's too much greed in men's hearts. I don't see freedom as a Christian ideal because Free Will isn't real. Do what God says or be punished for eternity; yeah, that's exactly like democracy. Wake up, people! Your God is a dictator. Though it may be a benevolent one, facts are facts. You don't worship the President, you worship the one holding your lives in the palm of their screwy hands (i.e. Cesar, Castro, Stalin, God). Yeah, I just compared God to a bunch of dictators. Read the Old Testament again. God was super pissed when ... who was it ... didn't wipe out everything as commanded? He saved the BEST of the enemy's to sacrifice to God. That's not what God had commanded and there was trouble for it. So, go ahead and elect a person who's of good moral Christian stock. They'll clearly support democracy.

Here's the dilemma: we need God in order to have a stable society. We need to have the idea of God more than anything else. We need to have something to believe in that we don't control. We control the money so we can't believe in that. We can't have faith in something we can see and touch and know the limitations of. If we did, as we are doing more and more every day, we'll fall apart. We need to have God in order to keep us looking to something better than ourselves. I am full of dichotomies, just stick around.

One of the reasons the Islamists are doing such a bang-up job (yeah, pun intended) is because they actually believe in what they're doing. They don't have the same distractions our life has. No, I don't condone it and I hope we crush them like the vermin they are, but you still have to understand what you're up against. You can't cower in a corner and say you're right and say you'll win the fight when you don't know who or what you're fighting. I've said it about 1500 times, you aren't proving or preventing anything by catching anyone in al Qaeda. You have dismantle it from the source; the money. It's all about the money in every society. The money to get what you want or the money to do what you want.

Why am I grumpy? Why isn't anyone else grumpy? Why isn't anyone else looking at the facts instead of looking to their truths? Why are we arguing about the gold standard when we're having new laws pushed into our faces not because we need them but because they won't enforce the old laws? Why do we spout the Freedom of Speech in the Constitution but complain when militias spout the 2nd Amendment? Where's the consistency in the hearts and minds of our people? There isn't any and I feel less and less deserving of whatever mercy whatever god happens to be showing us...

Hard to think I'm actually a happier person and seriously mysteriously suddenly enjoy the idea of procreation. Where's my fear? Simple, I have faith in something. I believe in the direction my mind has gone, and I have the knowledge I believe to back it up. Individual points can be sketchy, but the overlying message remains the same and I plan on putting more of that up in the coming days and weeks. This whole world needs a wakeup call and since I'm not cool enough to have my own publishing company and I hate being on camera I'll just plug up MySpace with more and more of my philosophies. For now, as I've been told recently, the Internet is the last real place where we can have a voice...

How long will that last...?

Why Religious Music Is Better

Now, for those who know me know I'm not a churchgoer and haven't been for some time. Not quite a generation but getting closer every day since I've stepped foot inside a church with the intention of worshipping or anything other than a wedding or a funeral (and the last funeral was a Catholic one). Still, I was talking with a friend today about music and I realized something that I hadn't thought about; the Christian music I grew up with is still better than most of the secular music I've grown to love. There are some exceptions of course, but there's a reason for it. Christian music says something.

It's true that some of the less-than-religious artists such as Tori Amos say quite a bit and I'm sure someone like L could easily add to this list, but the overall crux of money-makers don't say anything that's real or relevant. Whether you believe the Christian ethos is edifying or ignorant, it says something. Of course there are those out there who want to make a Holy Buck as opposed to the Devil Dollars of "the world", but let's really take a look at this.

Bands in the 60s were all saying the same thing; down with the war. This isn't an accurate statement but it's the overreaching generalization that will work for our argument. But they said what they believed in; this is when music was really more than commercialization; it was America's time to integrate music into our society the way other nations have existed with it for years and years. Of course we corrupted it and turned it into this play-doh money-making machine, but I digress.

As music went forward, we learned of new ways to irritate Mc and to make more money than we deserved, but there were artists who still said what they believed in. Either the singer-songwriter or the religious artist. I grew up on Petra, Phil Keaggy, Rich Mullins... I grew up on music that stood for something and they did a good job sharing what they believed. They weren't just out there trying to be a good Christian, they were out there trying to be the best damn musician they could be in the name of their God.

Read some stuff on Rich Mullins and Mark Heard and you'll understand what I mean. Even more than Petra these two stand out to me as true men of God who really sang what they believed and did it in the fashion accustomed to them and how they believed. Now, compare that to some of the stories of the secular bands who have made fortunes singing about nothing…

    I miss Rich and Mark…

You Big Asshole And Other Pet Names

There have been some complaints laid upon me that I don't talk enough about my wife. That's right, my wife's the one complaining. Well, they're not without their merit. You see, I prefer to write as little about other people as possible; it prevents some emotions and potential confrontations if I ever spoke of how I really felt or if there was ever a disagreement about my perspective and it's just something I can more easily avoid. Well, times have changed and since this is a blog, I am forced to give in to the stereotype and talk about my life as it is right now. Yes. A window into the reality of my life. Brought to you by my wife. Heh.

Alright. First, since we're on the subject of honesty and being real, it should be known that after 5 years being together, 3 of which were marriage, there have been changes and adjustments made, and some trouble. I've been going through some stuff emotionally and mentally and unfortunately my wife has had to bear the brunt of this. Questions and doubts abound, but I've come to my sense and know that K really is the best thing for me and the odds of there being anyone who can not only put up with me as I am but to love me and want to have my children besides... That's what real miracles are.

So, I'll give you the big skinny on how we met. This story is both good and bad, depending on how you look at it. We met on Yahoo. That's right. Yahoo. How, you ask? Simple. I was cruising for chicks (which I used to find lots...) and found a friend of hers online and started chatting it up. Well, K was there and started talking to me on her friend's account. We hit it off pretty well, but K was seeing someone at the time. Turns out they were barely seeing each other and she was really interested in me. Well her friend found out I played D&D (I'll get to that later, too) and thought I was too weird. Which is funny given that she turned out to be insane.

So. We started going out. By roughly our third month I was in love with her. After all, I had been with roughly a dozen different women. I would say... just about 5 of them I actually loved or wanted to be with. Things just didn't work out. They either weren't keepers or I just wasn't ready for something that serious. The rest? Well... Uh... Never mind that. The fact was K provided me with the emotional support and interest I just wasn't able to find anywhere else. For some reason, she thought I was just

- Perception Is Truth -

great, too. I still ask her what she was thinking, but she just loves me. So much it hurts us both sometimes. Relationships are work, people, don't let anyone tell you any different!

Well, I had this whole thing planned out for the proposal, which was really to trick her into driving someplace nice and I'd stop her when I found the perfect spot. We found the perfect spot someplace up north, I think on 119 or just off 119... Rassin frassin. We got out and walked around a bit. It was up a mountain and we had a grand view before us. Unfortunately it was black fly season and really, really buggy. This wasn't working out quite as well as I had hoped, but I was committed.

So, we got back into her car and talked for a few minutes. I told her how much I loved her and how much she meant to me and I asked her if she was interested in spending the rest of her life with me. She was crying by now, but I make her cry a lot when I'm sweet since it doesn't happen very often (I'm a big asshole, remember?). It looked like I was going to lean over and give her a kiss when I moved to the side and pulled a little container out of my pocket. Her eyes got wide and the tears were a-flowing. Inside was my great-grandmother's ring, bought by her husband around World War II (as memory serves; K will remember). She didn't think I was actually proposing, but I surprised her. Obviously, she said yes.

Next was the wedding. We had it at Searles Castle in Windham. Great spot. It was also the only nice day that whole week. It had rained and was cold up until the night before our wedding, then it rained the day after. Must have been a sign.

...

Well, it was not without its problems. Our wedding was supposed to be videotaped, but apparently that meant to tape us all gathering and K walking up to meet me, then taping us walking down the aisle. Nothing in between. Yes. That's right. Mc's wedding is NOT on moving, sound-making film. So, for that I do apologize to those who were not invited. I feel the need to apologize again for that. I'll tell the story.

Aside from the wedding not being televisable (which took about six months to figure out in the first place), there were also problems with the invitees. Different factions of people under one big tent outside of a castle is prone to create problems. Well, my computer geek friends and my role-playing geek friends were basically the only people

I invited besides family. This would ultimately end in failure and almost cost me some friendships I've had for almost a decade by that point. To this day I don't know what really happened but it's one of those things that, since I can't get the whole data, I can't do anything about it. The facts are a closely guarded secret because people don't want me to look back on my wedding with any bad memories. Too late for that. Not to mention some of my wife's friends are less than mature when you get them in groups. So, while I don't have my wedding on camera, I do have one of her friends thanking us for "the open fuckin bah". Yeah. Great. Thanks. People I could have not avoided. K' stepdad and I wanted to have a kegger in their backyard. Big parties are easier to segregate than assigned seating. Take it from a pro. So, again I apologize.

We bought a house, got a couple cats that we treat as our children, and have been trying to move out of this place for just about as long as we lived in it. Being in a condex (duplex with two owners) means having a neighbor. Which is mostly fine. But, I'm also concerned about how much noise we make, when I have too much stereo power to be concerned about anyone other than the FAA complaining about the noise. Really. I wanna blow stuff up with my stereo sometimes. So, that's the next plan.

We went to Bermuda for our honeymoon. I almost drowned while snorkeling. We went to Disney World, which really is a magical place. I tried the rocking roller coaster; first roller coaster I've ever been on... Got sick. Never again! We went to South Carolina and drove a Mustang convertible which was WAY too small for us. We're tall folk. Went to Colonial Williamsburg most recently. Got nauseous on a violent water slide. That's right, even water slides make me ill. Yay. How could anyone else want this beast?

That's the quick and dirty of how we met and got engaged and married and why we need to move. She's got the degree in history and I still have a GED. She tells me I'm the smartest man she knows, I tell her I know about 4 things really, really well. When I can change my oil (which I understand the principle of) and can mow the lawn (I hate my lawn with an undying passion) without complaining then come back to me and tell me I'm super smart. Heh...

So... Yeah. Quick look into me.

Latter Days

Debates, Debacles, or Debaucheries?

So, I watched some of last night's "debate" and I found myself questioning the entire concept. I've been part of debate teams in school, and I found that I was pretty decent at debates (some would say I was better at arguing than debating). So much so I would not only learn the point of view I was arguing, but I would get the other side's arguments and use it for ammo. I enjoyed it. A lot. The problem with "debates" and "political debates" is the person itself. To have a decent argument, you need to make your point and destroy their point. Simple stuff. A political debate should also be that simple, but there are some torrid extras we need to discuss.

I ordered tuna, why is my bill 300 pages?

Anyone can say they are against cancer or against tax increases for the poor or against the war (whichever war they want to be against at the time) or for health care, but then we find out from their opponent that the voted for a bill that not only raises taxes, but cuts social health care programs and funnels that tax money to researching cures for cancer while creating a suggested time table for the troops to come home... Bills, laws, whatever it is they vote on down there in DC, are not as cut-and-dry as people are lead to believe. They talk about pork barrel spending and earmarks, because bills are allowed to have in it whatever someone wants them to have in it, whether related or not. McCain votes against a bill that would give the troops more of what they need because of such a timetable, while Obama claims to have voted for it (he might have voted "present" it's hard to say). Again, we only know either the crux of the bill (if it's good for whoever's talking) or the extras on the bill (if it's bad for the other guy). We never know the whole bill, because it's just too damn long and they believe the American people are too ignorant to understand the whole thing (which is true but bulletin points work).

I ordered tuna, but I got dolphin-friendly chicken salad

Another problem is what the man stands for and what their point of view is. If you watch them, during the debates anyway, they seem to stick to their guns for the purpose of that debate at that time, but they all go flippety-flop at some point, leading me to believe that they truly have no convictions and ultimately will do whatever the special interests tell them. This is not true of everyone and indeed McCain has shown himself to be someone who will make a decision while Obama will wait to see what the polls say before making a choice. So, being someone who will make an unpopular decision is a better choice in terms of leadership, but if I don't agree with what the maverick's going to choose does that make him better than the spineless leading the blind? And does Obama's waiting make him a better legislature or puppet? It does appear that Obama is at least concerned with what the populace is thinking, but only the populace that sees the world as he sees it. Which is another problem; they're not after "the American people" they're after "those people who agree with me or at least don't agree with him". They're not out to prove themselves to all of us, because they can't. Lincoln knew that, which is part of what sets him aside from Obama in terms of experience. Lincoln clearly had a better understanding of leadership and not just politics. Sorry, Mr. O.

I ordered tuna on rye but got wheat germ

Then we have the blanket superiority complex one seems to need to have to get this close to a major office. Clearly they all know what's best for us and all their experts are more right than someone else's experts. Because the media is pressing that global climate change is real (it is) and that humans are to blame (maybe partly) for all of it (maybe partly), obviously they must be right even when there are as many climatologists (maybe more) saying it isn't our fault at all it's just part of the natural order of things. Of course the elected are going to believe them and mandate they make their policies based upon this "fact". then again, the odds are pretty good that whatever policies they make will, on the down-low, have climate-destroying initiatives in them that will come out only at the next election cycle. I'm sure the big-budget climate-cleaners will come forward, but will have provisions for earmarking that all of those legislators seem to call for, but there will be some failings, too.

Cthulhu in '08: the stars are right!

So, we're left with the lesser of two evils, which I always thought was a crock. We're still choosing evil, there's not a lesser evil (in comparison to the Great Old Ones maybe...). But, when both of them are going to do things that are ultimately going to hurt my way of life and the way I believe America should be going then I really am choosing evil, and the lesser of those evils is in relation to the lesser amount of evil they are going to plague upon me... But we're still screwed. I'm sorry, the hard-working taxpayers of America are screwed in all forms, while the shiftless and illegal are going to get my money to break the law and do as little as possible. I might wanna join that bandwagon when the time comes... Why work at all? The government's going to take care of me and as well they should.

I have one question: who's paying for that?

Disclaimer

When I first started asking questions I was just confused about why things were the way they were and why we were being told specific things from the pulpit and why it had to be that way and how friends of mine believed the same thing when it seemed so totally illogical to me. I wasn't one to push then, just be pushed. I grew up and the questions became something else, something I would find a way to argue against and just create chaos and irritation amongst Believers. Some of them stuck with me even through this period and they proved either their friendship or their devotion to Christian Duty during this time. However, none of them would engage me in an argument because it was fruitless and no one wants to argue with someone who refuses to back down. This wasn't entirely true; if you could prove to me pretty conclusively that I was wrong I'd totally back down. This happened often in real life but not in my intellectual life. What came next was more questions, but for myself and for the sake of knowing. I really started to re-discover things and ideas but I still held onto concepts and people from my past. Today, those things are behind me. I have been freed from that pretense and started my own pretense. I laud people for having faith and believing, but I loathe them for being so "right" about it all the time without taking the chance to admit they might be wrong or that perhaps something DID get lost in the translation. I just want people to really know what they're believing in and selling their soul to. Even the Bible says that Satan, the deceiver, will come as an angel of light... That's the simplest and most dangerous warning I can think of off the top of my head.

So, yeah, this is important to me because most of the people in my life have been Christian and I was one of them once, too, and I think that since no one else wants to take up this cause of really questioning their faith I will. And I will do it as maturely as possible. It's time everyone is free from the chains that bind them, including the chains they believe set them free...

Evolution vs. Creation vs. Other

So, I've been doing a lot of thinking about a lot of random things, mostly so I'm not so focused on work, and I've had some curious thoughts about the whole theory of evolution. Without having read Darwin's collected works my argument will not be as complete as it needs to be, so please bear with me. But, do not misunderstand me, I do not believe in the theory of evolution as presented in our public schools as actual science. It is as much a theory as the world being created by an all powerful deity. They are on the same level of possibility for me. I've had this discussion with some friends of mine who believe evolution more than creation, this is fine, but I'm told that it "makes more sense" than creation. I don't think that's the case. This is more what I'm going to inquire about than any specific treatise.

I have some specific questions that I feel everyone should be asking about evolution before they dare teach it to their children as legitimate fact. I fear the day comes that parenting will not be in the hands of the progenitors but in the hands of the state and the odds of us teaching our youth any sort of moral value that isn't taxpayer-funded goes away more and more as this country and our world joins the new religion of liberalism, which is masked socialism but that's in a different argument that I'm still putting together. With that sidetrack in mind, let's take a look at a couple things:

Why did everything evolve differently?

This may be a simple question to some, but I truly believe this is far more difficult than anything we could be asking. If we all evolved from the same tadpole soup in the same environment all over the world, how did we evolve into different things? Why did the same puddle evolve into things as varied as plants and animals, as roses and cockroaches and horses and my aunt? If we all were supposedly just trying to survive and we all came from the same basic place with the same basic problems, why did we evolve as different entities altogether? Cheetahs didn't evolve into speedy cats because they were trying to outrun the other single-cell organisms...

Why did we evolve?

This should probably be the first question, but I think that once people read this one they won't bother reading the rest. Anyway, what was the need for us to evolve? What was the need for us to grow from tadpole to person? If the whole point to evolution is for survival, what were we surviving against? What caused the very first amoeba to feel threatened enough that it needed to change its genetic structure so it would outlast said threat? It certainly wasn't another amoeba, was it? Was it a bully amoeba? Did the wind carry in a bit of salt that was a danger to it so it needed to grow a water sac so it could stay moist enough to outlive the salt particle? What purpose did evolving serve at the very beginning of it? The same question is asked of Creation; why did God create us? I'm not here to debate that, that'll take way too long.

It's easy to go back and try to fill why we are where we are, and since no one wants to ask important questions anymore, no one dares to ask why it happened the way it did. People don't want to look at the nuances of a theory or a lie, they just want to live in their ignorant bliss. Why face facts when we have enough distractions with television and everything that goes on and around our entertainment? Why ask yourself "why" something happened instead of just accepting "how" it happened...

I have heard an interesting idea as to why evolution is real, and even if the world was millions and millions of years old, it still doesn't explain the "why did we evolve" question, but it bears repeating. If you look at cockroaches, if you try a specific kind of pesticide, within four generations, that line of cockroaches will have developed an immunity to it. They evolved to protect themselves against that particular chemical compound. However, it does not pass to every single other cockroach in existence. Just because a family of a thousand cockroaches in New York are immune to Raid formula 687, does not mean that cockroaches in New Delhi are going to share the same immunity. Hell, the New Delhi cockroaches may still be susceptible to formula 142, I don't know.

So, even though evolution may exist on a smaller scale, such as building a resistance to a particular drug (interesting that we look down on our bodies for building immunities for drugs we "need"... do we really need those drugs after all?), it does not mean that a tadpole today will "evolve" or grow into something completely different.

PS This argument needs work, but you see what I'm driving at I hope.

From the site suggested by "Unapologetic Catholic":
Scientific theories are validated by empirical testing against physical observations.

Theories are not judged simply by their logical compatibility with the available data. Independent empirical testability is the hallmark of science—in science, an explanation must not only be compatible with the observed data, it must also be testable. By "testable" we mean that the hypothesis makes predictions about what observable evidence would be consistent and what would be incompatible with the hypothesis. Simple compatibility, in itself, is insufficient as scientific evidence, because all physical observations are consistent with an infinite number of unscientific conjectures. Furthermore, a scientific explanation must make risky predictions— the predictions should be necessary if the theory is correct, and few other theories should make the same necessary predictions.

I should point out that I did create a logical flaw with my discussion, but I write what I think and I'm not opposed to giving my detractors and potential detractors ammunition to work with. However, the above statement, in itself, doesn't make sense to me. Obviously I will need to continue reading this site and apparently grab some Darwin from my favorite used book store, or find it online (should be public domain by now). If we are to believe that the world is tens of millions of years old, how can we adequately test or predict macroevolution...? More to come!

F You, Black Friday

Yet another reason why Christmas as an American holiday should be banned... A 34-year-old Wal-Mart employee was murdered this very morning by throngs of frothing consumers yearning to tear down the doors (literally) to get cheap crap from a store that undercuts everyone so they can be the only game in town. Exploitation of the masses through commercialized holiday madness has caused yet another death at the hands of local humanity. I am disgusted with Wal-Mart for the organizational savvy of a bull in a china shop and wonder if we can get footprints off this poor guy's body and arrest some people for reckless disregard for human life and at the very least second-degree murder. This was more than an accident, my loyal reader(s), this was perpetuated in the name of our economic crisis and this insipid holiday that's gone on for too long unchecked. Ban Christmas shopping, donate to a charity. And for those who still believe that Christ is the reason for Christmas, let this story be a sad reminder that no holiday is what it started as, and no life is more important than great deals...

- Perception Is Truth -

Is Heaven Real?

Some of you may remember a little post I did where, with minimal research, it was pretty easy to disprove Hell the way it was taught for all those years. Well, I started doing some re-reading of that sacredest of books and I wondered what else I could find or stumble across or wonder what else was being taught that was, frankly, wrong, misguided, an area of deceit or just confusion and mistake. Seems that the opposite of Hell is now on the table. Be here for when I cut away the layers and tackle this interesting and difficult subject. My research is freely available online. Hit up some websites, do some research for yourself. If you're interested you won't just take my word for it, but I hope that I'll give you enough information that you'll see that I'm in this for the knowledge and not for anything else...

This proves to be an expansive research project. Feel free to follow along. Check the Pages at the right side, or click below to keep up. Please note that comments are not allowed for the research. If you have issues or questions feel free to post them with this thread. Thank you.

NOTES

02 July 2008

It's been suggested that Strong's isn't as good a concordance. Young's is better. I had heard that Strong's was... lacking... but it was the standard for so long I forgot. For the moment I will have to locate a Young's that I can work with, but I will continue to use the BlueLetterBible site for the translation comparisons. The first article [08064] will remain untouched but I may notate that Strong's was used. Thanks for joining the party!

04 July 2008

Hmm. I've done some generic sniffing around (Google), and determined why Strong's is... less than adequate. There are enough actual concerns about Strong's for its usage in what I'm trying to accomplish. Wikipedia actually has a pretty substantial entry about this. If you read the last couple paragraphs of the link, you can get a clearer picture as to what's up. So... Off to find a more conclusive concordance...

05 July 2008

- Latter Days -

So, I've been reviewing the problems with Strong's and my present accessibility of a different concordance of the electronic kind. Given that Strong's does still maintain the correct root word in Hebrew, I will continue my work with that tome. It will also keep the work consistent and since most of the Christian community utilizes that particular document it is what I shall also continue to use. If I do happen across another concordance before or after I am finished with this, I will write what changes should be made at that time.

Is Heaven Real? Pt 2

Heaven's an interesting topic; one that few people want to challenge. Some challenge it because they want to challenge the very notion of God or God's existence. They're troublemakers who want to sow chaos just because it'll get people riled up. I used to be that person, not anymore. There are others who don't want to know that Heaven may not exist, so they won't argue the point either. Some are Christians because their only hope is that when they die they will get treasures and eternal peace. Well, what treasures will Heaven have to offer? What use does my soul need of treasure anyway? Streets of gold and crowns with jewels and big houses and no tears... Why would a soul need any of those things in the first place? We as mankind give gold and jewels and crowns their worth, God doesn't. Why would God care about such things anyway? These are questions that have nagged me for years, but the idea of Heaven has always been too good a thing to want to mess with. Not anymore. Now, I need to understand. I need to know just what was intended by Heaven. Will I get to answer it here? Of course not. No one can answer this but God. However, it should be determined at the very least what the Bible entails about Heaven and what our part is within it. So, sit back and enjoy the ride...

Genesis 1:1

For anyone that's ever tackled Sunday school, this should be one of the easiest verses to remember, but which translation is best? Below are the various examples of what's available. Note that the King James and the New International Versions are the most widely used phrasings, and the Hebrew Names at the bottom uses a very generic word meaning land or country or anything ground-related. Very broad usage term the way we use little E "earth" today. [Remind me to look into the etymology of the word earth and how it became the name of our planet.]

- **KJV:** In the beginning God created the heaven and the earth
- **NIV:** In the beginning God created the heavens and the earth
- **Young:** In the beginning of God's preparing the heavens and the earth
- **HNV:** In the beginning God created the heavens and the eretz.

Let's take a look at the usage of the word "heaven" from the Hebrew: shamayim. This word has various meaning tied to it.

1) heaven, heavens, sky

    a) visible heavens, sky

        I) as abode of the stars

        ii) as the visible universe, the sky, atmosphere, etc

    b) Heaven (as the abode of God)

Notice how capital H "Heaven" is a secondary meaning, if you consider sub-meanings of the primary meaning to be still primary. At any rate, it was not the initial intention of this word's usage to be used as the home of God, Elohiym. It must have been decided upon later to describe God's location for there could have been no words to describe where the Creator of all things would reside. After all, until Elohiym was named and declared Elohiym, how could we have a word meaning "Elohiym's House"?

Now for the etymology:

Old English *heofon* "home of God," earlier "sky,"

- possibly from Proto-Germanic **khemina-*

- from Proto-Indo-European base **kem-/*kam-* "to cover"

- Plural use in sense of "sky" is probably from Ptolemaic theory of space composed of many spheres, but it was also formerly used in the same sense as the singular in Biblical language, as a translation of Classical Hebrew plural *shamayim*. Heavenly "beautiful, divine" is from 1460, often (though not originally) with reference to the celestial "music of the spheres;" weakened sense of "excellent, enjoyable" is first recorded 1874.

This states pretty plainly that the word "Heaven" in its "home of God" usage is not from the Classical Hebrew, which begs the question I'm asking presently. This may be a bit of a stretch logically speaking, but put aside all that you know and all that you believe about Heaven and Hell and the Bible and God and all the hang-ups that go along with that. Good or bad. Let's take this one step at a time, for that's how I'm taking it. I realize this will not be construed as a well-researched document, but I expect detraction throughout this whole process.

Ptolemy is also mentioned here which brings up another point. We let a lot of philosophy get thrown into the belief system and the dogma of the Christian faith as a way to reach the masses or to at least help them to understand and relate to concepts that were new and exciting but still keep the Bible relevant. I wonder how much of it got filtered in there, and I wonder what else I'm going to find.

Alright, let's set the word itself aside for a second. We all know that the first argument I should receive with any cadence is related to the evolution of language and the translation of the words from the original Hebrew into whatever native tongue we happen to have had at the time: Latin, Old English, etc. Keep in mind that the translations we are working from, mostly, come from European history. Translated into the Latin Vulgate by Jerome in the 400s from the Hebrew Tanakh, which is pretty impressive considering up until that time everything had come from the Greek Septuagint. Hebrews don't write in Greek, though. Keep that in mind as this progresses.

A quick search relating back to the Strong's Concordance shows that the word "heaven" in the aforementioned usage(s) occurs 374 times in the King James Version. This is strictly Old Testament as everyone in Sunday School knows that the Bible is Hebrew OT and Greek NT. This isn't actually true but we'll get to that later. For now, let's talk about the usage throughout the Old Testament. The word "heaven" shows up 82 times in the Torah, the Pentateuch, or the Chumash, which consists of the first five books of the Bible as we have it today. What's interesting is a word search of "heaven" (by itself and not coupled with the usage given above) gives different numbers. A scavenger hunt! Oh, boy!

Genesis

-"heaven" occurs 30 times in 29 verses in Gen of the KJV

-"heaven" [08064] occurs in 31 verses in Gen of the KJV

Comparing the search from above, most of Genesis uses heaven to mean sky, the are above us, where the clouds and the fowls and the stars reside (obviously the stars do NOT reside here but from the ground it sure is a hard point to argue). It appears that in Genesis 28 things are slightly different, specifically the area of Jacob's dream, but careful reading proves this is not so and heaven still remains merely the sky. In Gen 28:17, where he states "this [is] none other but the house of God, and this [is] the gate of heaven" he is not referring to the sky as the house of God. Continue reading. Gen 28:22 "And this stone, which I have set [for] a pillar, shall be God's house: and of all that thou shalt give me I will surely give the tenth unto thee." It was the rocks that Jacob presumed to be the house of God, not heaven.

The discrepancy noted above is because the usage of "heaven" [08064] may include the word "air" or possibly "sky". Let's move away from Genesis.

Exodus

Exodus has the listing counted 14 times. Exodus does seem to link God more and more to heaven, but does not delineate any special mention of it being where God specifically resides. God gave bread from heaven (16:4), talks to Moses from heaven (20:22), and Moses often reaches to heaven to perform the miracles of God. While this does come closer to placing God as being in heaven, at least when needed, this does not speak to a permanent location nor does it talk about heaven being where we go when we die. Let's continue.

Leviticus

Just 1 entry. 26:19. It doesn't look to be a happy usage either, but it is still strictly for the sky with no secondary meaning even alluded to. Huh. One more book left.

Deuteronomy

38 entries. This gets more promising. 4:39 "Know therefore this day, and consider [it] in thine heart, that the LORD he [is] God in heaven above, and upon the earth beneath: [there is] none else." This is curious. Let's look at the Hebrew used for this verse.

English	Strong's	Hebrew (Root form)
Know	[03045]	yada`
therefore this day,	[03117]	yowm
and consider	[07725]	shuwb
[it] in thine heart,	[03824]	lebab
that the LORD	[03068]	Y@hovah
he [is] God	[0430]	'elohiym
in heaven	[08064]	shamayim
above,	[04605]	ma`al
and upon the earth	[0776]	'erets

beneath: [there is] none else.

Strange. The phrasing "in heaven" here is inconsistent. Look at "beneath: [there is] none else" doesn't exist in the original Hebrew. Where did it come from? Hey... Read it without that addition. "Know therefore this day, and consider [it] in thine heart, that the LORD he [is] God in heaven above, and upon the earth". This again does NOT relate God to living in Heaven, merely that the LORD is God in heaven *above* and *upon* the earth. Let's see what else we got.

26:15 "Look down from thy holy habitation, from heaven, and bless thy people Israel, and the land which thou hast given us, as thou swarest unto our fathers, a land that floweth with milk and honey." From thy holy habitation, from heaven. Is this separate but equal? Let's look. (Is anyone actually having fun yet? I'm totally fascinated.)

English	**Strong's**	**Hebrew (Root form)**
Look down	[08259]	shaqaph
from thy holy	[06944]	qodesh
habitation,	[04583]	ma`own
from heaven,	[08064]	shamayim
and bless	[01288]	barak
thy people	[05971]	`am
Israel,	[03478]	Yisra'el
and the land	[0127]	'adamah
which thou hast given	[05414]	nathan
us, as thou swarest	[07650]	shaba`
unto our fathers,	[01]	'ab
a land	[0776]	'erets
that floweth	[02100]	zuwb
with milk	[02461]	chalab
and honey.	[01706]	d@bash

So, according to our findings, habitation is just a dwelling or a refuge (of jackals?), and its use in the Bible is consistent with this. Also note that "from thy holy" indicates a definite separateness, not just a holy place. This would indicate to me a place we cannot get to or are not allowed, but that is yet unproven and would take more research into a tangent thought. But, it may prove to be necessary on the next foray into this topic.

Let's make a note of it.

So far, this seems to be the only definitive mention of God residing in heaven, but this still is in the sky. So God dwells in the sky at this point. Also, this is our last real good piece of information in the Torah regarding "heaven". Should we move on? I didn't think so; let's close out the "holy" loop real quickly if we can.

Hm. I'm not sure we can... Not sure it's an open loop at the moment. May be a new piece, a continuation of this one? How marvelous!

Conclusion?

So, from the findings of the word "heaven" [08064], it may be where God dwells. This usage does not discuss whatsoever the idea of us going there after death. We may have to look for another phrasing or do a specific search for Heaven later in the Bible and try to backtrack it.

Mixed Messages From Gloucester

I've been following this story rather haphazardly when it first hit the local radar. It's been all over the web, apparently from here to Australia (though I'm having trouble tracking down those sources). There's been a score of people supporting and lambasting the girls for their choice, the school system, the members of the school board which include the Mayor and the Principal, the governor, President Bush, even other planets have been blamed for this. All in all, there's the usual "blame game" going on and everyone trying to get their attention by demanding no attention at all. I'm still not certain what I'm supposed to think about all this; should I feel bad for the girls and the situation they are in? If they made a pact to have children and to keep them and to have their own parties and to have someone love them unconditionally... Should I be angry at them for making such a childish decision about such an adult responsibility? Should I be angry at their families for not keeping better tabs on their little girls? Should I be angry at the culture in Gloucester from the good Catholic fishing folk for giving these girls really nothing better to look forward to? Or can I just blame the media for zeppelin-ing a situation right into a flaming ball of hydrogen?

Seriously, the more I read about this and the more I consider the current state of affairs in this country and most of the "civilized" world I have to wonder: what choice did these girls have? What hope did they have for their lives to be anything other than what we are starting to expect from Gloucester; fisher-families. Mothers raising boys to fish or girls to raise boys, etc. I'm sure it's not this simplistic, but I presume this is the growing national and international belief on this small, fisher-family town, given what's being reported. Further, it's teenage girls in a sleepy, Catholic town; let the stereotypical jokes begin. Oh, and from what I've heard on local talk radio, the girls in Gloucester are known for their promiscuity anyway; no pact required.

But, what are we talking about? We're treating pregnancy like it's a disease that we need to fight on one hand, and on the other hand it's the most wonderful thing ever that we shouldn't encourage but we shouldn't resist if it happens. We're listening to how there's a daycare at that school and how they cannot give contraceptives to the students or lose funding and supplies; they're not given a choice. Abstinence in this day and age is also being treated like an unrealistic disease. Why? Why are we giving up on the old way of doing things just because popular culture and modern urban living seems to denounce any form of rules as religious pondering?

They don't want the girls to have sex, because they're Catholic. They certainly don't want them protecting themselves from pregnancy, because they're Catholic. That same protection is supposed to help protect against other dangers of the sexual lifestyle, though some studies suggest it really doesn't help at all or that the percentage that you will be protected is actually pretty low and not worth the aggravation. They cannot use any such protection for any such reason. What I don't understand is if they're having sex out of wedlock they're already breaking the rules, so perhaps they should be using contraceptives since they're already breaking the rules. Clearly, there is intent in this action which puts the onus squarely on the girls. Not the boys or men (though they were complicit in this activity), or even the parents or the school or the government or any outside factors. It's the choices of these girls that have brought them into this situation. None of them were raped from what I've heard so there was no forced entry, as it were.

I'm also confused how the girls are supposed to see life. From what I've been reading and hearing, the general consensus is that most people who grow up in Gloucester "never cross the bridge", raise their families and die there. I don't know any exact statistics which I'm sure someone will come to me and say I don't know anything because I don't have statistics, but statistics are used all the time to prove and disprove ideas. I'm more interested in what people who are willing to talk about it have to say, and what they're saying isn't very hopeful, and I don't even know if that's an appropriate term. The expected lifestyle, as stated above, is to perpetuate the fishing community of Gloucester, MA, plain and simple. College is not only an unexpected option but also an unlikely one for these girls, and since their lot in life is to raise families why not let them get started as soon as the pipes work? Clearly they're old enough to have children physically, and since that's their sole purpose, just let them get started. Why waste all this time worrying about them when that's all they're going to do anyway? They're going to, what, go to school for a couple more years and get a diploma that they won't need because who needs geometry when you're balancing a checkbook or changing a diaper or other "woman's work"? They'll never cross that bridge to the mainland, so they won't really need to learn how to drive for more than an evening at a neighbor's house or to get groceries, but I'm sure they can use whatever menial public transportation the great state of Mass has provided them. After all, they're due to get funds from the state for being underage mothers and they have their families to support them and state taxes are funding the day care so they can finish school to get a diploma they aren't really going to use...

What are we supposed to do about that? The culture of the place isn't hopeless or wrong, it's just different from the way much of the American population understands or sees it. They see things like this and immediately jump to there being a problem in Gloucester, but what's the problem? We've tossed morals out the window years ago; sex is a game but if they get pregnant it's a problem? Is that was forming life is now, a problem? Some have suggested that we need more teenage abortions. How is that a solution? That is technically only resolving a symptom of the problem, like a cough syrup or a band-aid. In this instance, the "symptom" is pregnancy, and the "cough syrup" is an abortion. The problem is much deeper than that but no one will ever admit to it because no one will ever believe me when I say it: fear.

We're watching fear unfold in such a manifest way that I can't believe no one's seeing it, but I'm also not surprised things are happening the way they are. Some people are scared it's an epidemic that will sweep the nation because of the all the media hype and movies like Juno and Knocked Up and any other movie where there's a pregnancy and hilarity ensues; even if there is some realistic drama intertwined. I heard someone actually say that unlike the movies, the girls of Gloucester aren't going to have their children adopted by Jennifer Garner. Some are scared that this will allow the government more control of our schools and our childrens' reproductive organs because of the fear of this spreading to their schools. Some people are afraid that God will smite them for being so promiscuous but forgive because they kept their pregnancies. A few Hail Mary's, some repentant benediction, and away you go. Maybe it'd be simpler if we just went back to Indulgences... And from what I can fathom, the girls are afraid of being unloved. At least, that's what the "experts" are saying in these reports. No matter how you slice it, there's fear all around.

So, what are we to do about it? Number one, round up the father who are legally adults and put them in jail for statutory rape. Consent or coercion, they made the choice to impregnate these girls and should be held accountable for it. That's really the biggest thing that I can say right away and without any real philosophical argument. They broke the law; they need to be punished appropriately. What comes next is trickier because of the situation we are in and continue to be in. What to do with the girls?

I don't even know where to begin with them. They didn't make a mistake, they made a bad choice. There's a difference. A mistake would be going to the prom without your purse. A bad choice would be to go without your underwear so you can sit on Billy the Bad Kid in the bathroom to celebrate becoming a woman without having to get your hair messed up. These girls made a specific choice to go this direction, but what can you do? Taking the kids away won't do anything but create more heartache in an already tense and confusing situation. But, leaving the kids could lead to a worse situation if the girls realize they were stupid and became bitter and didn't properly care for the child. Obviously, they need to be educated and their families need to get involved. Oh, and if the family should denounce their child and the child that's being brought into this world they need a good ass-kicking. Remember what your Savior said about love and forgiveness. Explain the mistake they made and acknowledge your own mistakes as parents. No, the parents didn't make the choice and the parents didn't allow it to happen, but the attention they paid to their daughters (and sons) and the lack of familial talk about sex and why they should or shouldn't have it is a travesty that cannot be forgiven by religious zealotry.

This exposes yet another problem with the reigns of religion over the population. People allow it to be their excuse for not conversing with their children about a topic and often causes parents to drive their heads deep in the sand. This exposes a fear that adults of a selfish age have about their children. Children want guidance, but not a heavy hand. Be respectful of them growing into adults but be firm in the belief system if you have one. If you don't have one but still pretend to be morally responsible I'd like to say hi because I don't know anyone like you. We're allowing children to run this place because psychology says we're supposed to and the government enforces that notion because obviously those people have gone to school forever and clearly know the best way to raise a child. Remember, Dr Spock's own son committed suicide; just because you're educated doesn't mean you know anything. Don't be afraid of your kids and don't be afraid to talk them about things. Just talk, don't lecture. Answer questions truthfully. It can be uncomfortable, but don't avoid it because you're scared and don't pretend to hide behind the Bible because that won't do you any better.

All I'm saying is this could have been avoided if we stopped being afraid of stepping on peoples' toes. Not everything they learn is going to be something they like. Better they hear it from someone who's supposed to love them than some homeless guy off the street...

Update 08 July 2008

I guess we're up to 18 girls now and various towns in the area are making fun of the girls. Good? Is mockery a tool or a weapon? Should we just be making fun of them so they get a thick skin and an attitude rather than trying to explain to them why they should be ashamed of such activity? Should we further delve into their general environment and determine why they made this choice in the first place? Hmm. Where should the shame go?

Pride

I stopped off at my closest Dunkin Donuts this morning as I do most mornings, and again I was greeted by a trashcan overflowing with junk. I realize this should be seen as nothing particularly new or interesting, but what audacity do you have to have to see that the trash is so full there's already stuff on the ground and yet you still have to try and cram in your cup? Oh, and there isn't any real "cramming" going on. It looks like they're just setting their cups into the existing pile of garbage and hoping the whole thing doesn't come crashing out onto the side of their vehicle. Naturally, much like everything else, this got me thinking.

Our levels of pride have absolutely no boundaries at all, do they? We figure that since this is someone else's trash receptacle it's now their problem and not ours. We figure that since they're getting paid to provide me service they should be grateful that part of the job is picking up whatever I happen to try and fit, and if it doesn't they should be on their hands and knees kissing my feet for the privilege of cleaning up after me because I'm too lazy to take my trash somewhere else. I see this all over the place. But, it doesn't stop there.

As already indicated, I see it in churches and in the religious or those people who are practicing religion but call it something else. I see it in myself every time I start a blog or every time I think that I'm doing the right thing over someone else. I see it on television from our commentators to our commentated. I see it when I drive as people cut me off or change lanes without a blinker. I see it when Manny Ramirez pushes an old guy for not giving him all the tickets he wants. I see it everywhere I look in the ole U S of A. I see it globally, too. I see it in those terrorists who think they're worshipping Allah correctly as Mohammed taught them. I see it in those Sinn Fein guys who used to blow stuff up. I see it in the eyes of every world leader. On the other side, I see it in people who have "problems" like anorexia and stress and depression and ADD. I see it in people who are in pain and who cause pain.

There is a similarity between the above examples and all the other examples I could possibly give: opinion. Merely opinion. I tried to throw money in there or power, but really it's about opinion or how someone perceives their own situation in relation to someone else's. It's more than just knowing something more than someone else, or having more stuff than someone else, or being able to do more things than someone else, or being able to make someone else do what you say or having more problems than someone else. It's about this feeling inside that you're better than someone else, for any reason. It's not just about ME being right, but it's about ME being more right than YOU, which is a big difference. You can be right and not be a dick about it, but if you're a dick about it you're just trying to prove your own worth to yourself and to everyone else who happens to be "lucky enough" to be in your presence. It's sickening, really. I know a few people who are right about a lot of things but they don't put it in your face. In fact, when they ARE right I tend to get upset that I wasn't the one who was right. It's like being a child again and telling your parents they don't know what they're talking about. They're not always right as parents but you're not always right as children either.

This is why my two major points for my own brand of philosophical living involves humility. I'm not the only one to have this as an idea, but you have to consider that things aren't new because we as humans are only so creative. Eventually, ideas overlap or repeat themselves. I'm also working on this day to day, but some days I really don't care about being humble because no one else is. What rules are we following anymore? Are we following any rules at all? Just remember people, everyone has their own opinion, and yours might be wrong. It will help you greatly when interacting with people of any belief system. Seriously. Try it out sometime. I dare you...

Superman Sucks

I've always been interested in how people react to things. Even when I was small I would not take naps because I had to see what was going on. I was naturally inquisitive of people and why they were in my house or lived on my street or why the neighbors across the street wouldn't talk to me. I spent some years trying to figure out some of those questions and I still find myself asking questions. I find very few answers, of course. You see, everyone else seems to know why things are they way they are and how to fix it. Or, at the very least, why it can't be fixed. I have played the game of being right as often as anyone else, probably more so now that I have this blog up and running again. Obviously, anyone who wants to list "blogger" as their profession or at least part of their resume have the ego to spread their own words as truth and hope that everyone else believes them. I wonder how many of us "bloggers" have self-esteem issues and need to spread our words to every corner of the globe as impressively as possible just to find someone who'll listen. I wonder how many of us really are unique and alone in the world. I wonder what's really going on in the minds of everyone.

There has been several discussions amongst my various groups of friends about which super powers we would want. This is a crazy question with limitless possibilities, but often we try to be "mature" about our selections. The simplest thing would be to choose "omnipotence", but that's far too unrealistic, so we try to find bits and pieces from heroes we already know and like. Superman, Spiderman, Luke Skywalker. Batman doesn't really fit the list as he's just a rich kid with emotional problems. Really. And I like Batman; he's my favorite. But let's be serious. His folks get killed and he has to take it out on every single criminal in the world? Talk about prejudice... I can't wait to see "The Dark Knight"...

Anyway, this has been an easy question for me but it always had with it some problems. I would choose immortality every time. If I only had one, it would be immortality. With this immortality would have to be some kind of limb regeneration or cellular regeneration so lost limbs and old age wouldn't take its toll on my body. Like Wolverine and either of the Highlanders. No more sickness or disease. I'd never have to eat because, well, I'm immortal. My body will work forever whatever I do to it. I could smoke, drink, have random sex with garden equipment and everything would still function (not that I would). I could also see the rise and fall of everything I ever knew and loved, and I could learn to predict its outcomes with the wisdom of the ages. How many of us can really know or believe in their hearts that they could see everything they've ever known turn to dust and move forward? I would have to: I am immortal after all...

Secondarily, telepathy and invisibility were always things that I enjoyed. Flying became a tertiary objective, along with teleportation or incorporealness. Although, immortality and a Green Lantern ring would kick major ass, too... Oh, I would want just mind reading telepathy, not mind control. If I knew what people wanted, with my wisdom, I could find a way to negotiate or convince them to give me what I want in exchange for what they wanted. Invisibility for when they realize they got screwed. Ha! I would just want to disappear sometimes. I do that. I don't think I would screw people over, but the temptation would certainly be there. I can see myself growing bored with humanity on the whole very quickly. Ever wonder if God feels the same way...?

But, are these really superhero traits or just comic book hero traits? Is there really a difference? What about those people who willingly put their lives on the line every day? Police, firefighters, soldiers, anyone in any of the volunteer armed forces. The ability to face their fears and come out alive and victorious in battle is pretty heroic. Is an advanced ability to kill heroism, or just the ability to defeat? Do we even know what heroism is anymore? Is it just an epic tale or saving a life? Can it be both?

The thing about heroes that always impressed me is their ability to maintain their composure in the heat of battle. Way I hear it, if you're not afraid when you're in combat, you're either an idiot or you have a death wish. We can't agree on anything, can we?

Who are your heroes? Why? They can be anyone from The Crow to The Christ, doesn't matter to me. I'm still just that little kid wondering why people do or say or think what they do. And why Superman is as much a national pastime as baseball.

The Bible Is Relevant

I feel the need to explain this is minor detail for any of my potential detractors. It is important that this is understood. I don't care if you believe it or you don't believe it; it's relevant. It serves a purpose and has been a major part of global history for centuries. Millennia even. What is said inside this collection of documents may be real or fake, right or wrong, but its existence and importance cannot be questioned. Without the Bible our world would look very different. Believe that if you want, but it's simply fact. Would there have been a need for Christ if there was no Law in the first place? If there was no explanation of God would we be doing the things we have been doing? Wouldn't we have skipped the Middle Ages entirely without the Bible? Would we have Islam if there was no Bible for Mohammed to relate his stories to? Would there be Catholicism at all? Where would our world be without the Bible? I'm not here to argue if it'd be better off or not; we have no way to answer that question. What I am here to do is tackle its "secrets". I feel stupid even using that word. It's not a secret, we've all just been too busy being told what it means that we don't take in what it says. What. It. Says. So yes, if you feel the Bible isn't relevant then you're irresponsible and I fear we won't like each other much because I'm liable to call you names. You have to believe IN the Bible but you don't have to agree with WHAT is in the Bible. That is all...

Whatever You Say

Poe wrote about a singular effect in his work and George Carlin knew that language was often our biggest holdup. Both of these men were speaking about a simple concept that plagues me every single day: consistency, specifically of thought. I look to the world around me and for a while I was searching for help inside of it, but there isn't any. Just watch the news sometime, really pay attention to what's going on and what's being said and you'll get what I mean. We're told to trust our politicians when they openly lie to us but we vote them into office anyway. We scold children for having sex without protection because of AIDS but when they get pregnant it's just an inconvenience and encourage them to have abortions. We're not allowed to state that most of modern terrorism is being performed by Muslims because it might offend them but they're already offended by our very existence! Oh, and if you don't think this isn't a holy war you're off your rocker. It is to them. Do some research.

We're in a society where it's no longer polite to say anything about anyone because it's racist or sexist or otherwise bigoted, unless it's against white European Christian males; then it's just acceptable payback. It's not consistent! I could give more examples but I don't really want to ramble (even though that seems to be my best hobby). I wish it wasn't this way, but we've allowed language to "evolve" by making it so totally overcomplicated that we don't know what anything means anymore. We water down our language by creating fake words or mixing words with other languages to compound our confusion. Words can't just mean something, they have to mean multiple things and apply based upon context. What about homonyms? What purpose do they serve besides confounding small children?

We're allowing words to carry more weight than just communication, and we're assuming that everyone else is, too. In all my reading I have yet to come across a whinier nation than America* in the entire globe. Sure, there a problems and there are people catching on to the fact that in America it's no longer "sticks and stones may break my bones but words will never hurt me" it's "hey, you can't say that about {insert whatever group you can think of}, that's {insert bigot synonym}". What are we doing? Are we evolving ourselves into wimps and whiners who can't accept any criticism? Does no one see this as weakening our mental facilities and our emotional barriers? Are we supposed to all cry and go to therapists and take drugs to get through life? They tell us to feel a certain way then they give us pills because we feel that way. What? "Feel bad because no one likes you, Tommy? Oh, you're the popular kid? Well, that's a lot of pressure. You should take these pills so you can cope with being so popular, that's quite a burden."

Are we overmedicating our society or just over stupidizing** it? Where does it end? The more we learn the more fear we seem to have. The more words we have the less we can say. The more problems we diagnose in people the more drugs we create. Is it just a business decision...?

We can't talk about the Muslims because it will offend them, but go ahead and lambaste the Catholic church because of their litany of mistakes and cover-ups including pedophilia and the Dark Ages. Sure, that's consistent. We're supposed to admit our problems to strangers but don't dare talk about it to friends and family. They're talking to the same therapist saying the same thing giving them the same prescription for anxiety when there wasn't any before you started seeing the therapist because that's what people do. Blame your parents for your choices even though they're not the ones putting the gun in your hand to go to your place of employment to level your co-workers in a single final act of stupidity.

Guns aren't the problem, drugs aren't the problem, even religion isn't the problem***... Anyone care to take a stab? I didn't think so. We are the problem. People and their stupid fear and pride. It's everywhere. I can almost taste it in the air when I'm around the right people. They speak of humility but ooze superiority. They act like macho idiots when they're really terrified inside. They talk about how smart they are when they only know what's in the world they've created for themselves - no, I'm not talking about me. They talk about other people's self-centeredness when they're so bitter they don't believe anyone else has their problems. They live inconsistent lives in a hope of distracting themselves from the fears they refuse to face because of fear or pride or both. I'm not any better, because it can be a hard road if you've avoided it long enough, but I recognize my weakness and am trying to work on it each and every day. Got to be willing to admit your faults if you expect to defeat them. Medication won't help you. Hell, if you're depressed take this anti-depressant and you might become suicidal...

- Perception Is Truth -

What?

Doesn't make any sense, but we do it on a daily basis. And so few seem to notice...

*maybe Canada, but with all that snow what else is there to do?

** yeah, it's a fake word, but it means to make stupider

***who believes they'd ever hear me say that?

Work

Work. All I remember. Work. Computers. Printers. Servers. Users. Work. I can't help. I can't fix anything. My brain stopped. Work. The music. The bells? The phone rings. I answer. What's my name? I'm the tech. Your problem? You can't print? Work. My head pounds. Her voice; annoying. Her name? I can't tell. Thick southern accent. Did she login? She logged in. Can she restart? No. No? She needs help. Restart. No. Humor me. She restarts. She logs in. Can she print? Not ready. Boss has a question. Where's what laptop? Oh. I don't know. I didn't do it. What name is there? That's not my name. Work. Can she print? No. From anything? Still? Can she open files? She can. Can I print? I can't either. I can see the printer. I can't see the printer? I see print server. Is the printer connected? It is. Unplug it. The print server. Wait a minute. Plug it back in. Yes, the lights blink. They always blink. What? You just don't look. Work. Work, damn you. Can you print? No. Still? Check the printer. Anything on the screen? It's dark. What do you mean dark? It's not on? Turn it on. Wait a minute. Can you print? You can print. Why was it off? You turn it off. Every night. You forgot? Oh. You were late. You thought someone else would. They didn't. Right. You're welcome. Work.

Same every day. Every single day. I talk. I question. I answer. I hate. They call. They question. They backpedal. They answer. I get orders. I start. I'm told to wait. Decisions haven't been made. Manager needs more time. Manager made request. Manager needs more time. My head hurts. It pulses. Work. Work. Work. Ibuprofen should do it. 600mg does the trick after 20 more minutes. Work. Work... work... ...work...

I write. I read. I wait. They call. I answer. I question. I can't help. I don't care. I won't help. My mind breaks. Work. Bills to pay. Games to play. Work today. Work. That word again. The agony is back. Is it lunchtime? It's after lunch? I missed lunch. I didn't bring lunch. Cafeteria's closed. Work. The pulsing is back. Work. Work. Work... What to do? What can I do? Work. Is that an answer? I want to go home. I can't go home. I have to work. Hours. Four hours. Four and a half hours. Wonderful.

The phone rings. I don't answer. I don't question. I don't help. I go home. I get fired.

References

"Perception Is Truth"

- Allers, C. T., & Golson, J. (1994). Multiple Personality Disorder: Treatment from an Adlerian Perspective. *Individual Psychology, 3,* 262-270.
- Brown, M. T. (2001). Multiple personality and personal identity. *Philosophical Psychology, 4,* 435-447.
- Dunn, G. E., & Paolo, A. M., & Ryan, J. J., & Van Fleet, J. N. (1994). Belief in the existence of multiple personality disorder among psychologists and psychiatrists. *Journal of Clinical Psychology, 3,* 454-457.
- Kennett, J., & Matthews, S. (2002). Identity, control and responsibility: the case of Dissociative Identity Disorder. *Philosophical Psychology, 4,* 509-526.
- Myers, D. G. (2004) Psychology (7th ed). Holland: Worth.
- Rosik, C. H. (2003). Critical issues in the dissociative disorders field: Six perspectives from religiously sensitive practitioners. *Journal of Psychology and Theology, 2,* 113-128.
- Sinnott-Armstrong, W., & Behnke, S. (2000). Responsibility in cases of multiple personality disorder. *Philosophical Perspectives, 14,* 301-323.

- References -
"Heretical Reason"

- Kaufmann, Walter. The Portable Nietzsche. New York, New York: Viking Penguin. 1976
- Lewis, C. S. Mere Christianity. New York, New York: Touchstone. 1980.
- Martindale, Wayne and Jerry Root, eds. The Quotable Lewis. Wheaton, Illinois: Tyndale House. 1989.
- Schaeffer, Francis A. A Christian Manifesto. Westchester, Illinois: Crossway Books. 1981.
- ---. How Should We Then Live? The Rise and Decline of Western Thought and Culture. Westchester, Illinois: Crossway Books. 1976.
- ---. The Francis A. Schaeffer Trilogy. Wheaton, Illinois: Crossway Books. 1990.
- Stein, Murray. Jung On Christianity. Princeton, New Jersey: Princeton University Press. 1999.
- Ephemera of Francis August Schaeffer - Collection 220. 15 November 2003. Manchester, NH. 03 March 2001. <http://www.wheaton.edu/bgc/archives/GUIDES/220.htm>
- Francis Schaeffer – Portraits of Great Christians – In Touch Ministries. 15 November 2003. Manchester, NH. Unknown. <http://www.intouch.org/myintouch/mighty/portraits/ francis_schaeffer_ 213605.html>
- God Is Dead: Killing God. 16 November 2003. Manchester, NH. 2003. <http://atheism.about.com/library/weekly/aa042600a.htm>
- Nietzsche Chronology. 16 November 2003. Manchester, NH. 09 May 1995. <http://www.usc.edu/~douglast/bio.html>
- Chronology of the Life of C. S. Lewis. 16 November 2003. Manchester, NH. Unknown. <http://www.cslewis.org/about/>
- Carl Jung. 16 November 2003. Manchester, NH. 1997. <http://www.ship.edu/~cgboeree/jung.html>
- IAAP. 01 December 2003. Manchester, NH. 01 December 2003. <http://www.iaap.org/joseph_henderson.html>

- Perception Is Truth -
"Edgar's Esoteric Explication"

- Andros, Gus D. and Minn, Michael. "Marie Sallé, (1707 - 1756)". *Andros on Ballet.* 21 Nov 2006. <http://www.michaelminn.net/andros/index.php?salle_marie>
- "Astrotrain" et al. "Royal coat of arms of Scotland." *Wikipedia: The Free Encyclopedia.* 20 Nov 2006. <http://en.wikipedia.org/wiki/Royal_coat_of_arms_of_Scotland>
- [Baltimore] The Edgar Allan Poe Society of Baltimore, Inc. *The Edgar Allan Poe Society of Baltimore.* "Berenice." & "Poe's Original Burial Place". 20 & 24 Nov 2006. <http://www.eapoe.org/works/index.htm>
- [Baltimore 2] (qtd. from) Mabbott, T.O., ed. *The Collected Works of Edgar Allan Poe.* 1978. p. 219, title note.
- Charters, Ann, ed. *The Story and Its Writer: An Introduction to Short Fiction, 7th Edition.* Taunton: Bedford/St. Martin's, 2007.
- Clute, John and Grant, John, eds. *The Encyclopedia of Fantasy.* New York: St. Martin's Griffin, 1997.
- Dictionary.com. "dis-", "dissimulation", "immolation", "sagacity", "simulation", "superinduced". *The American Heritage® Dictionary of the English Language, Fourth Edition.* Houghton Mifflin Company, 2004. 21 Nov. 2006. <http://dictionary.reference.com/browse/immolation>
- Gmoser, Stefan. "Berenice", "The Raven", "The Philosophy of Composition". *The Work of Edgar Allan Poe.* 20 Nov 2006. <http://bau2.uibk.ac.at/sg/poe/Work.html>
- Pulju, Timothy J. "History of Latin: An irreverent but true chronology." 20 Nov 2006. <http://www.ruf.rice.edu/~kemmer/Words04/structure/latin.html>

www.ingramcontent.com/pod-product-compliance
Lightning Source LLC
Chambersburg PA
CBHW032101090426
42743CB00007B/200